NIGHT'S DOMINION™

VOLUME 2

AN ONI PRESS PUBLICATION

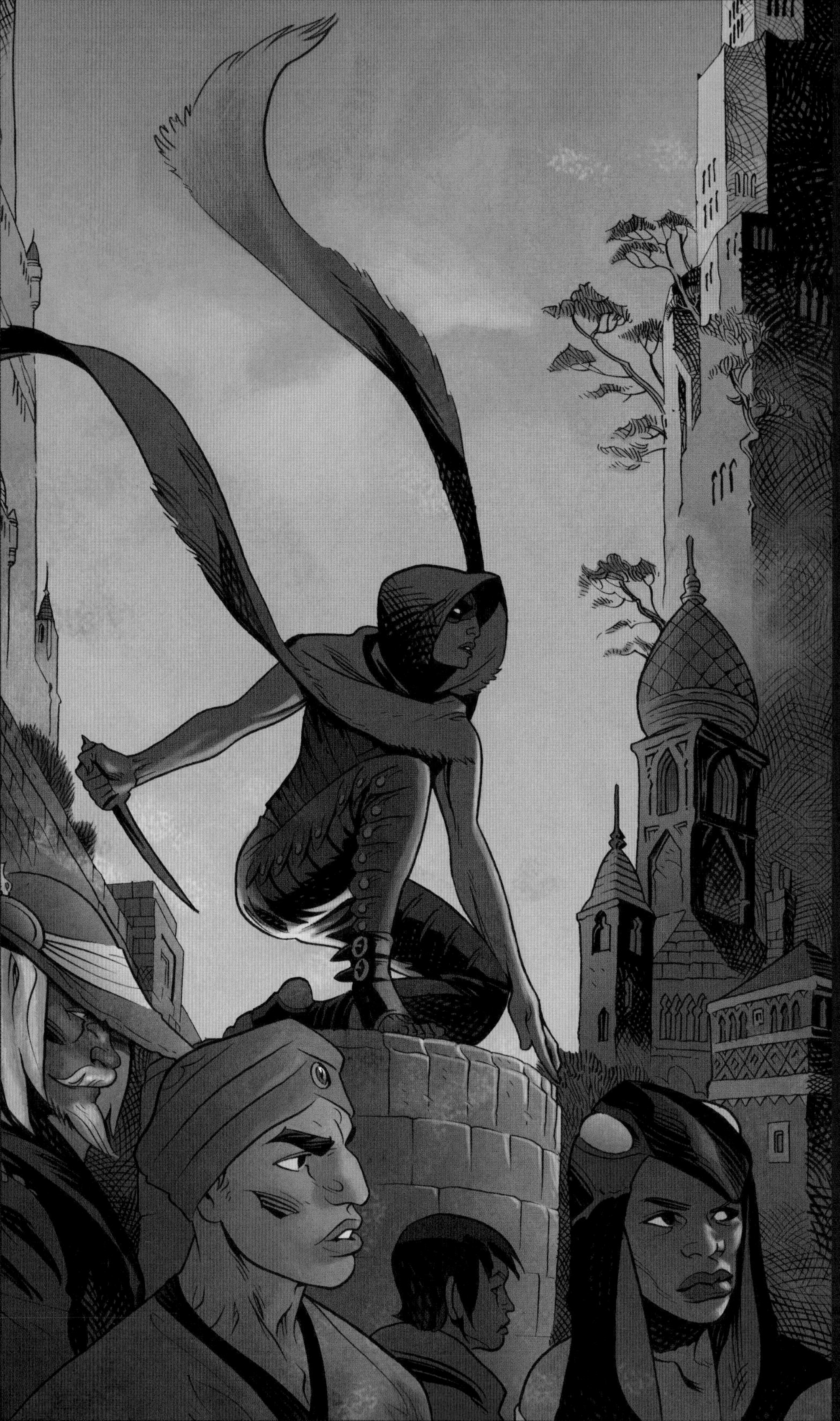

NIGHT'S DOMINION

VOLUME 2

WRITTEN & ILLUSTRATED BY
TED NAIFEH

LETTERED BY
ADITYA BIDIKAR

EDITED BY
ROBIN HERRERA

DESIGNED BY
KEITH WOOD

PUBLISHED BY ONI PRESS, INC.

JOE NOZEMACK founder & chief financial officer

JAMES LUCAS JONES publisher

CHARLIE CHU v.p. of creative & business development

BRAD ROOKS director of operations

RACHEL REED marketing manager

MELISSA MESZAROS publicity manager

TROY LOOK director of design & production

HILARY THOMPSON senior graphic designer

KATE Z. STONE junior graphic designer

ANGIE KNOWLES digital prepress lead

ARI YARWOOD executive editor

ROBIN HERRERA senior editor

DESIREE WILSON associate editor

ALISSA SALLAH administrative assistant

JUNG LEE logistics associate

Oni Press, Inc.
1319 SE Martin Luther King Jr. Blvd.
Suite 240
Portland, OR 97214
USA

First edition: May 2018

onipress.com
facebook.com/onipress • twitter.com/onipress
onipress.tumblr.com • instagram.com/onipress

@tednaifeh • tednaifeh.com

Originally published as issues 1-4 of the Oni Press comic series *Night's Dominion: Season Two.*

ISBN 978-1-62010-496-5 • eISBN 978-1-62010-497-2

Library of Congress Control Number: 2017956257

10 9 8 7 6 5 4 3 2 1

PRINTED IN CHINA.

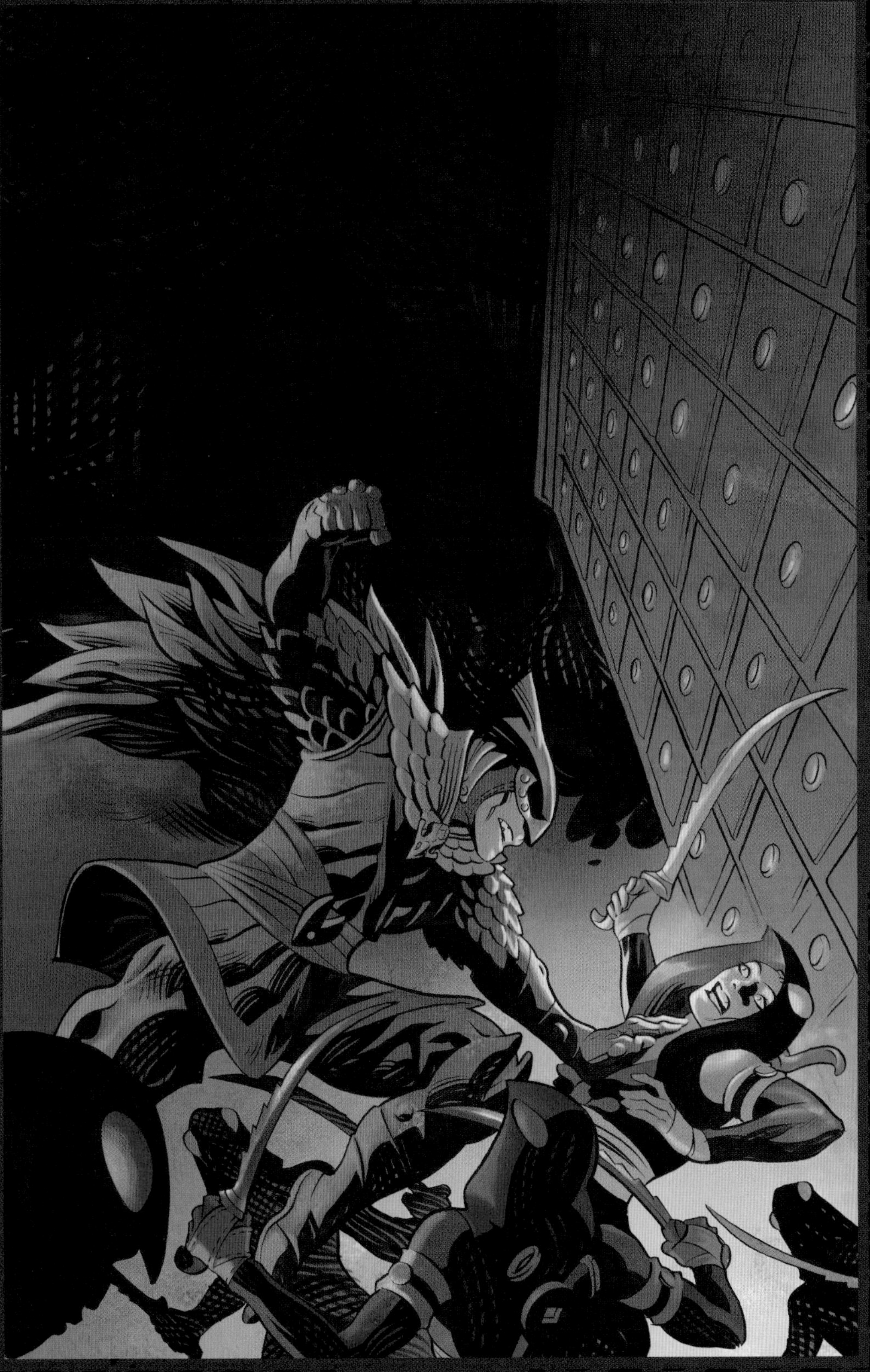

Chapter 1

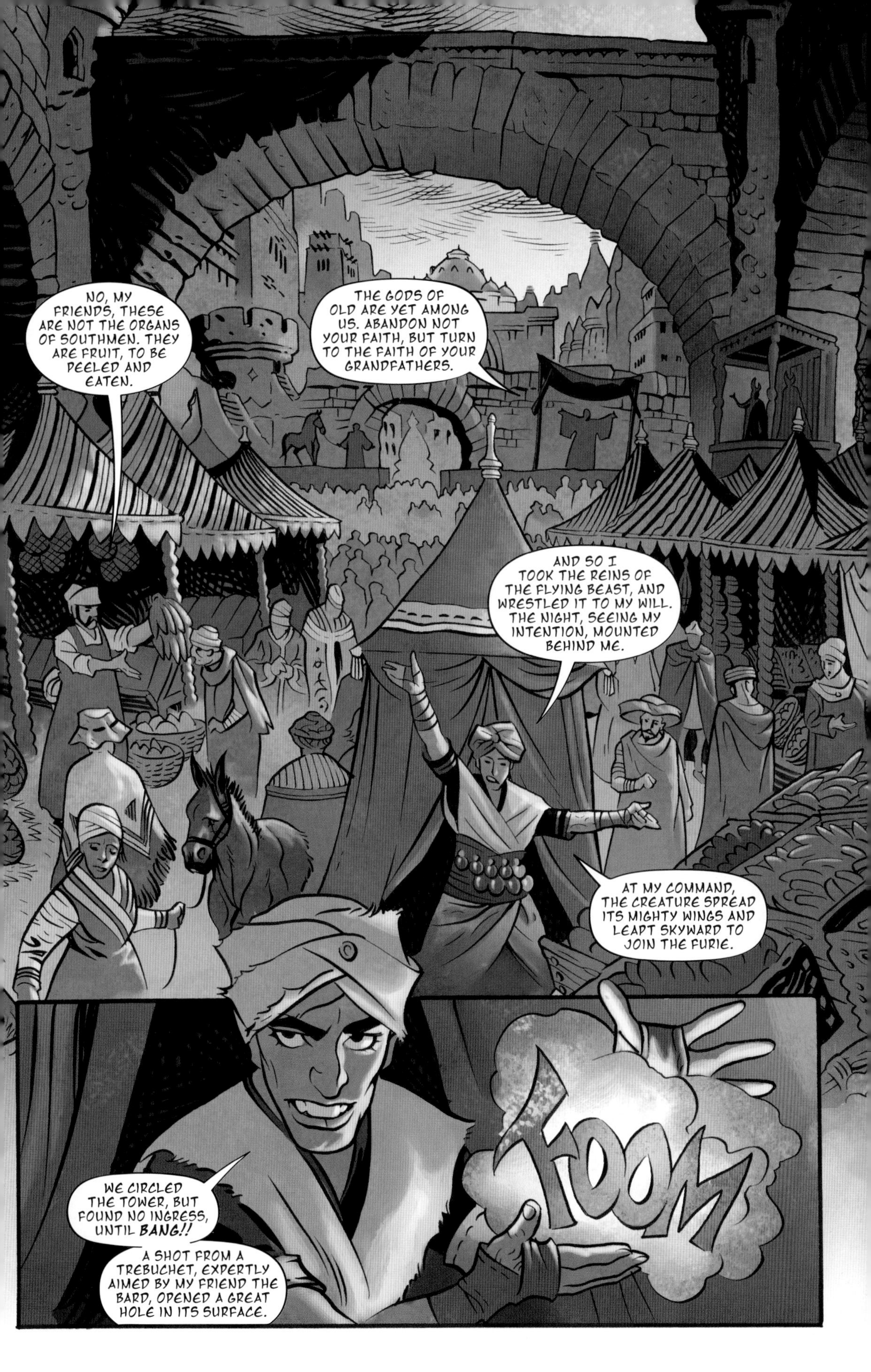
NO, MY FRIENDS, THESE ARE NOT THE ORGANS OF SOUTHMEN. THEY ARE FRUIT, TO BE PEELED AND EATEN.
THE GODS OF OLD ARE YET AMONG US. ABANDON NOT YOUR FAITH, BUT TURN TO THE FAITH OF YOUR GRANDFATHERS.
AND SO I TOOK THE REINS OF THE FLYING BEAST, AND WRESTLED IT TO MY WILL. THE NIGHT, SEEING MY INTENTION, MOUNTED BEHIND ME.
AT MY COMMAND, THE CREATURE SPREAD ITS MIGHTY WINGS AND LEAPT SKYWARD TO JOIN THE FURIE.
WE CIRCLED THE TOWER, BUT FOUND NO INGRESS, UNTIL *BANG!!*
A SHOT FROM A TREBUCHET, EXPERTLY AIMED BY MY FRIEND THE BARD, OPENED A GREAT HOLE IN ITS SURFACE.
FOOM

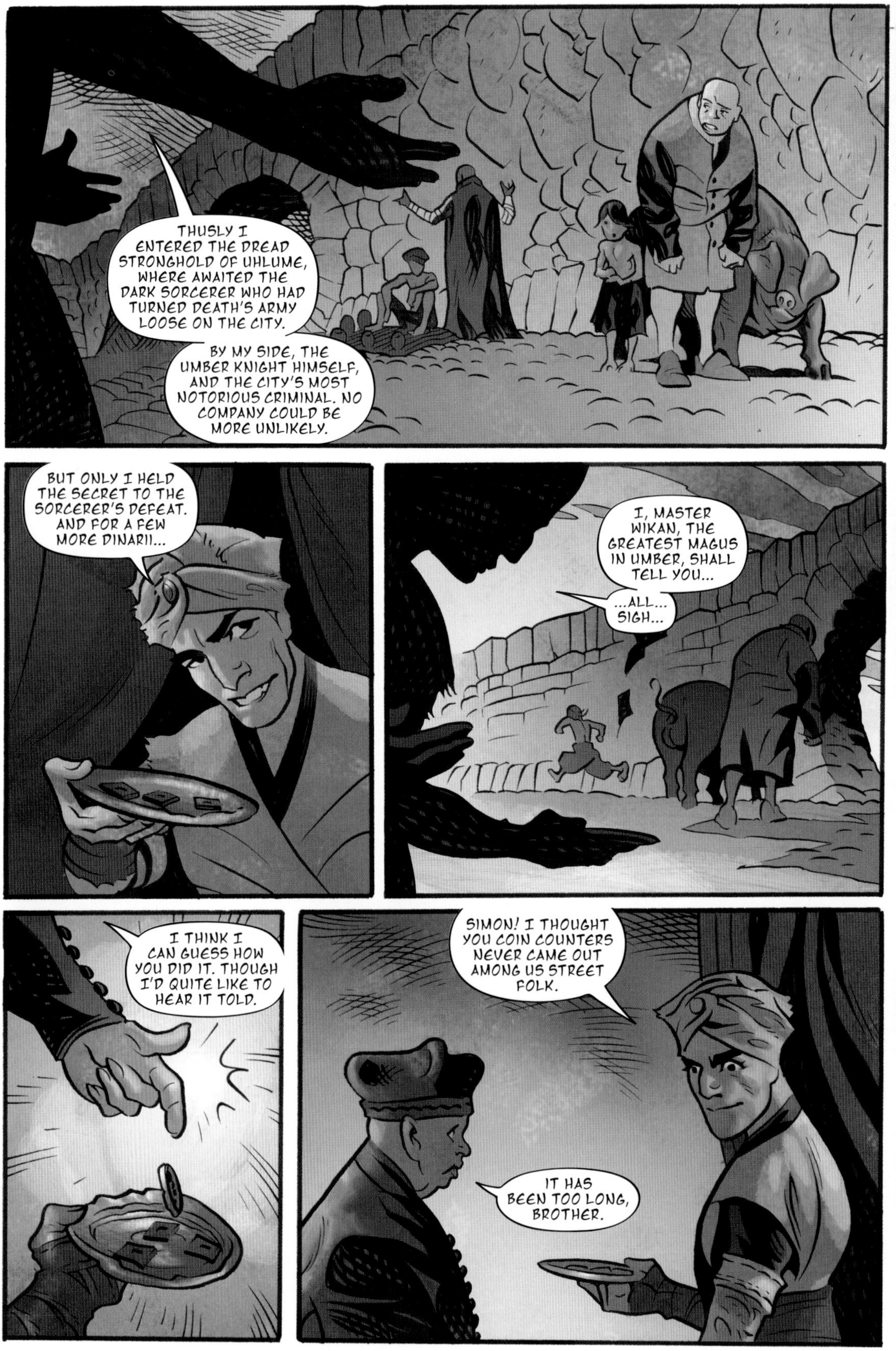
THUSLY I ENTERED THE DREAD STRONGHOLD OF UHLUME, WHERE AWAITED THE DARK SORCERER WHO HAD TURNED DEATH'S ARMY LOOSE ON THE CITY.
BY MY SIDE, THE UMBER KNIGHT HIMSELF, AND THE CITY'S MOST NOTORIOUS CRIMINAL. NO COMPANY COULD BE MORE UNLIKELY.
BUT ONLY I HELD THE SECRET TO THE SORCERER'S DEFEAT. AND FOR A FEW MORE DINARII...
I, MASTER WIKAN, THE GREATEST MAGUS IN UMBER, SHALL TELL YOU...
...ALL... SIGH...
I THINK I CAN GUESS HOW YOU DID IT. THOUGH I'D QUITE LIKE TO HEAR IT TOLD.
SIMON! I THOUGHT YOU COIN COUNTERS NEVER CAME OUT AMONG US STREET FOLK.
IT HAS BEEN TOO LONG, BROTHER.

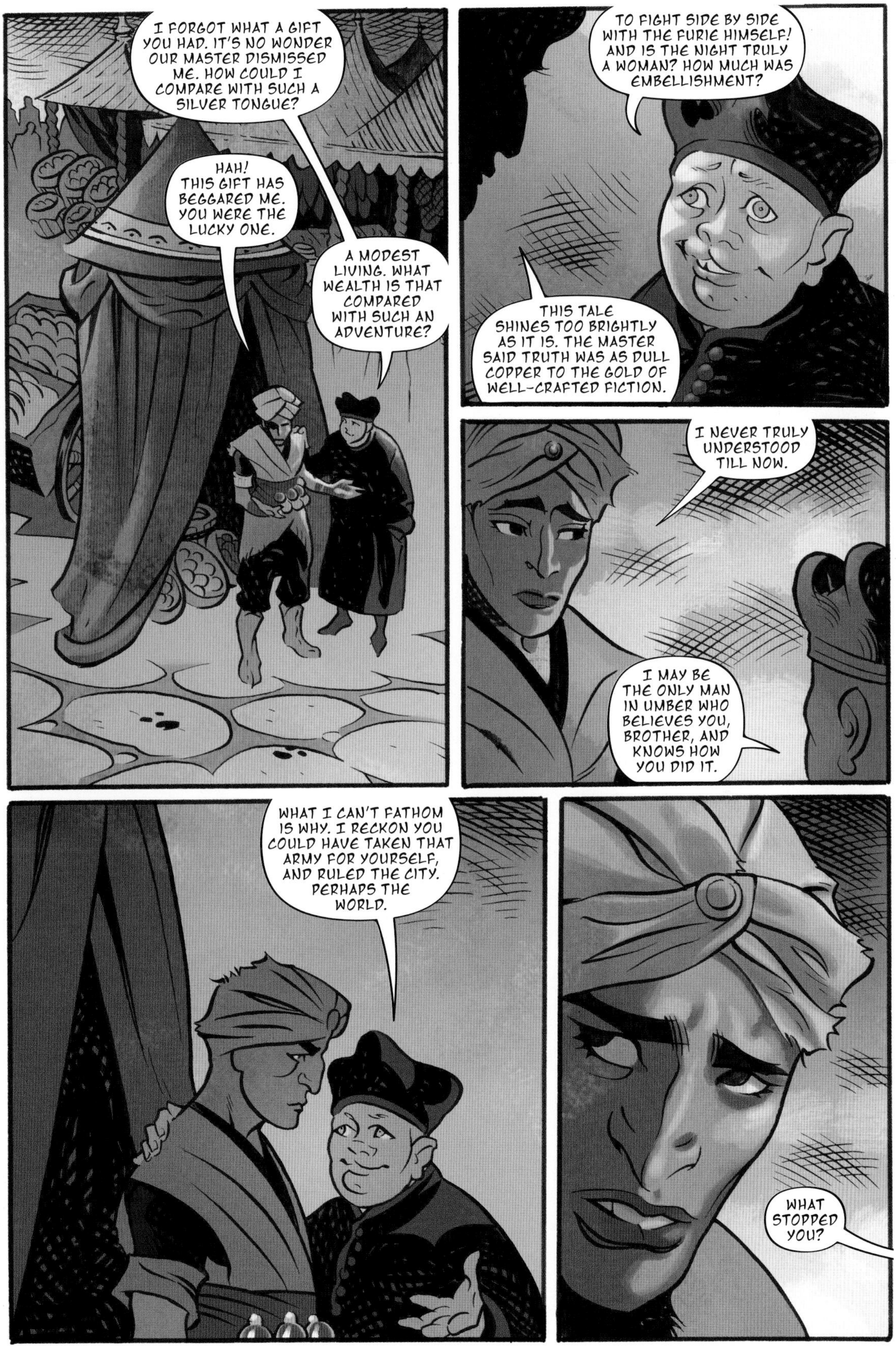
I FORGOT WHAT A GIFT YOU HAD. IT'S NO WONDER OUR MASTER DISMISSED ME. HOW COULD I COMPARE WITH SUCH A SILVER TONGUE?
HAH! THIS GIFT HAS BEGGARED ME. YOU WERE THE LUCKY ONE.
A MODEST LIVING. WHAT WEALTH IS THAT COMPARED WITH SUCH AN ADVENTURE?
TO FIGHT SIDE BY SIDE WITH THE FURIE HIMSELF! AND IS THE NIGHT TRULY A WOMAN? HOW MUCH WAS EMBELLISHMENT?
THIS TALE SHINES TOO BRIGHTLY AS IT IS. THE MASTER SAID TRUTH WAS AS DULL COPPER TO THE GOLD OF WELL-CRAFTED FICTION.
I NEVER TRULY UNDERSTOOD TILL NOW.
I MAY BE THE ONLY MAN IN UMBER WHO BELIEVES YOU, BROTHER, AND KNOWS HOW YOU DID IT.
WHAT I CAN'T FATHOM IS WHY. I RECKON YOU COULD HAVE TAKEN THAT ARMY FOR YOURSELF, AND RULED THE CITY. PERHAPS THE WORLD.
WHAT STOPPED YOU?

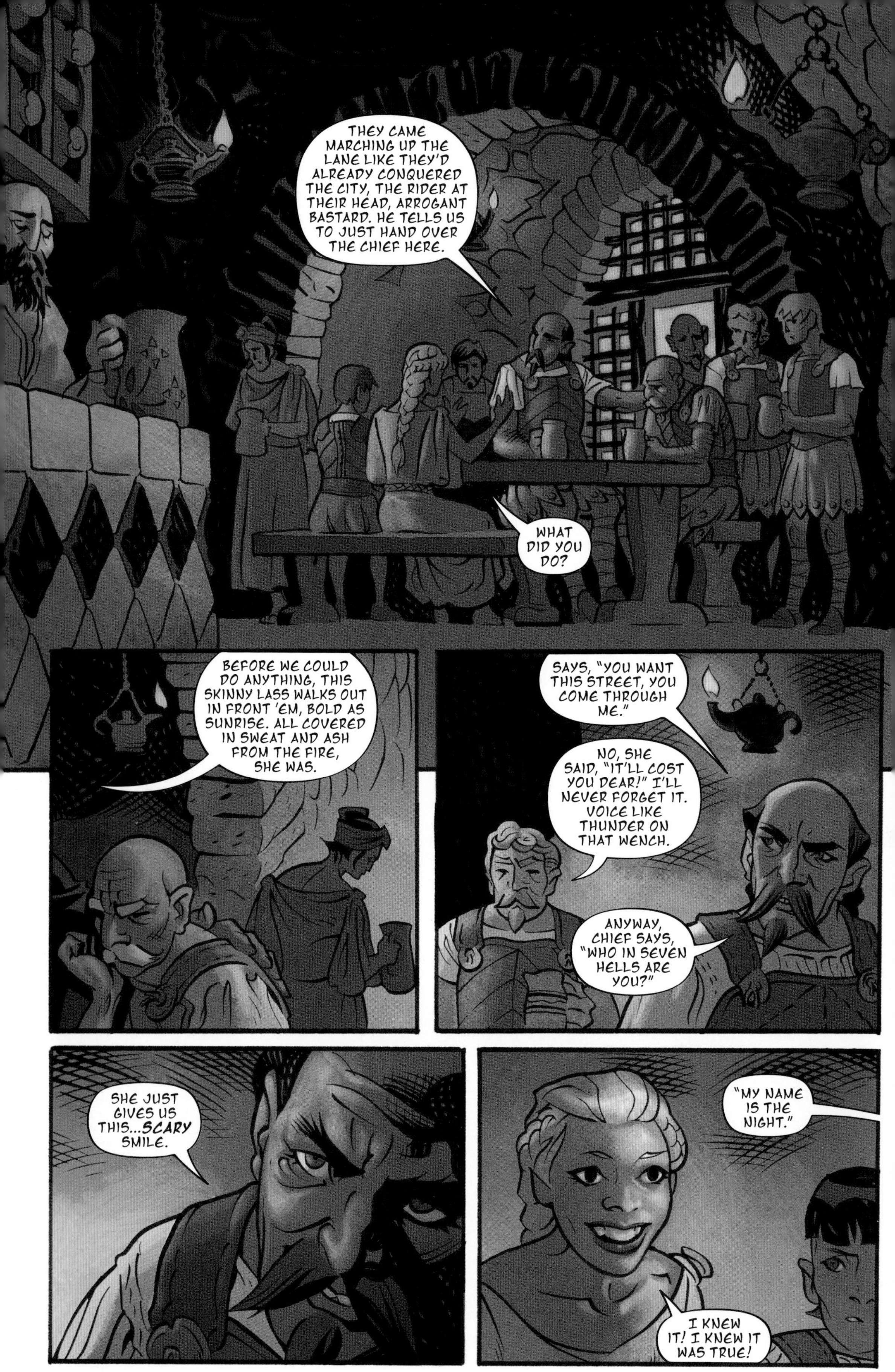

THEY CAME MARCHING UP THE LANE LIKE THEY'D ALREADY CONQUERED THE CITY, THE RIDER AT THEIR HEAD, ARROGANT BASTARD. HE TELLS US TO JUST HAND OVER THE CHIEF HERE.
WHAT DID YOU DO?
BEFORE WE COULD DO ANYTHING, THIS SKINNY LASS WALKS OUT IN FRONT 'EM, BOLD AS SUNRISE. ALL COVERED IN SWEAT AND ASH FROM THE FIRE, SHE WAS.
SAYS, "YOU WANT THIS STREET, YOU COME THROUGH ME."
NO, SHE SAID, "IT'LL COST YOU DEAR!" I'LL NEVER FORGET IT. VOICE LIKE THUNDER ON THAT WENCH.
ANYWAY, CHIEF SAYS, "WHO IN SEVEN HELLS ARE YOU?"
SHE JUST GIVES US THIS...**SCARY** SMILE.
"MY NAME IS THE NIGHT."
I KNEW IT! I KNEW IT WAS TRUE!

STARTS TEARING THOSE SKULL-HEADED JACKALS APART.

I DON'T KNOW WHO SHE WAS, BUT SHE WASN'T THE NIGHT.

I'VE MET THE NIGHT, REMEMBER?

WHAT? YOU NEVER TOLD ME THAT!

NOT THIS AGAIN. YOU BARELY REMEMBER IT YOURSELF.

I RECALL WELL ENOUGH.

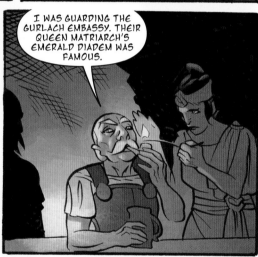

I WAS GUARDING THE GURLACH EMBASSY. THEIR QUEEN MATRIARCH'S EMERALD DIADEM WAS FAMOUS.

"STILL, I DIDN'T RECKON ANYONE BOLD ENOUGH, OR FOOLISH ENOUGH, TO MAKE AN ATTEMPT. SO I INDULGED A BIT. I INDULGED A LOT IN THOSE DAYS.

"I WAS ABOUT TO LEARN A HARD LESSON."

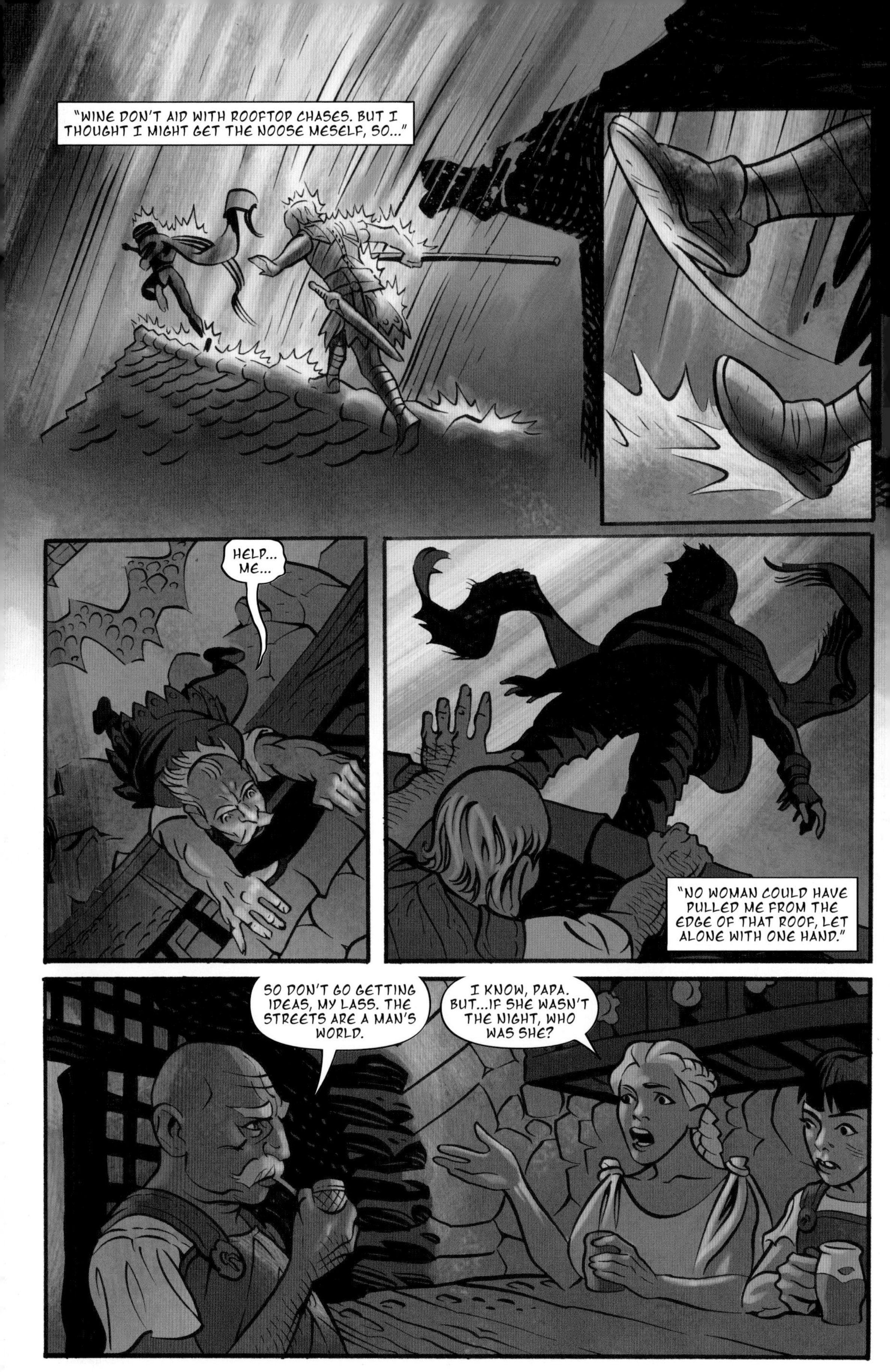
"WINE DON'T AID WITH ROOFTOP CHASES. BUT I THOUGHT I MIGHT GET THE NOOSE MESELF, SO..."
HELP... ME...
"NO WOMAN COULD HAVE PULLED ME FROM THE EDGE OF THAT ROOF, LET ALONE WITH ONE HAND."
SO DON'T GO GETTING IDEAS, MY LASS. THE STREETS ARE A MAN'S WORLD.
I KNOW, PAPA. BUT...IF SHE WASN'T THE NIGHT, WHO WAS SHE?

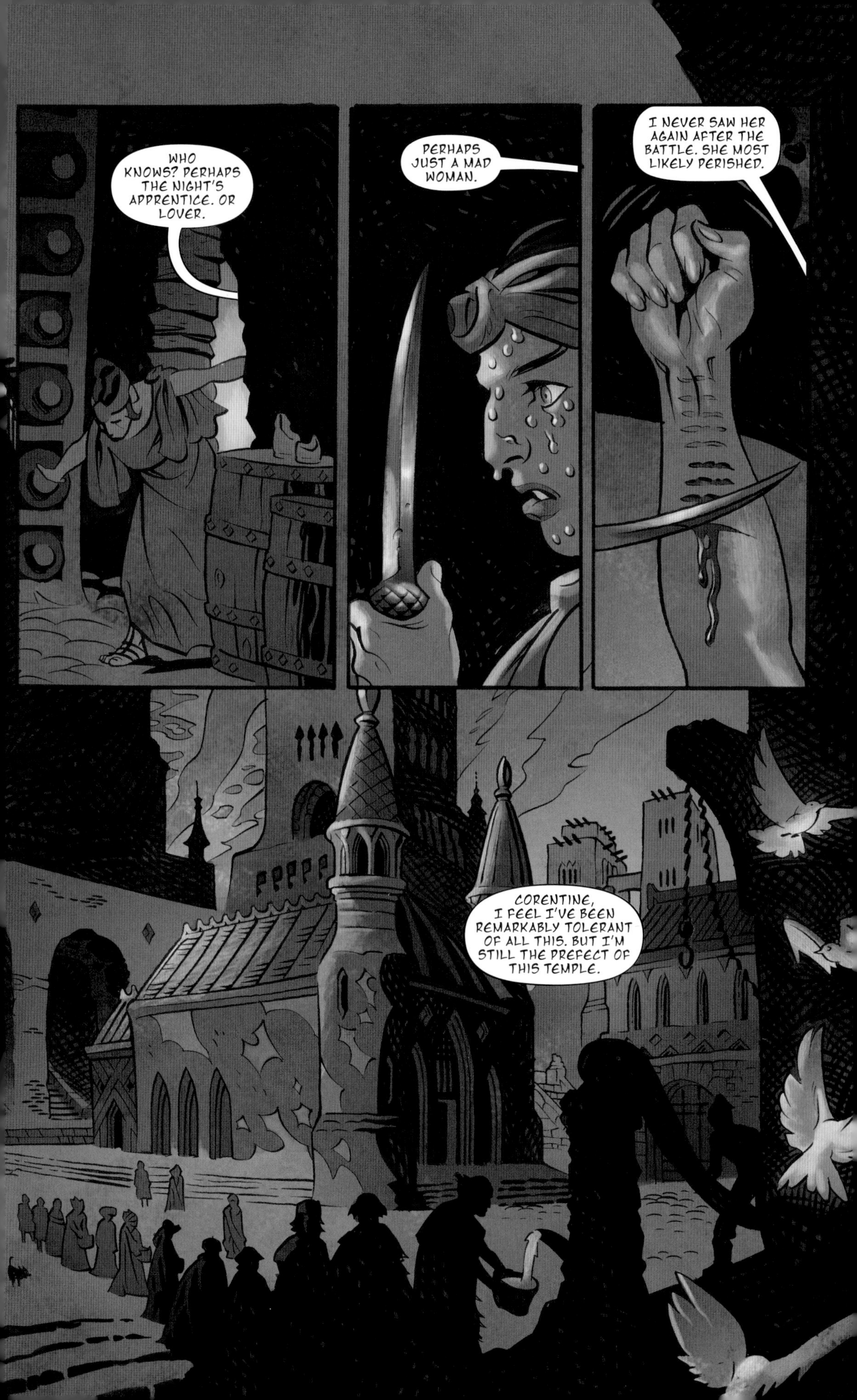
WHO KNOWS? PERHAPS THE NIGHT'S APPRENTICE. OR LOVER.
PERHAPS JUST A MAD WOMAN.
I NEVER SAW HER AGAIN AFTER THE BATTLE. SHE MOST LIKELY PERISHED.
CORENTINE, I FEEL I'VE BEEN REMARKABLY TOLERANT OF ALL THIS. BUT I'M STILL THE PREFECT OF THIS TEMPLE.

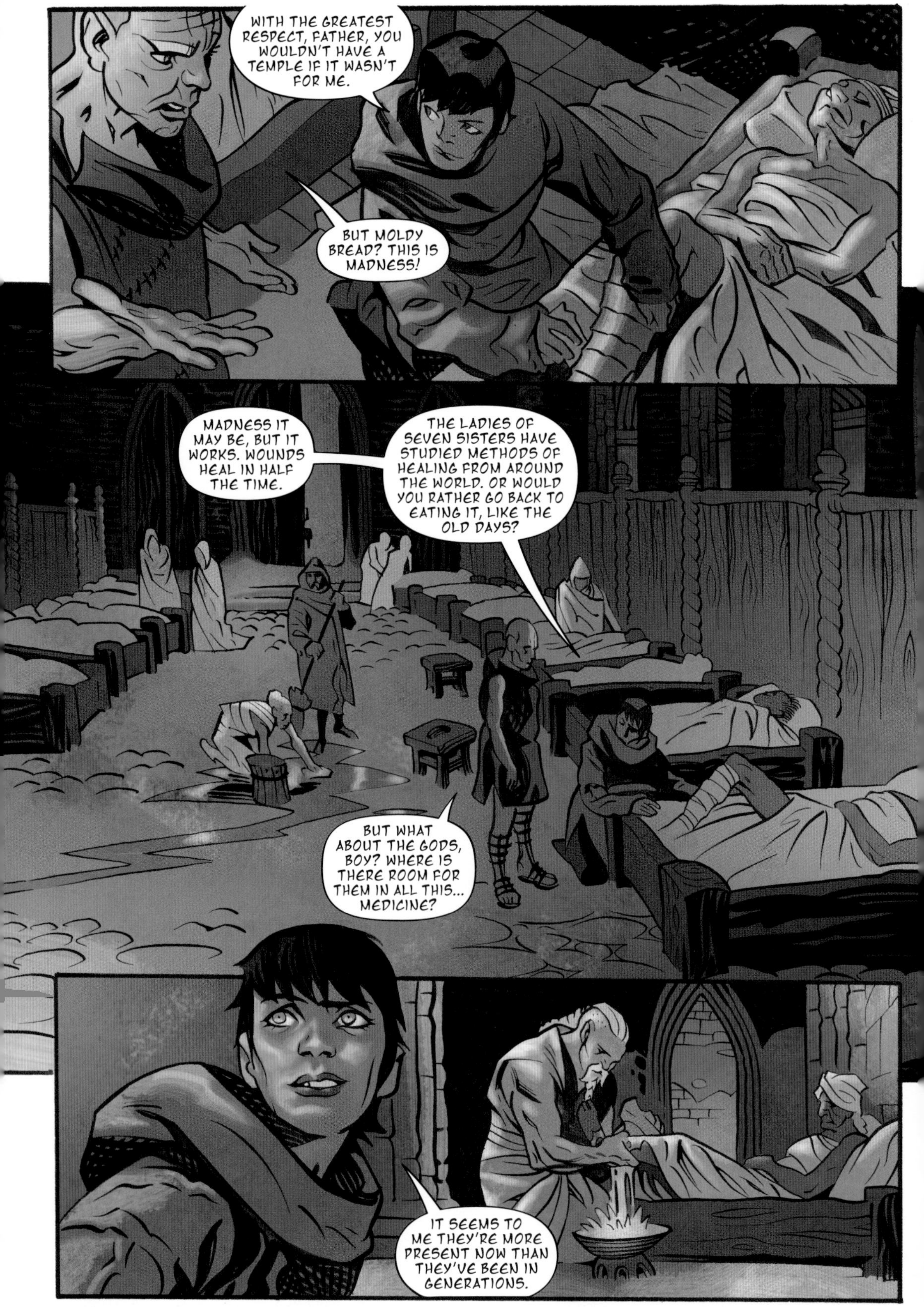
WITH THE GREATEST RESPECT, FATHER, YOU WOULDN'T HAVE A TEMPLE IF IT WASN'T FOR ME.
BUT MOLDY BREAD? THIS IS MADNESS!
MADNESS IT MAY BE, BUT IT WORKS. WOUNDS HEAL IN HALF THE TIME.
THE LADIES OF SEVEN SISTERS HAVE STUDIED METHODS OF HEALING FROM AROUND THE WORLD. OR WOULD YOU RATHER GO BACK TO EATING IT, LIKE THE OLD DAYS?
BUT WHAT ABOUT THE GODS, BOY? WHERE IS THERE ROOM FOR THEM IN ALL THIS... MEDICINE?
IT SEEMS TO ME THEY'RE MORE PRESENT NOW THAN THEY'VE BEEN IN GENERATIONS.

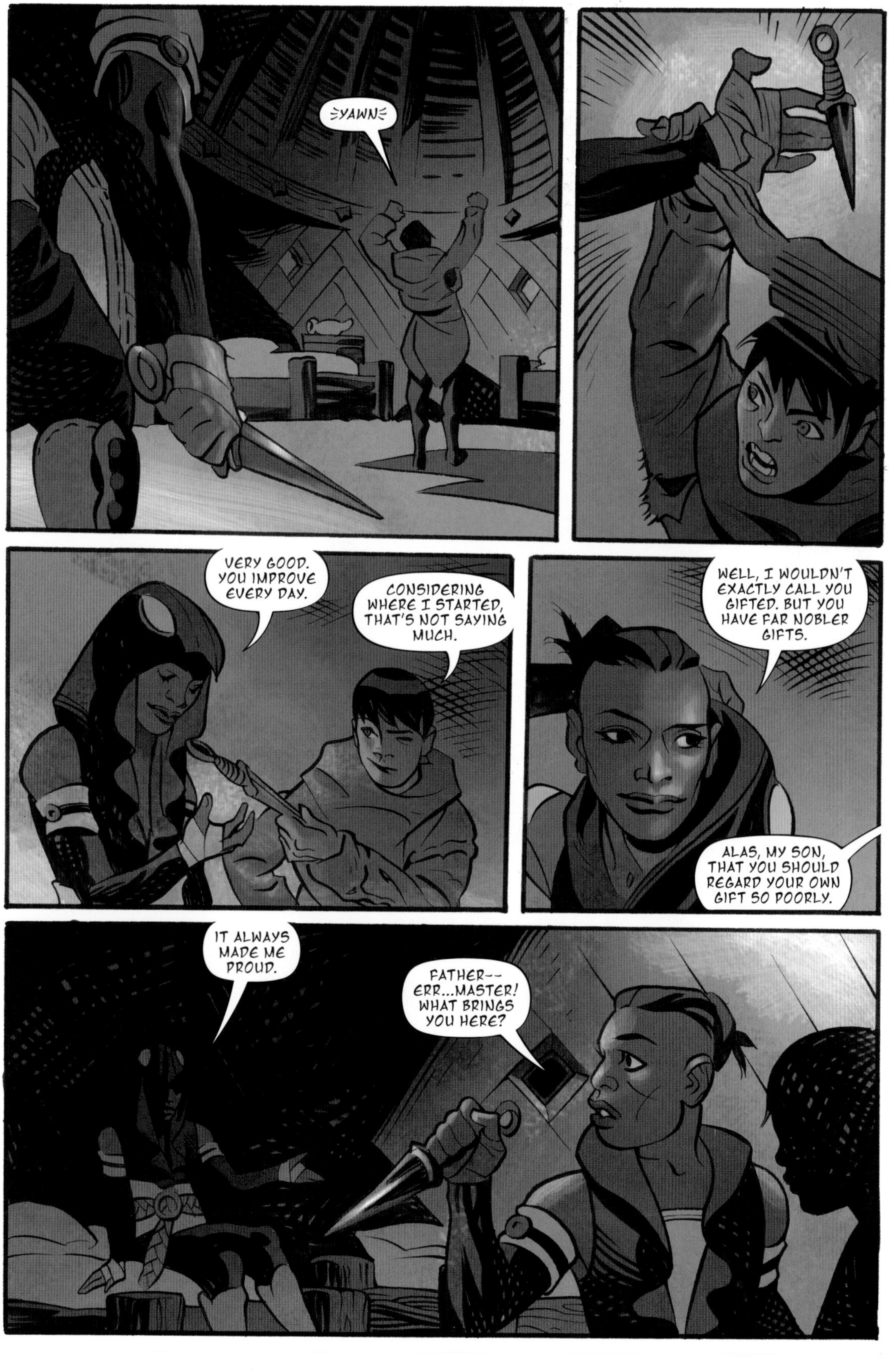
YAWN
VERY GOOD. YOU IMPROVE EVERY DAY.
CONSIDERING WHERE I STARTED, THAT'S NOT SAYING MUCH.
WELL, I WOULDN'T EXACTLY CALL YOU GIFTED. BUT YOU HAVE FAR NOBLER GIFTS.
ALAS, MY SON, THAT YOU SHOULD REGARD YOUR OWN GIFT SO POORLY.
IT ALWAYS MADE ME PROUD.
FATHER-- ERR...MASTER! WHAT BRINGS YOU HERE?

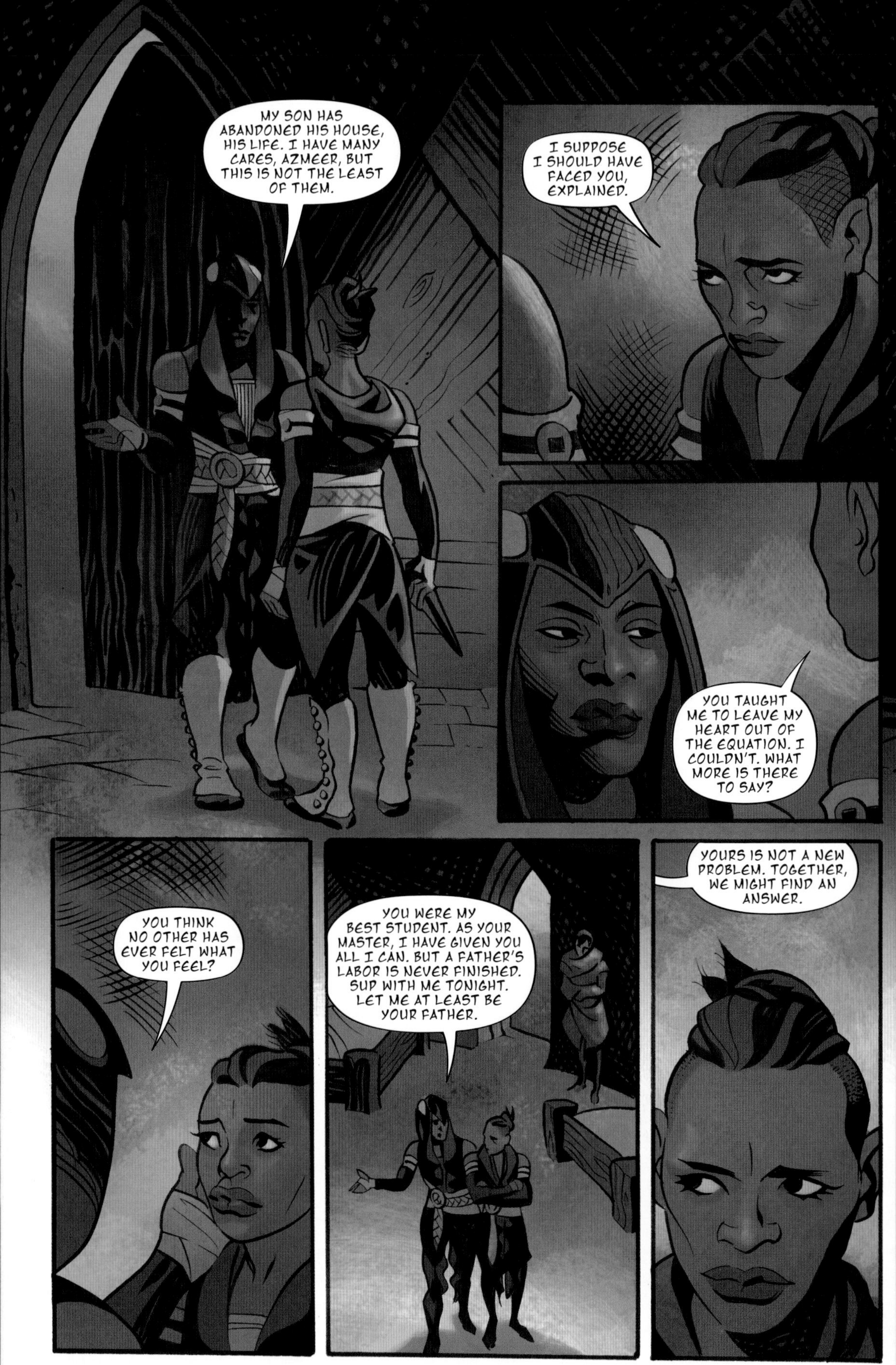
MY SON HAS ABANDONED HIS HOUSE, HIS LIFE. I HAVE MANY CARES, AZMEER, BUT THIS IS NOT THE LEAST OF THEM.
I SUPPOSE I SHOULD HAVE FACED YOU, EXPLAINED.
YOU TAUGHT ME TO LEAVE MY HEART OUT OF THE EQUATION. I COULDN'T. WHAT MORE IS THERE TO SAY?
YOU THINK NO OTHER HAS EVER FELT WHAT YOU FEEL?
YOU WERE MY BEST STUDENT. AS YOUR MASTER, I HAVE GIVEN YOU ALL I CAN. BUT A FATHER'S LABOR IS NEVER FINISHED. SUP WITH ME TONIGHT. LET ME AT LEAST BE YOUR FATHER.
YOURS IS NOT A NEW PROBLEM. TOGETHER, WE MIGHT FIND AN ANSWER.

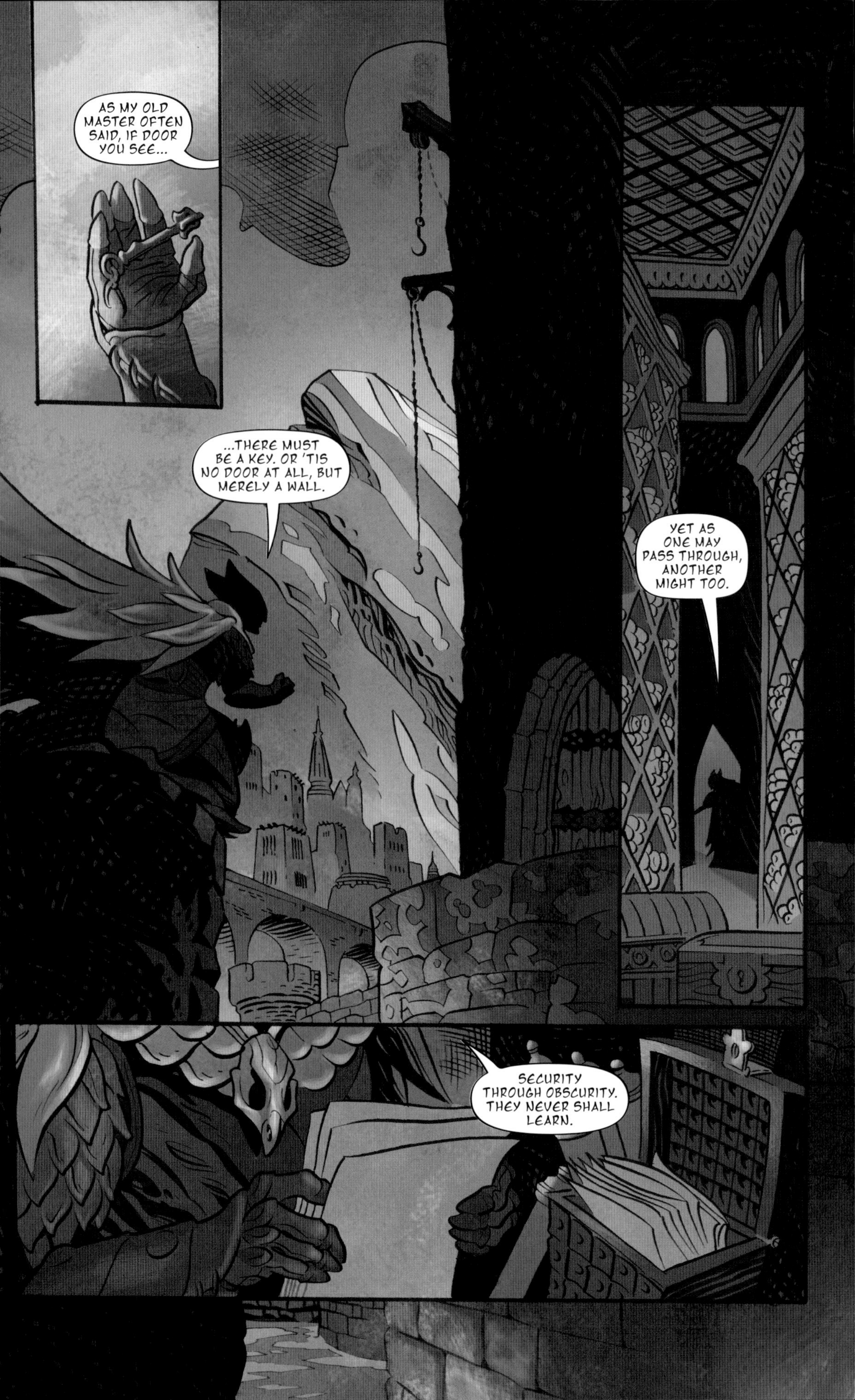
AS MY OLD MASTER OFTEN SAID, IF DOOR YOU SEE...
...THERE MUST BE A KEY. OR 'TIS NO DOOR AT ALL, BUT MERELY A WALL.
YET AS ONE MAY PASS THROUGH, ANOTHER MIGHT TOO.
SECURITY THROUGH OBSCURITY. THEY NEVER SHALL LEARN.

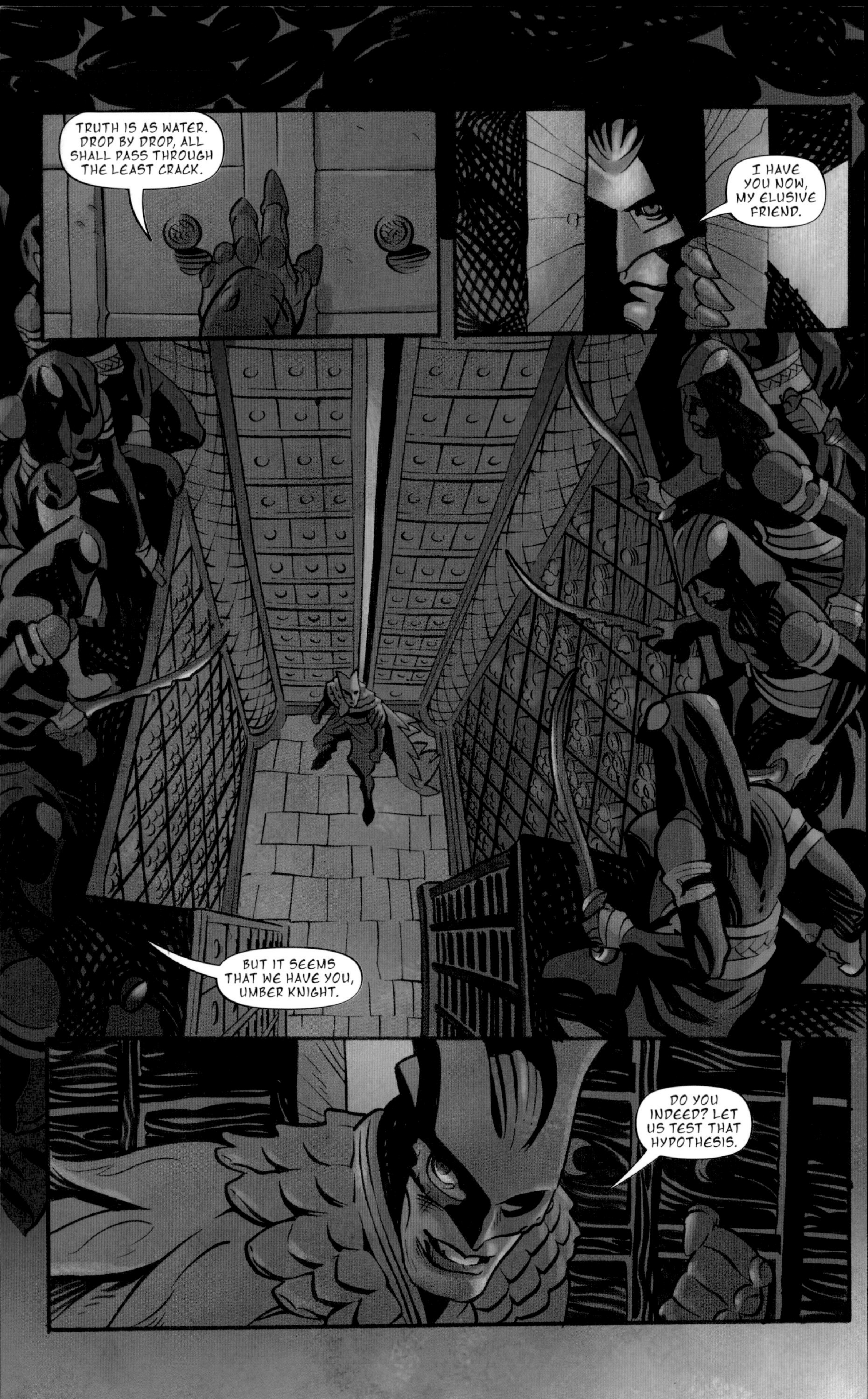
TRUTH IS AS WATER. DROP BY DROP, ALL SHALL PASS THROUGH THE LEAST CRACK.
I HAVE YOU NOW, MY ELUSIVE FRIEND.
BUT IT SEEMS THAT WE HAVE YOU, UMBER KNIGHT.
DO YOU INDEED? LET US TEST THAT HYPOTHESIS.

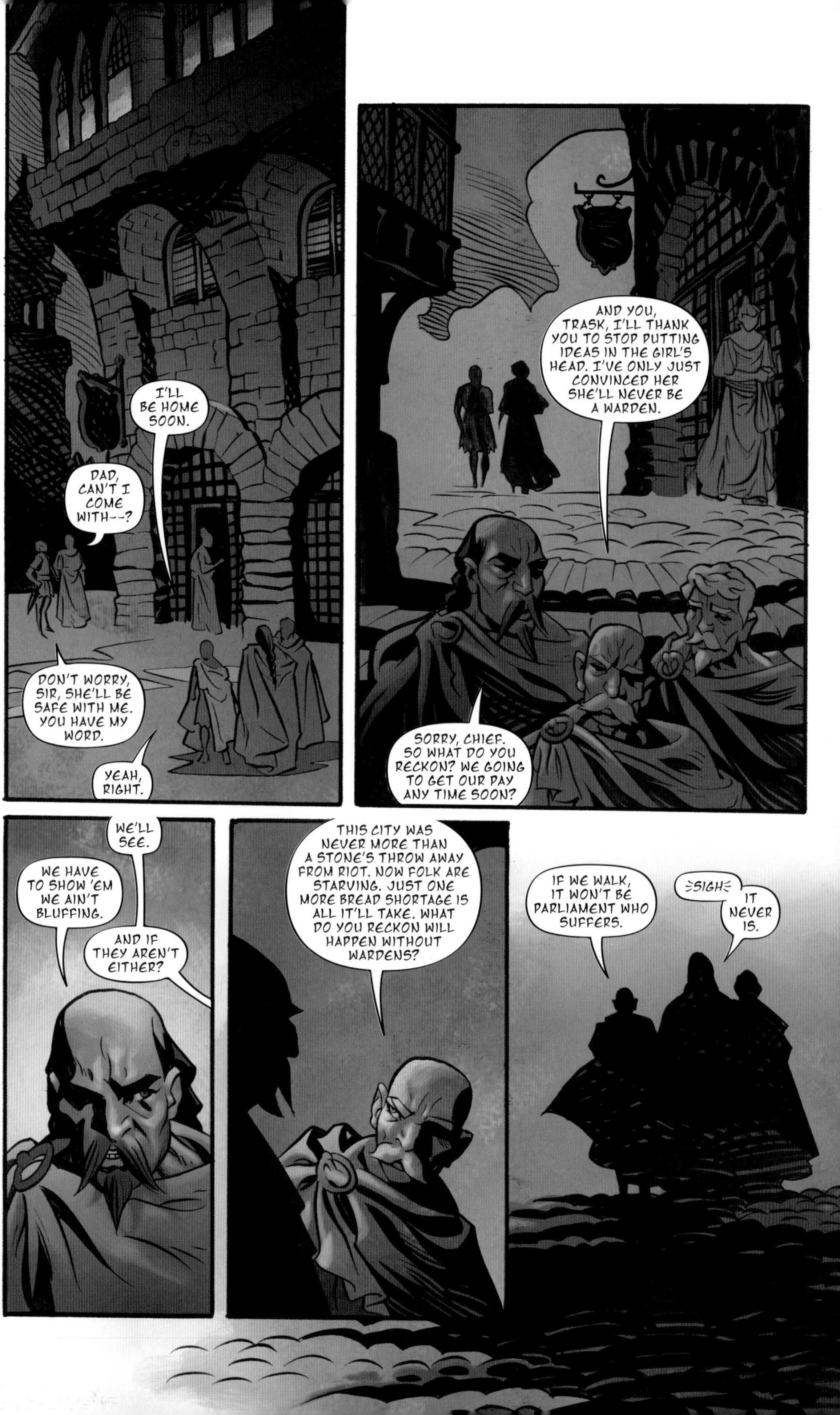
DAD, CAN'T I COME WITH--?
I'LL BE HOME SOON.
DON'T WORRY, SIR, SHE'LL BE SAFE WITH ME. YOU HAVE MY WORD.
YEAH, RIGHT.
AND YOU, TRASK, I'LL THANK YOU TO STOP PUTTING IDEAS IN THE GIRL'S HEAD. I'VE ONLY JUST CONVINCED HER SHE'LL NEVER BE A WARDEN.
SORRY, CHIEF. SO WHAT DO YOU RECKON? WE GOING TO GET OUR PAY ANY TIME SOON?
WE'LL SEE.
WE HAVE TO SHOW 'EM WE AIN'T BLUFFING.
AND IF THEY AREN'T EITHER?
THIS CITY WAS NEVER MORE THAN A STONE'S THROW AWAY FROM RIOT. NOW FOLK ARE STARVING. JUST ONE MORE BREAD SHORTAGE IS ALL IT'LL TAKE. WHAT DO YOU RECKON WILL HAPPEN WITHOUT WARDENS?
IF WE WALK, IT WON'T BE PARLIAMENT WHO SUFFERS.
SIGH
IT NEVER IS.

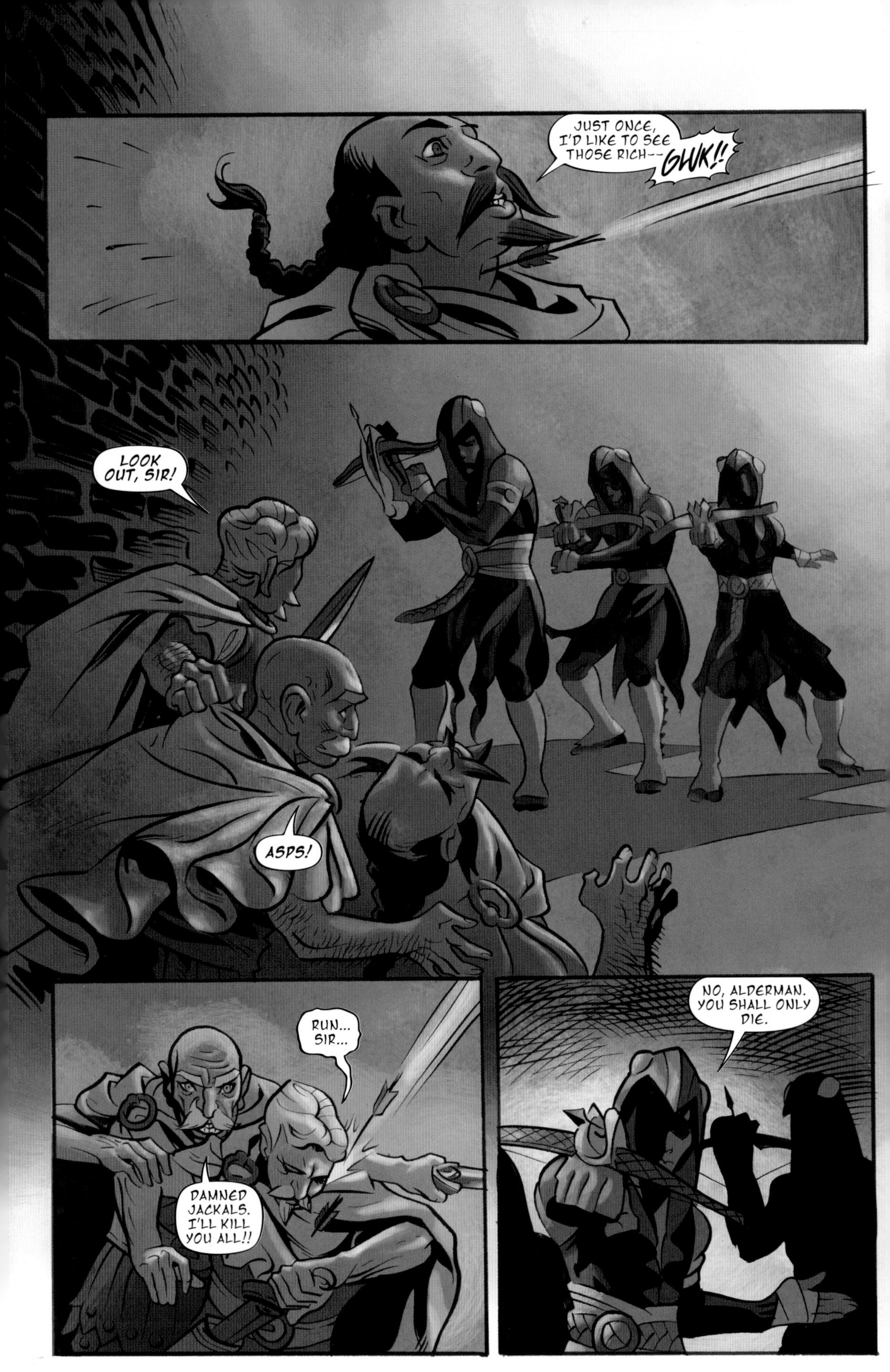
JUST ONCE, I'D LIKE TO SEE THOSE RICH--
GWK!!
LOOK OUT, SIR!
ASPS!
RUN... SIR...
DAMNED JACKALS. I'LL KILL YOU ALL!!
NO, ALDERMAN. YOU SHALL ONLY DIE.

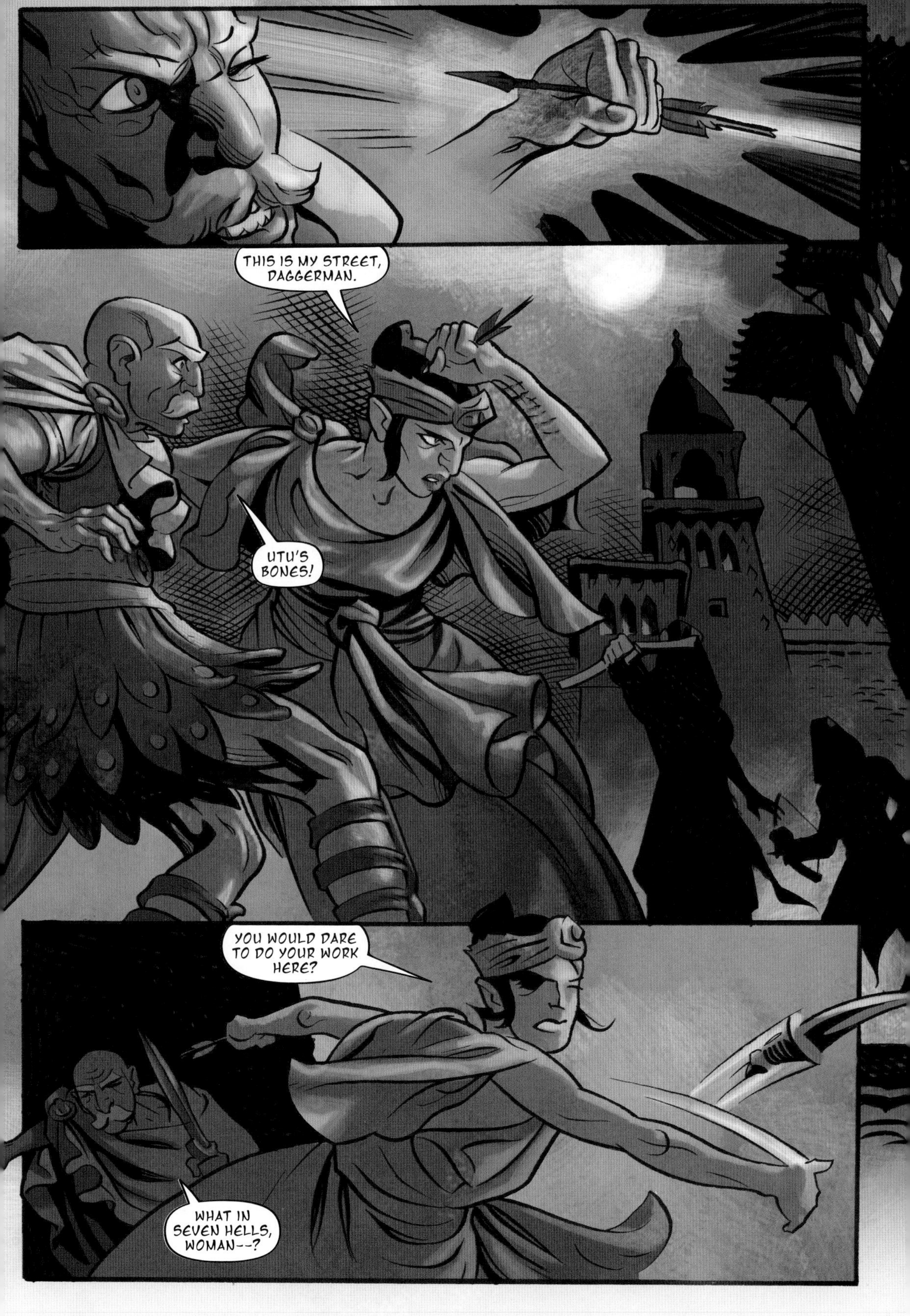
THIS IS MY STREET, DAGGERMAN.
UTU'S BONES!
YOU WOULD DARE TO DO YOUR WORK HERE?
WHAT IN SEVEN HELLS, WOMAN--?

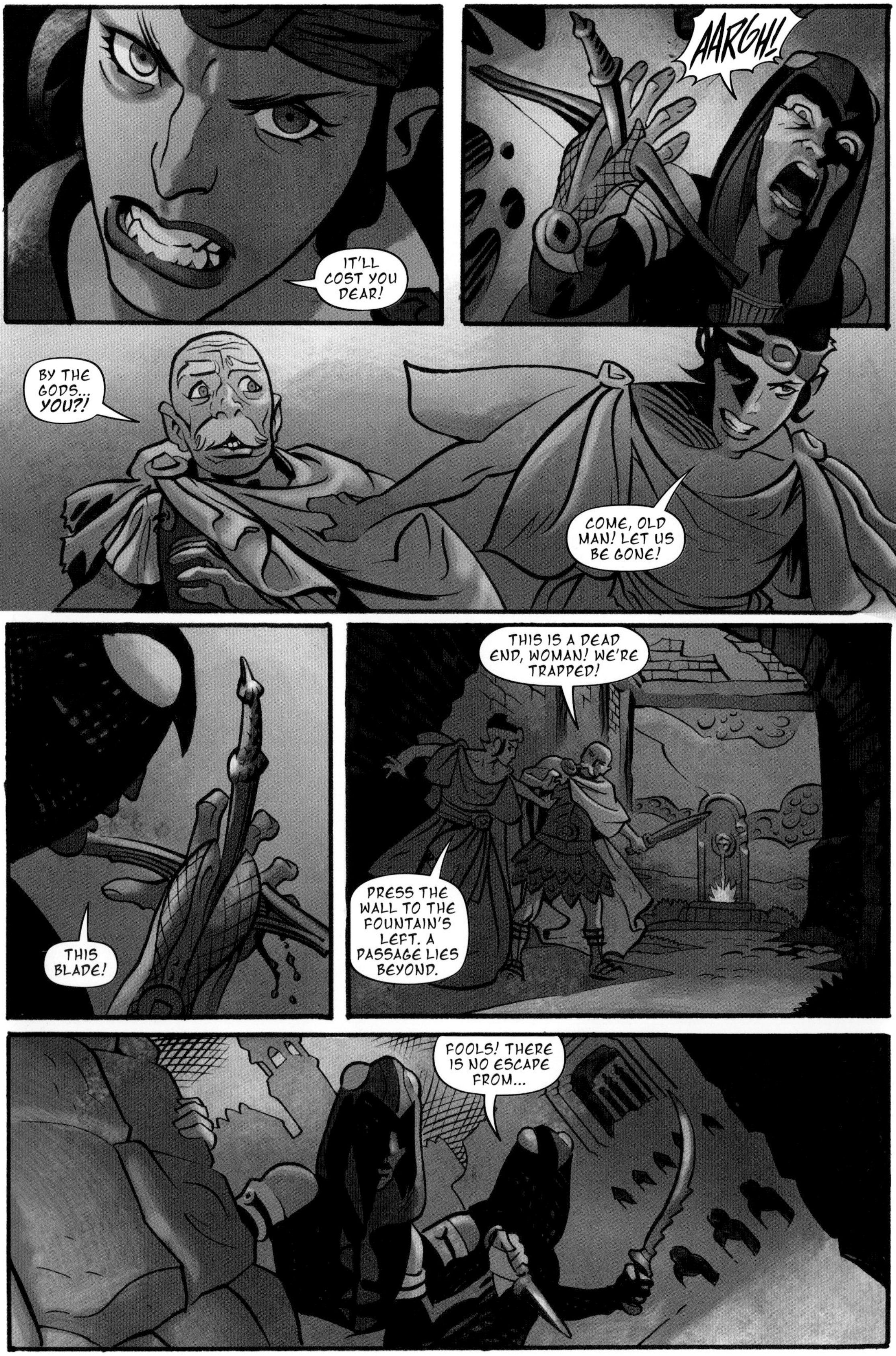
IT'LL COST YOU DEAR!
AARGH!
BY THE GODS... YOU?!
COME, OLD MAN! LET US BE GONE!
THIS BLADE!
THIS IS A DEAD END, WOMAN! WE'RE TRAPPED!
PRESS THE WALL TO THE FOUNTAIN'S LEFT. A PASSAGE LIES BEYOND.
FOOLS! THERE IS NO ESCAPE FROM...

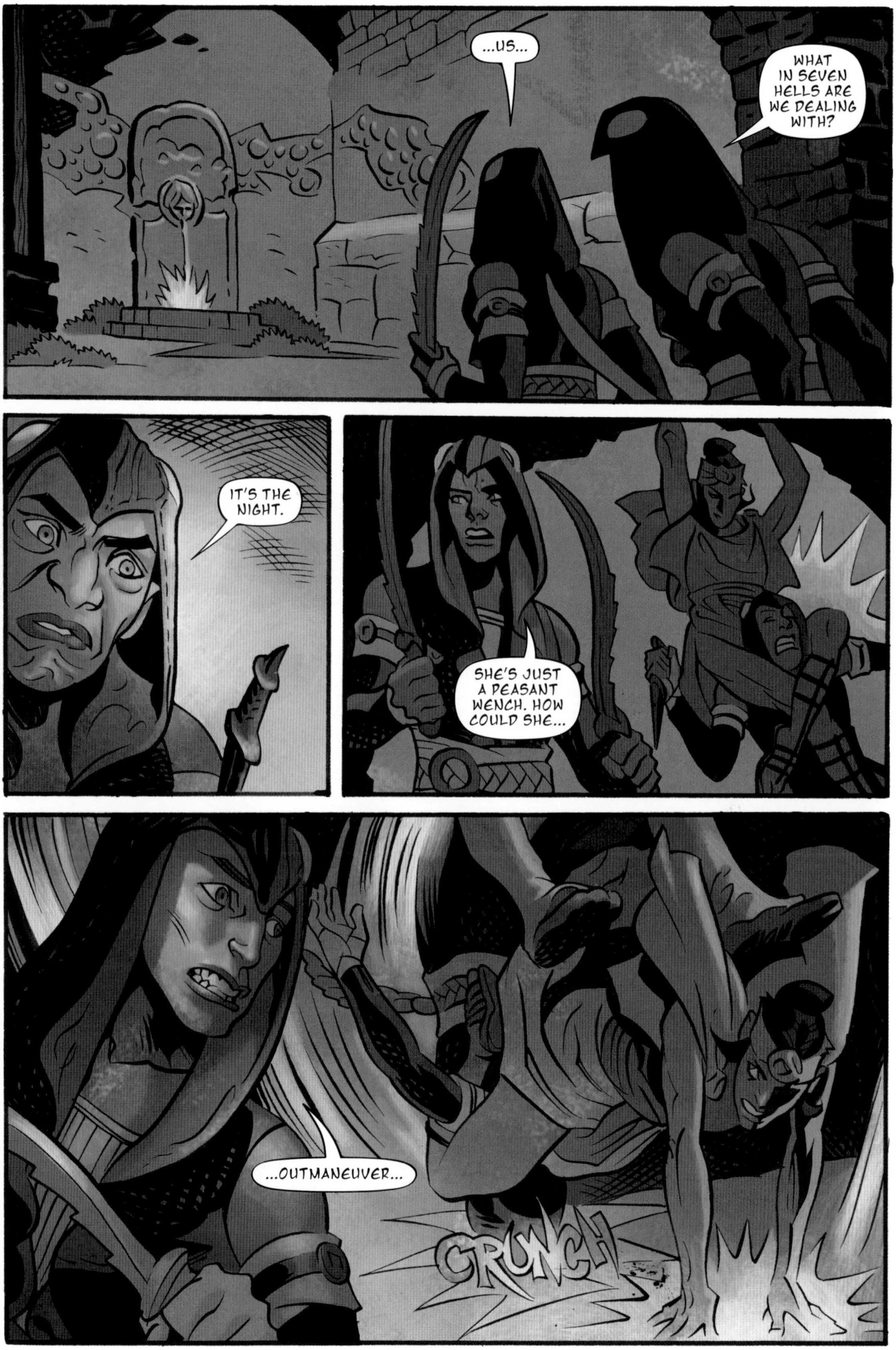
...US...
WHAT IN SEVEN HELLS ARE WE DEALING WITH?
IT'S THE NIGHT.
SHE'S JUST A PEASANT WENCH. HOW COULD SHE...
...OUTMANEUVER...
CRUNCH

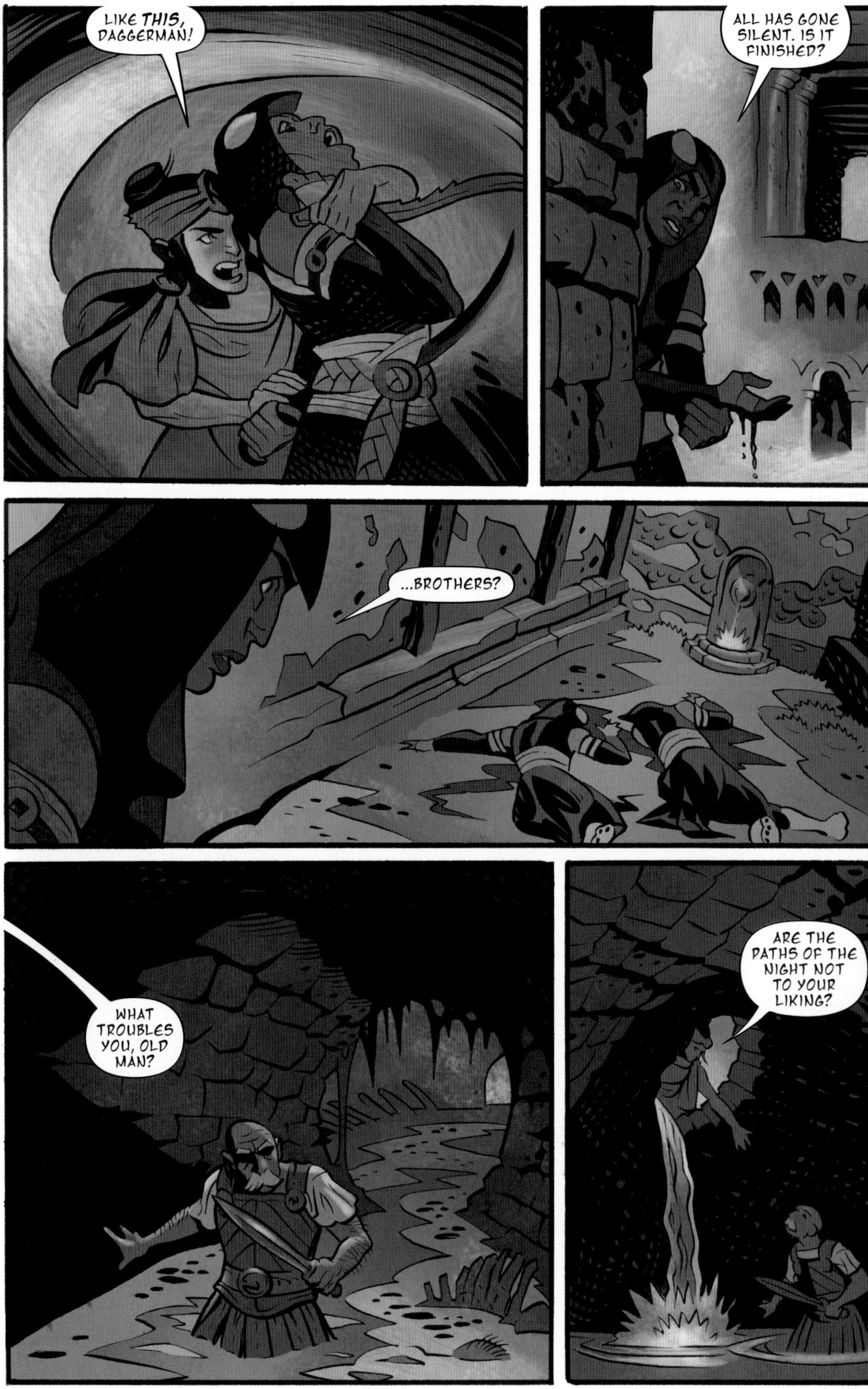
LIKE THIS, DAGGERMAN!
ALL HAS GONE SILENT. IS IT FINISHED?
...BROTHERS?
WHAT TROUBLES YOU, OLD MAN?
ARE THE PATHS OF THE NIGHT NOT TO YOUR LIKING?

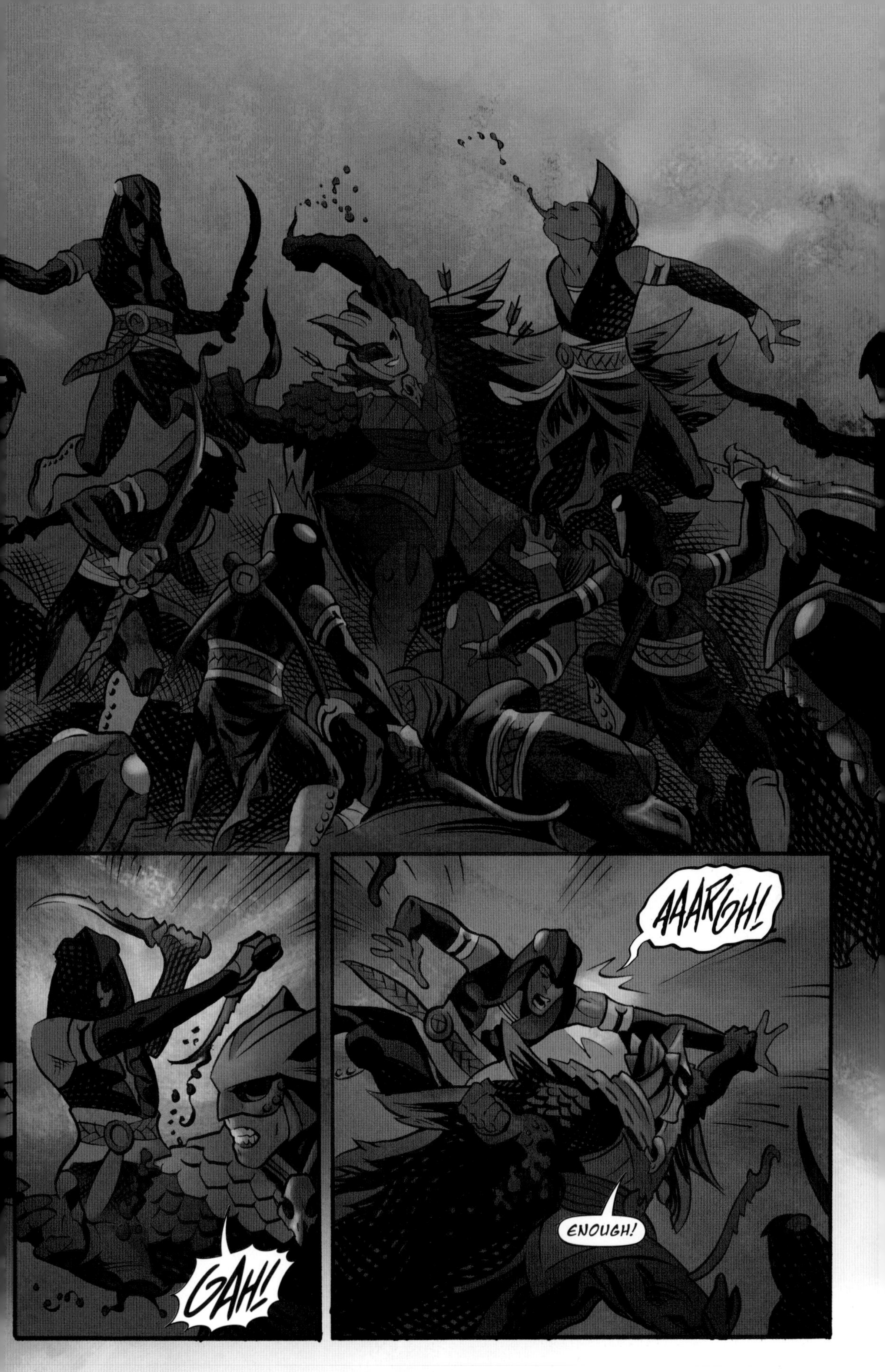
GAH!
AAARGH!
ENOUGH!

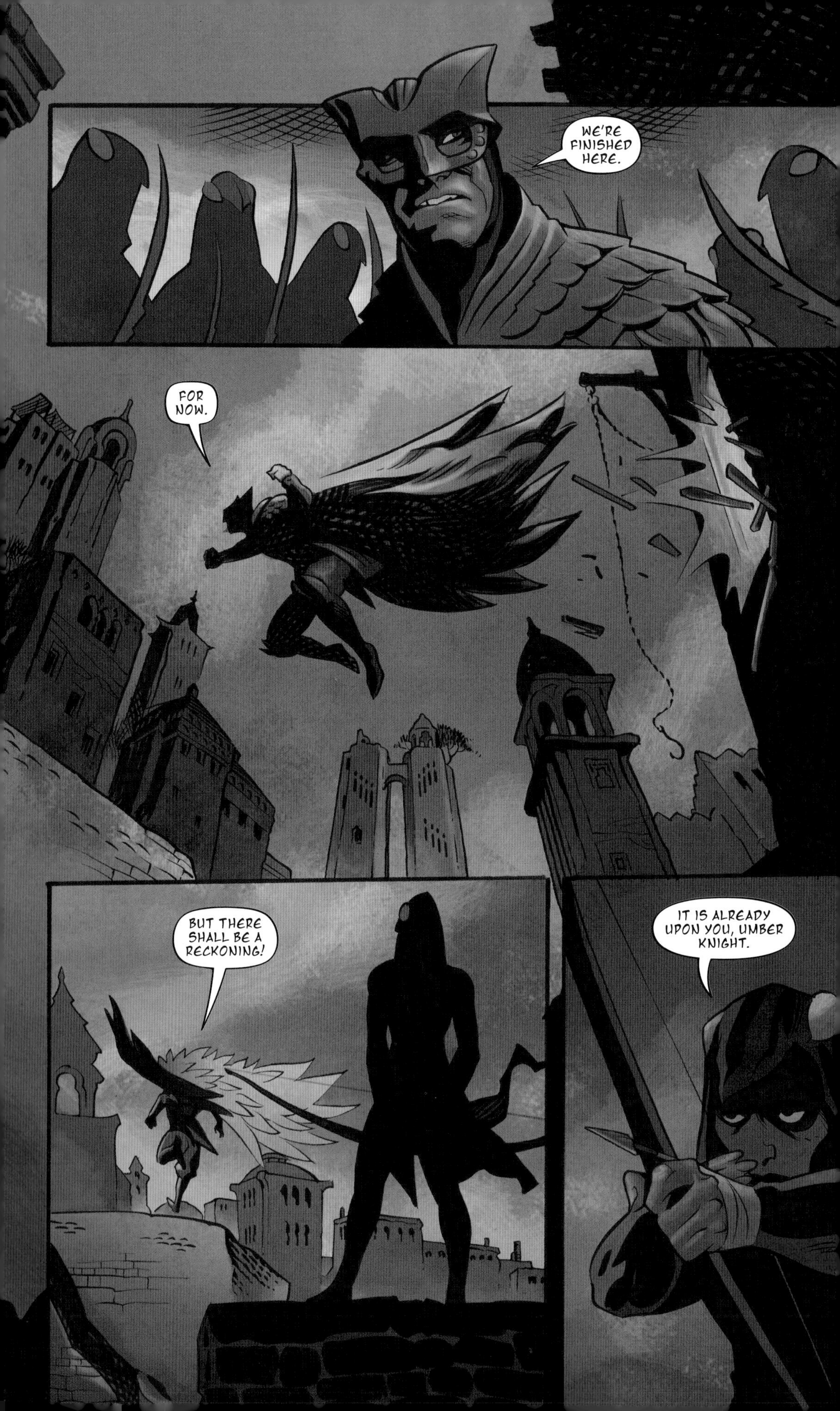

WE'RE FINISHED HERE.
FOR NOW.
BUT THERE SHALL BE A RECKONING!
IT IS ALREADY UPON YOU, UMBER KNIGHT.

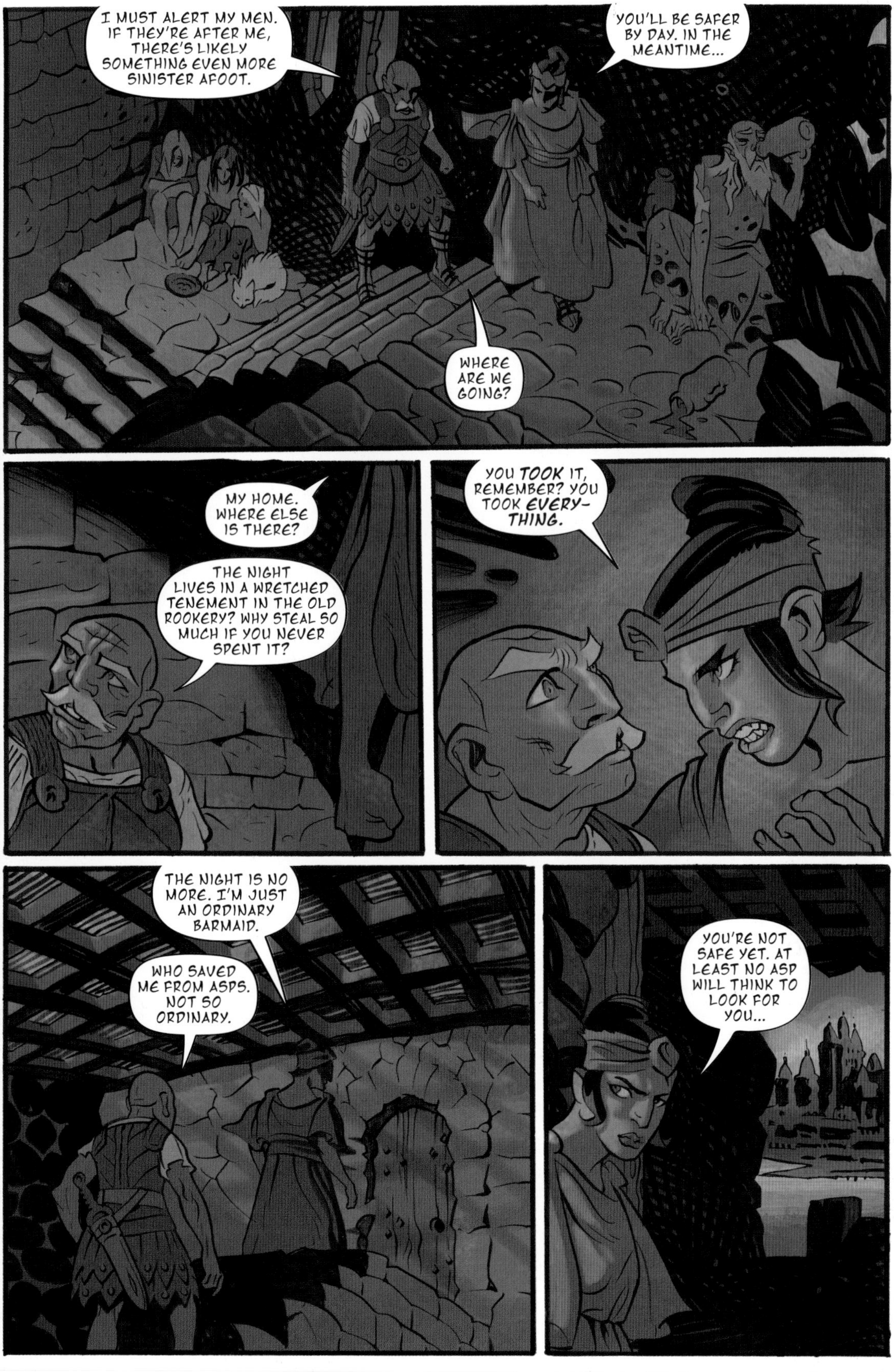
I MUST ALERT MY MEN. IF THEY'RE AFTER ME, THERE'S LIKELY SOMETHING EVEN MORE SINISTER AFOOT.
YOU'LL BE SAFER BY DAY. IN THE MEANTIME...
WHERE ARE WE GOING?
MY HOME. WHERE ELSE IS THERE?
THE NIGHT LIVES IN A WRETCHED TENEMENT IN THE OLD ROOKERY? WHY STEAL SO MUCH IF YOU NEVER SPENT IT?
YOU *TOOK* IT, REMEMBER? YOU TOOK *EVERY-THING.*
THE NIGHT IS NO MORE. I'M JUST AN ORDINARY BARMAID.
WHO SAVED ME FROM ASPS. NOT SO ORDINARY.
YOU'RE NOT SAFE YET. AT LEAST NO ASP WILL THINK TO LOOK FOR YOU...

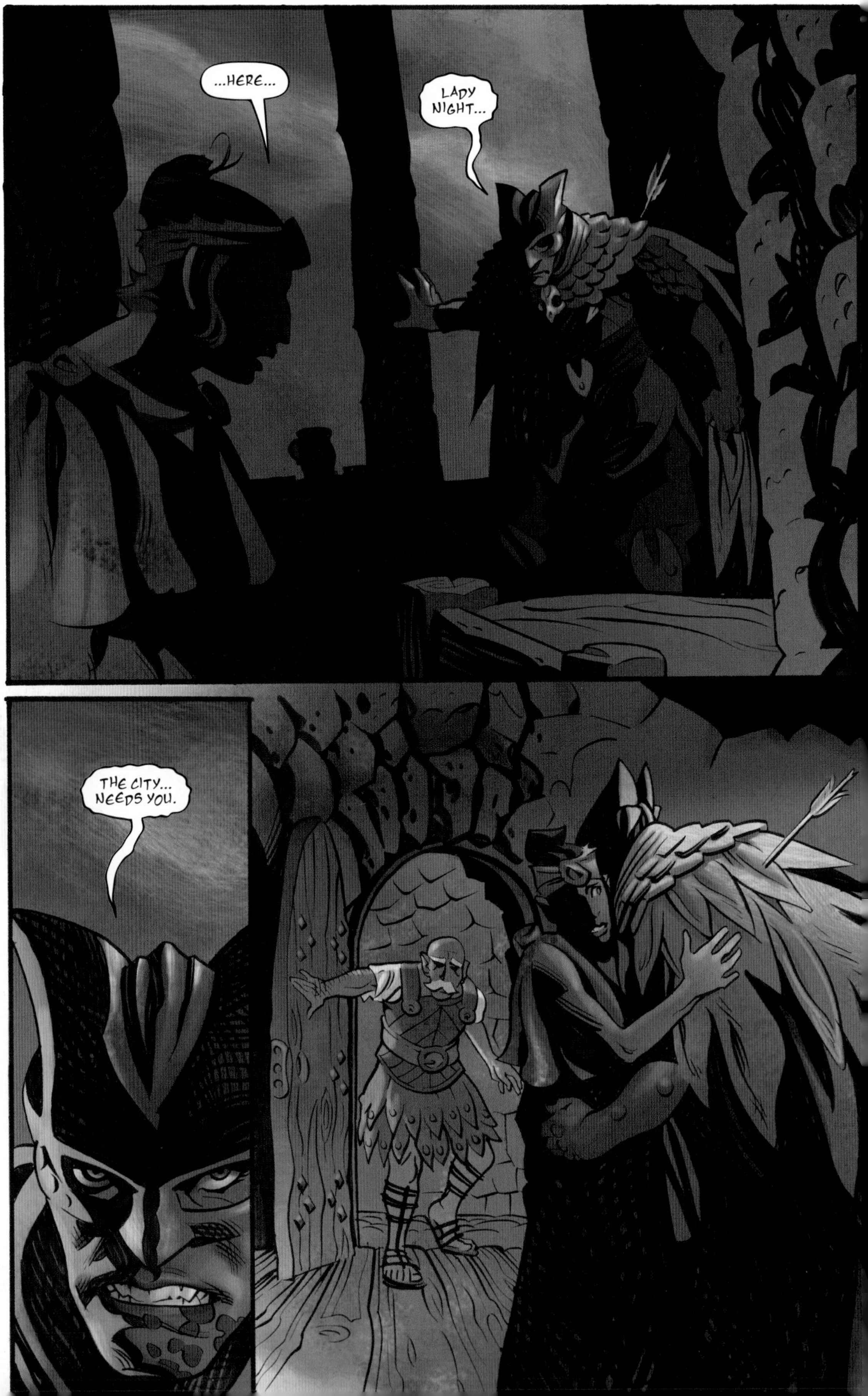
...HERE...
LADY NIGHT...
THE CITY... NEEDS YOU.

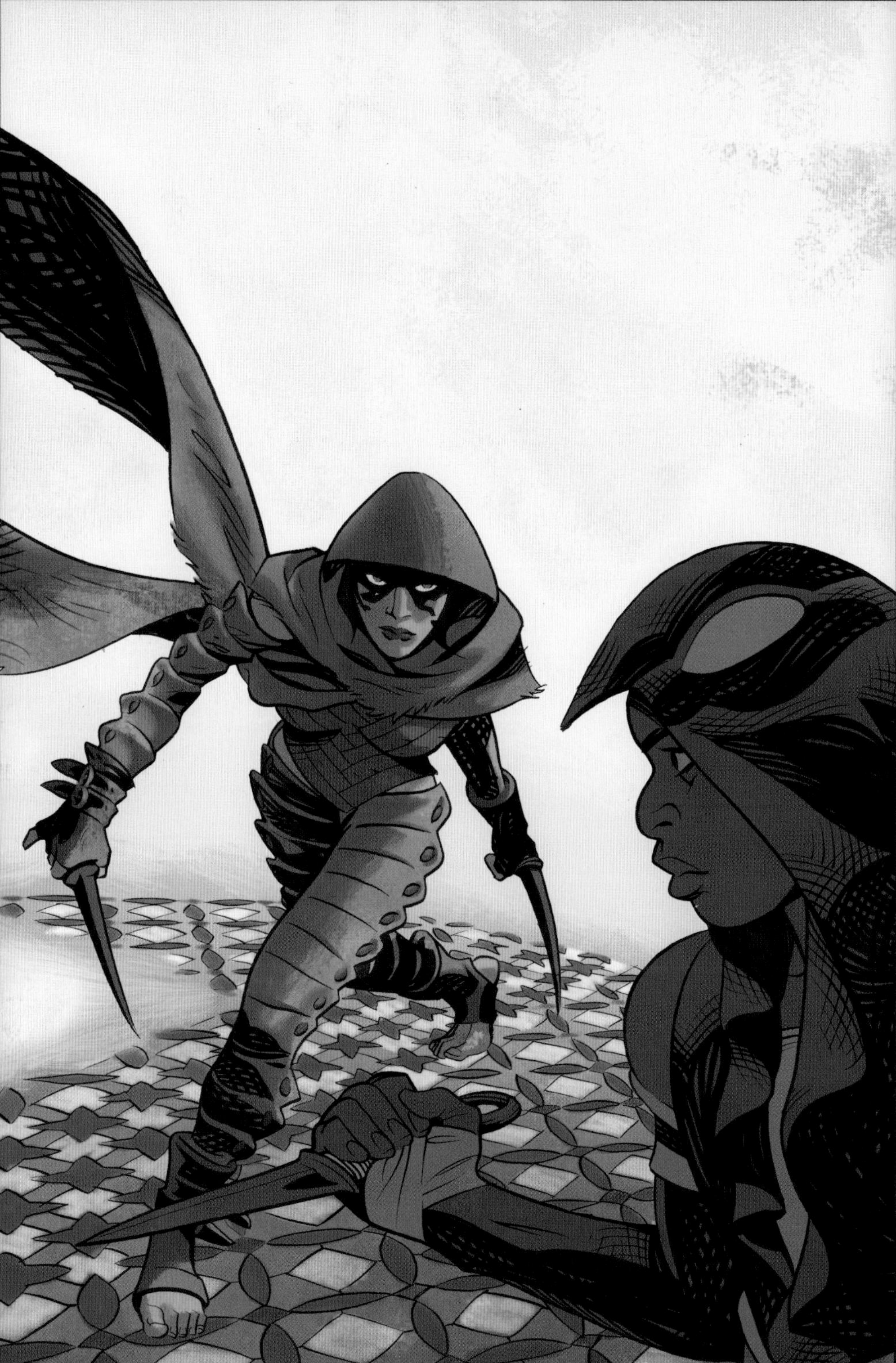

Chapter 2

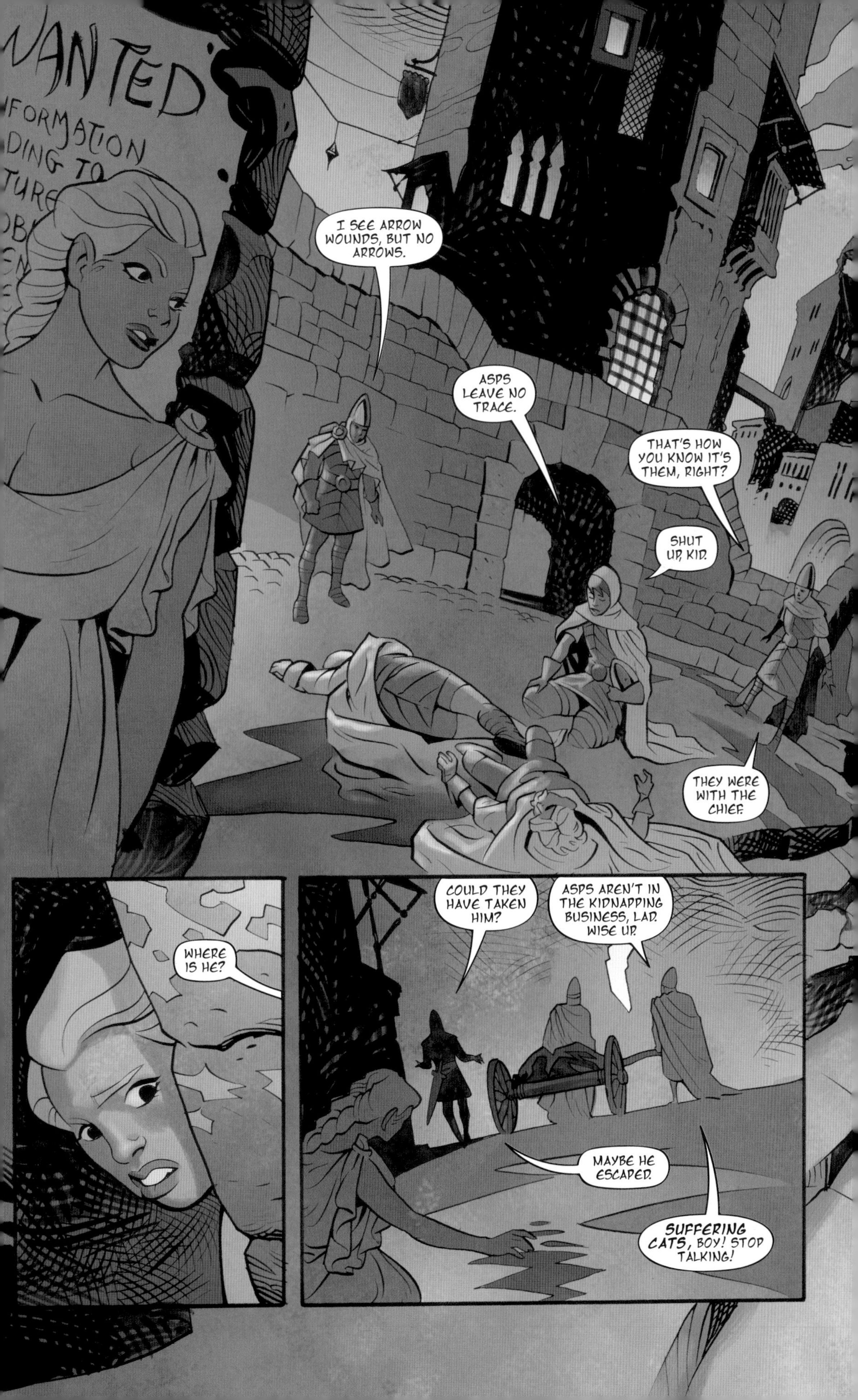
I SEE ARROW WOUNDS, BUT NO ARROWS.
ASPS LEAVE NO TRACE.
THAT'S HOW YOU KNOW IT'S THEM, RIGHT?
SHUT UP, KID.
THEY WERE WITH THE CHIEF.
WHERE IS HE?
COULD THEY HAVE TAKEN HIM?
ASPS AREN'T IN THE KIDNAPPING BUSINESS, LAD. WISE UP.
MAYBE HE ESCAPED.
SUFFERING CATS, BOY! STOP TALKING!

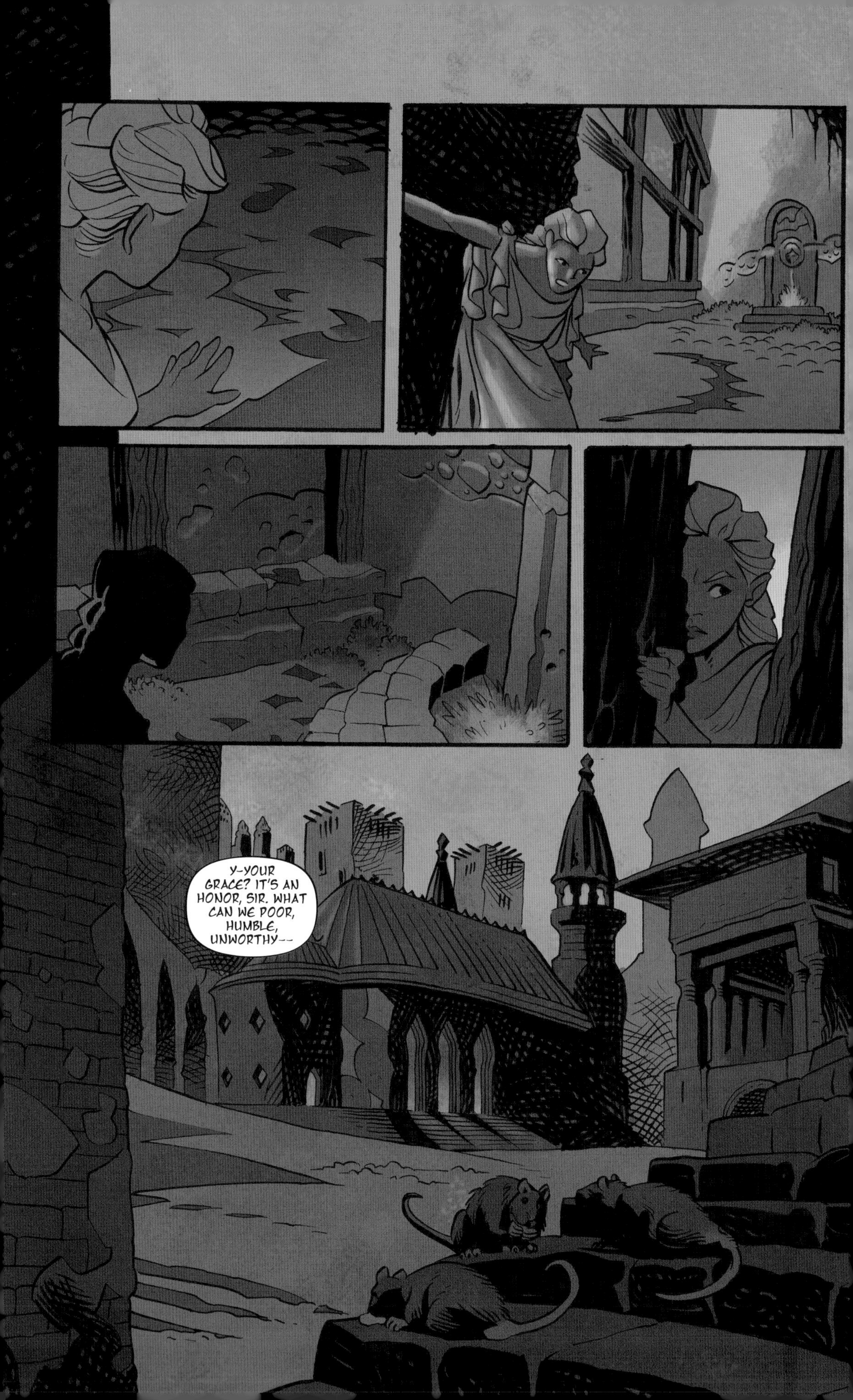
Y-YOUR GRACE? IT'S AN HONOR, SIR. WHAT CAN WE POOR, HUMBLE, UNWORTHY--

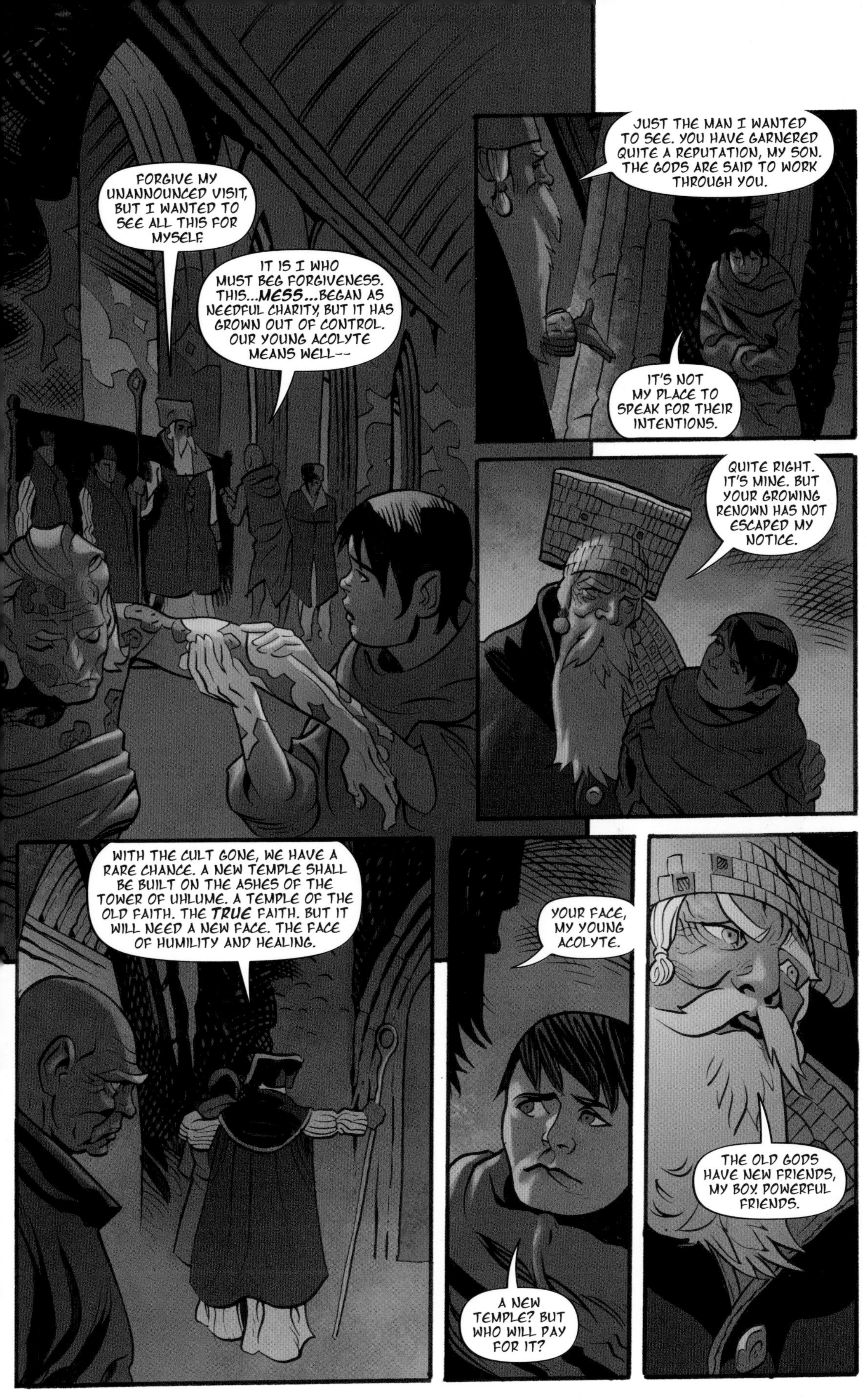
FORGIVE MY UNANNOUNCED VISIT, BUT I WANTED TO SEE ALL THIS FOR MYSELF.
IT IS I WHO MUST BEG FORGIVENESS. THIS...MESS...BEGAN AS NEEDFUL CHARITY, BUT IT HAS GROWN OUT OF CONTROL. OUR YOUNG ACOLYTE MEANS WELL--
JUST THE MAN I WANTED TO SEE. YOU HAVE GARNERED QUITE A REPUTATION, MY SON. THE GODS ARE SAID TO WORK THROUGH YOU.
IT'S NOT MY PLACE TO SPEAK FOR THEIR INTENTIONS.
QUITE RIGHT. IT'S MINE. BUT YOUR GROWING RENOWN HAS NOT ESCAPED MY NOTICE.
WITH THE CULT GONE, WE HAVE A RARE CHANCE. A NEW TEMPLE SHALL BE BUILT ON THE ASHES OF THE TOWER OF UHLUME. A TEMPLE OF THE OLD FAITH. THE TRUE FAITH. BUT IT WILL NEED A NEW FACE. THE FACE OF HUMILITY AND HEALING.
YOUR FACE, MY YOUNG ACOLYTE.
A NEW TEMPLE? BUT WHO WILL PAY FOR IT?
THE OLD GODS HAVE NEW FRIENDS, MY BOY. POWERFUL FRIENDS.

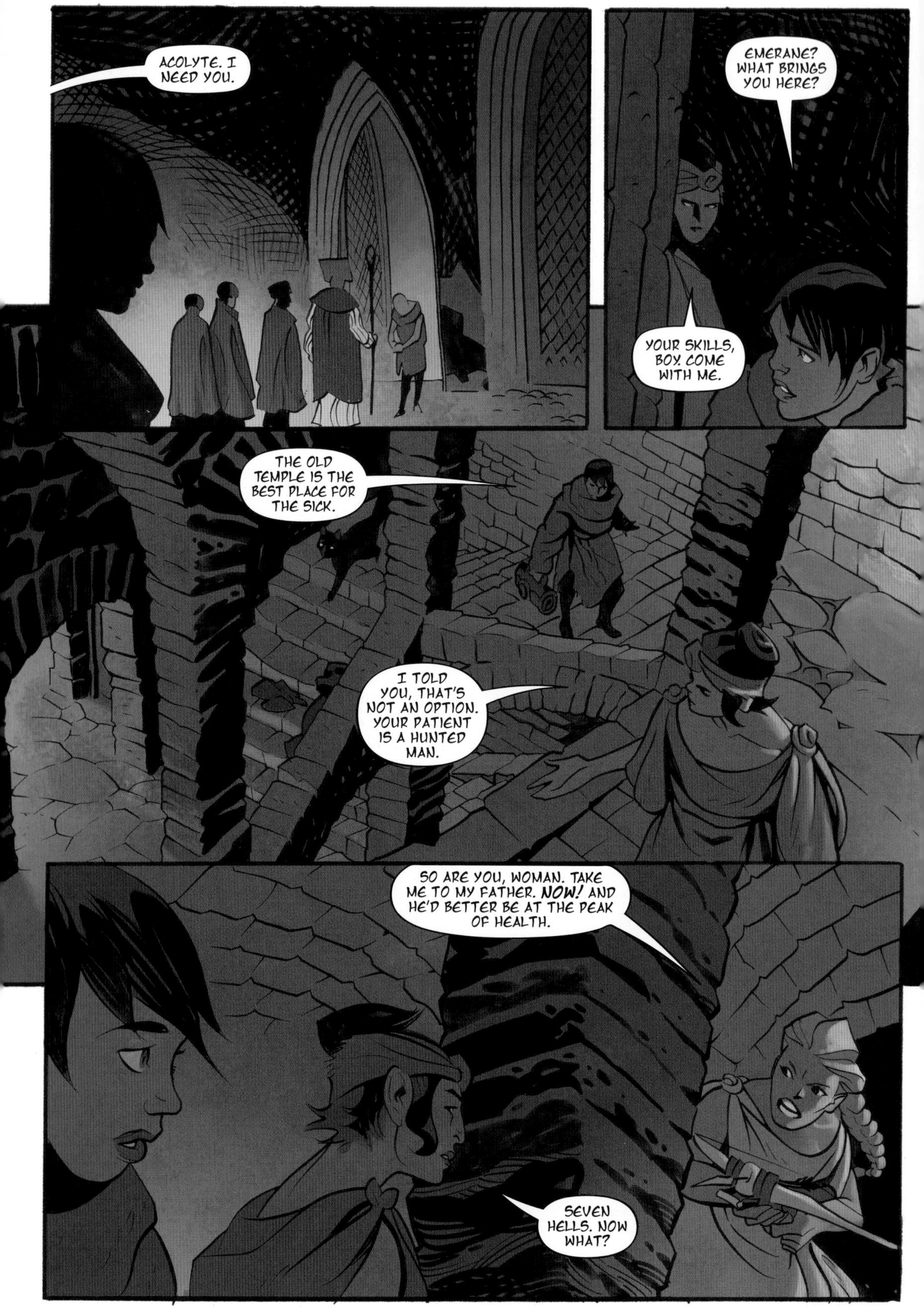
ACOLYTE. I NEED YOU.
EMERANE? WHAT BRINGS YOU HERE?
YOUR SKILLS, BOY. COME WITH ME.
THE OLD TEMPLE IS THE BEST PLACE FOR THE SICK.
I TOLD YOU, THAT'S NOT AN OPTION. YOUR PATIENT IS A HUNTED MAN.
SO ARE YOU, WOMAN. TAKE ME TO MY FATHER. NOW! AND HE'D BETTER BE AT THE PEAK OF HEALTH.
SEVEN HELLS. NOW WHAT?

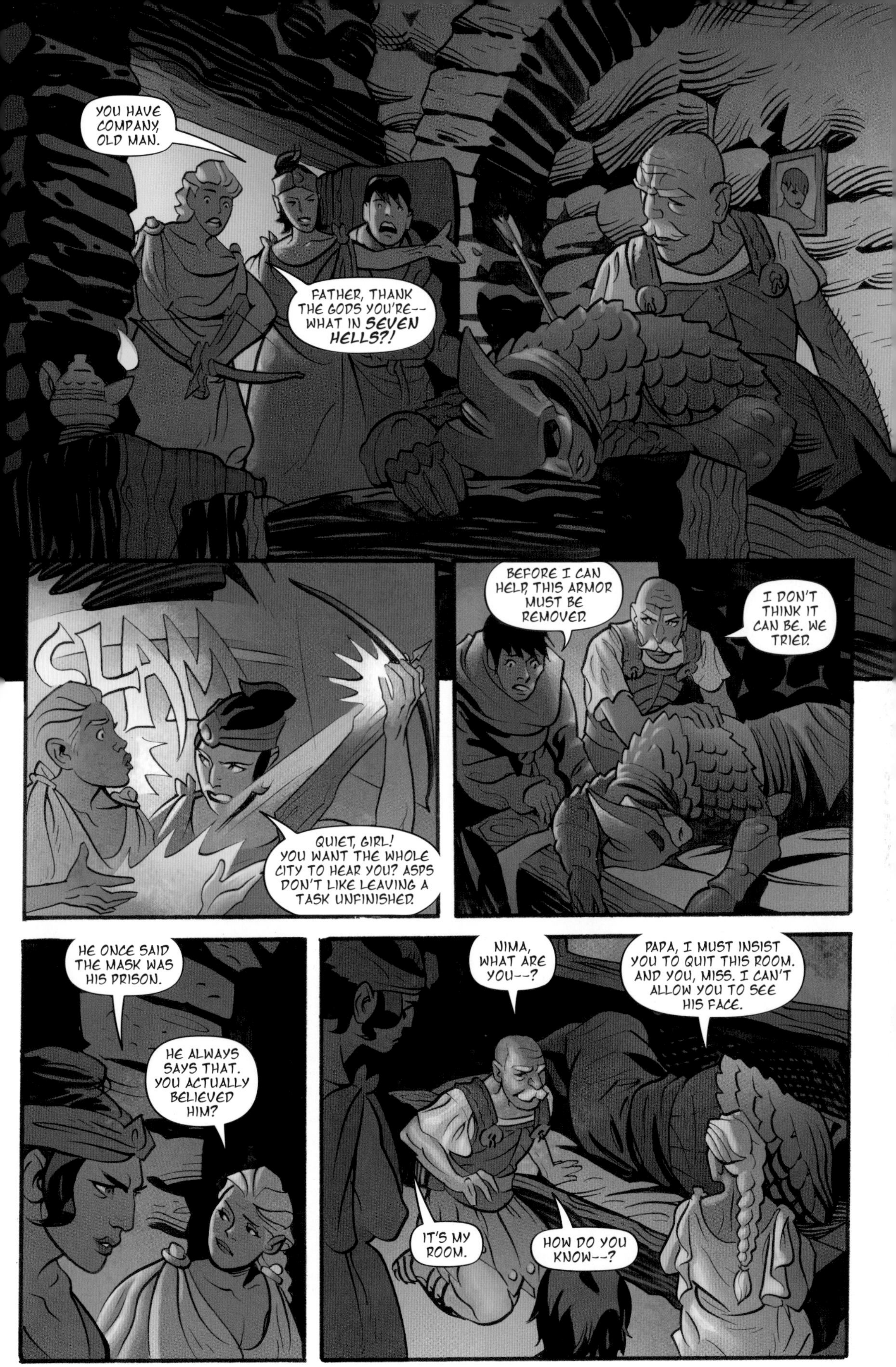
YOU HAVE COMPANY, OLD MAN.
FATHER, THANK THE GODS YOU'RE-- WHAT IN SEVEN HELLS?!
SLAM
QUIET, GIRL! YOU WANT THE WHOLE CITY TO HEAR YOU? ASPS DON'T LIKE LEAVING A TASK UNFINISHED.
BEFORE I CAN HELP, THIS ARMOR MUST BE REMOVED.
I DON'T THINK IT CAN BE. WE TRIED.
HE ONCE SAID THE MASK WAS HIS PRISON.
HE ALWAYS SAYS THAT. YOU ACTUALLY BELIEVED HIM?
NIMA, WHAT ARE YOU--?
PAPA, I MUST INSIST YOU TO QUIT THIS ROOM. AND YOU, MISS. I CAN'T ALLOW YOU TO SEE HIS FACE.
IT'S MY ROOM.
HOW DO YOU KNOW--?

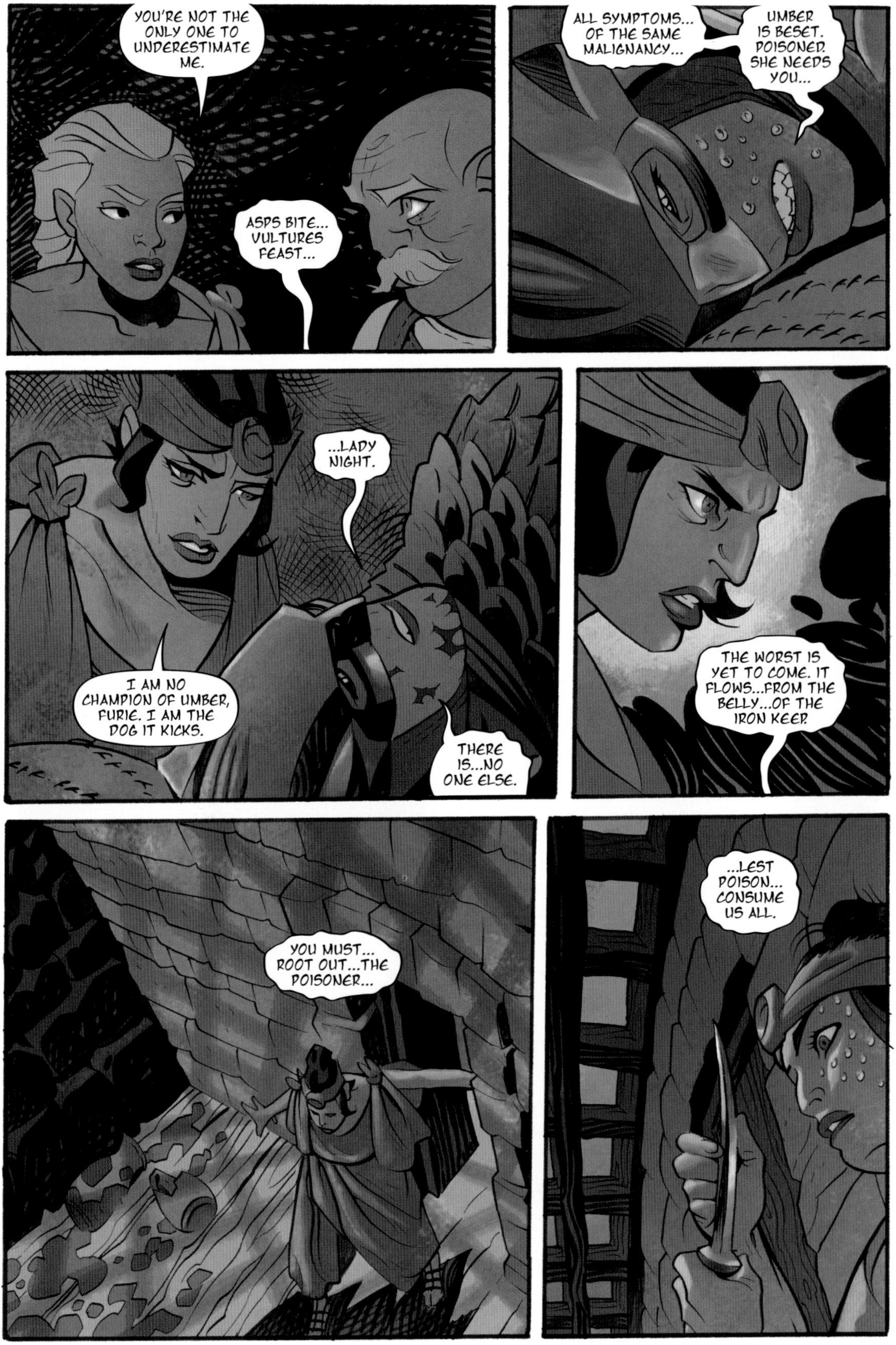
YOU'RE NOT THE ONLY ONE TO UNDERESTIMATE ME.
ASPS BITE... VULTURES FEAST...
ALL SYMPTOMS... OF THE SAME MALIGNANCY...
UMBER IS BESET. POISONED. SHE NEEDS YOU...
...LADY NIGHT.
I AM NO CHAMPION OF UMBER, FURIE. I AM THE DOG IT KICKS.
THERE IS...NO ONE ELSE.
THE WORST IS YET TO COME. IT FLOWS...FROM THE BELLY...OF THE IRON KEEP.
YOU MUST... ROOT OUT...THE POISONER...
...LEST POISON... CONSUME US ALL.

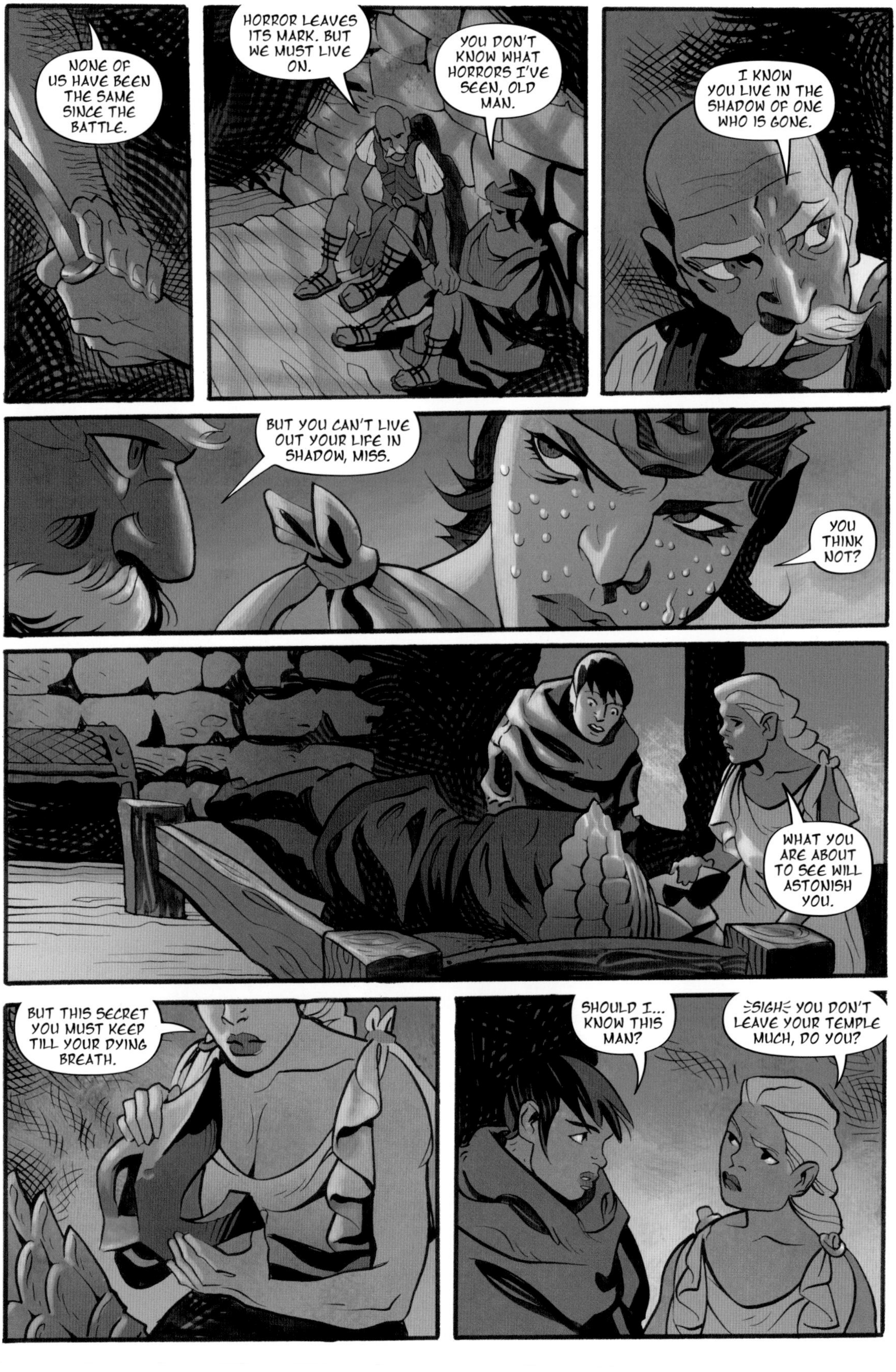
NONE OF US HAVE BEEN THE SAME SINCE THE BATTLE.
HORROR LEAVES ITS MARK. BUT WE MUST LIVE ON.
YOU DON'T KNOW WHAT HORRORS I'VE SEEN, OLD MAN.
I KNOW YOU LIVE IN THE SHADOW OF ONE WHO IS GONE.
BUT YOU CAN'T LIVE OUT YOUR LIFE IN SHADOW, MISS.
YOU THINK NOT?
WHAT YOU ARE ABOUT TO SEE WILL ASTONISH YOU.
BUT THIS SECRET YOU MUST KEEP TILL YOUR DYING BREATH.
SHOULD I... KNOW THIS MAN?
=SIGH= YOU DON'T LEAVE YOUR TEMPLE MUCH, DO YOU?

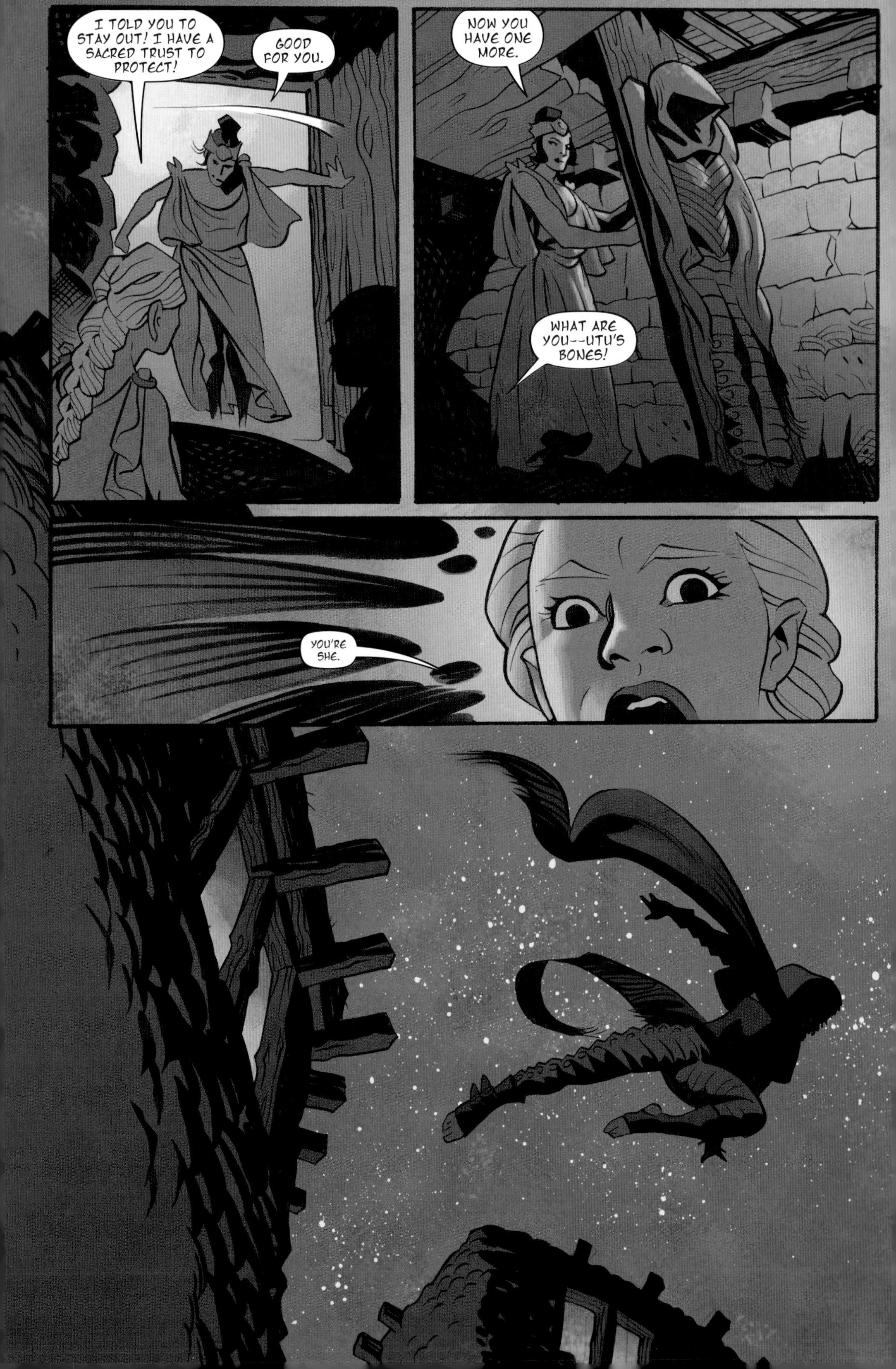
I TOLD YOU TO STAY OUT! I HAVE A SACRED TRUST TO PROTECT!
GOOD FOR YOU.
NOW YOU HAVE ONE MORE.
WHAT ARE YOU--UTU'S BONES!
YOU'RE SHE.

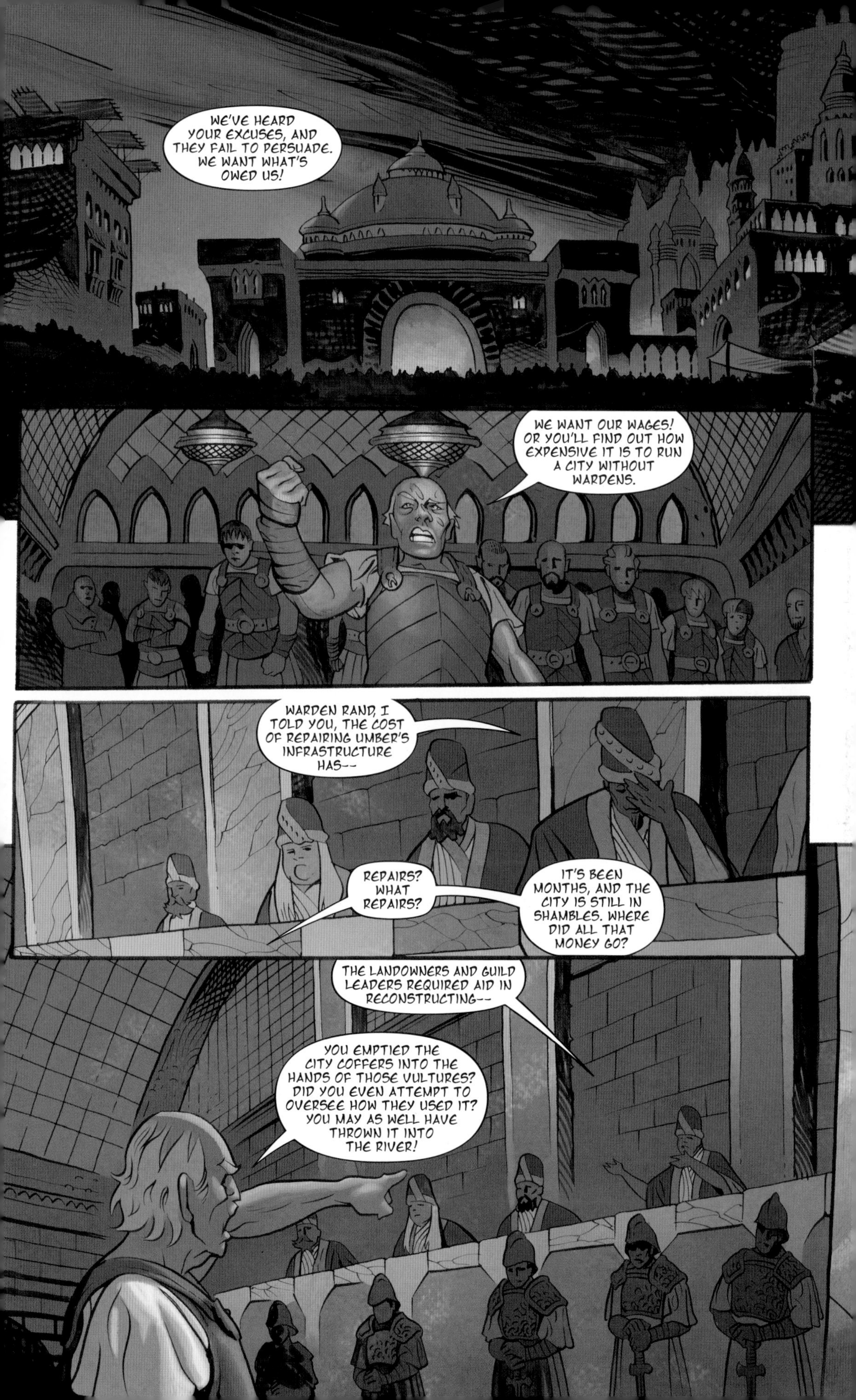
WE'VE HEARD YOUR EXCUSES, AND THEY FAIL TO PERSUADE. WE WANT WHAT'S OWED US!
WE WANT OUR WAGES! OR YOU'LL FIND OUT HOW EXPENSIVE IT IS TO RUN A CITY WITHOUT WARDENS.
WARDEN RAND, I TOLD YOU, THE COST OF REPAIRING UMBER'S INFRASTRUCTURE HAS--
REPAIRS? WHAT REPAIRS?
IT'S BEEN MONTHS, AND THE CITY IS STILL IN SHAMBLES. WHERE DID ALL THAT MONEY GO?
THE LANDOWNERS AND GUILD LEADERS REQUIRED AID IN RECONSTRUCTING--
YOU EMPTIED THE CITY COFFERS INTO THE HANDS OF THOSE VULTURES? DID YOU EVEN ATTEMPT TO OVERSEE HOW THEY USED IT? YOU MAY AS WELL HAVE THROWN IT INTO THE RIVER!

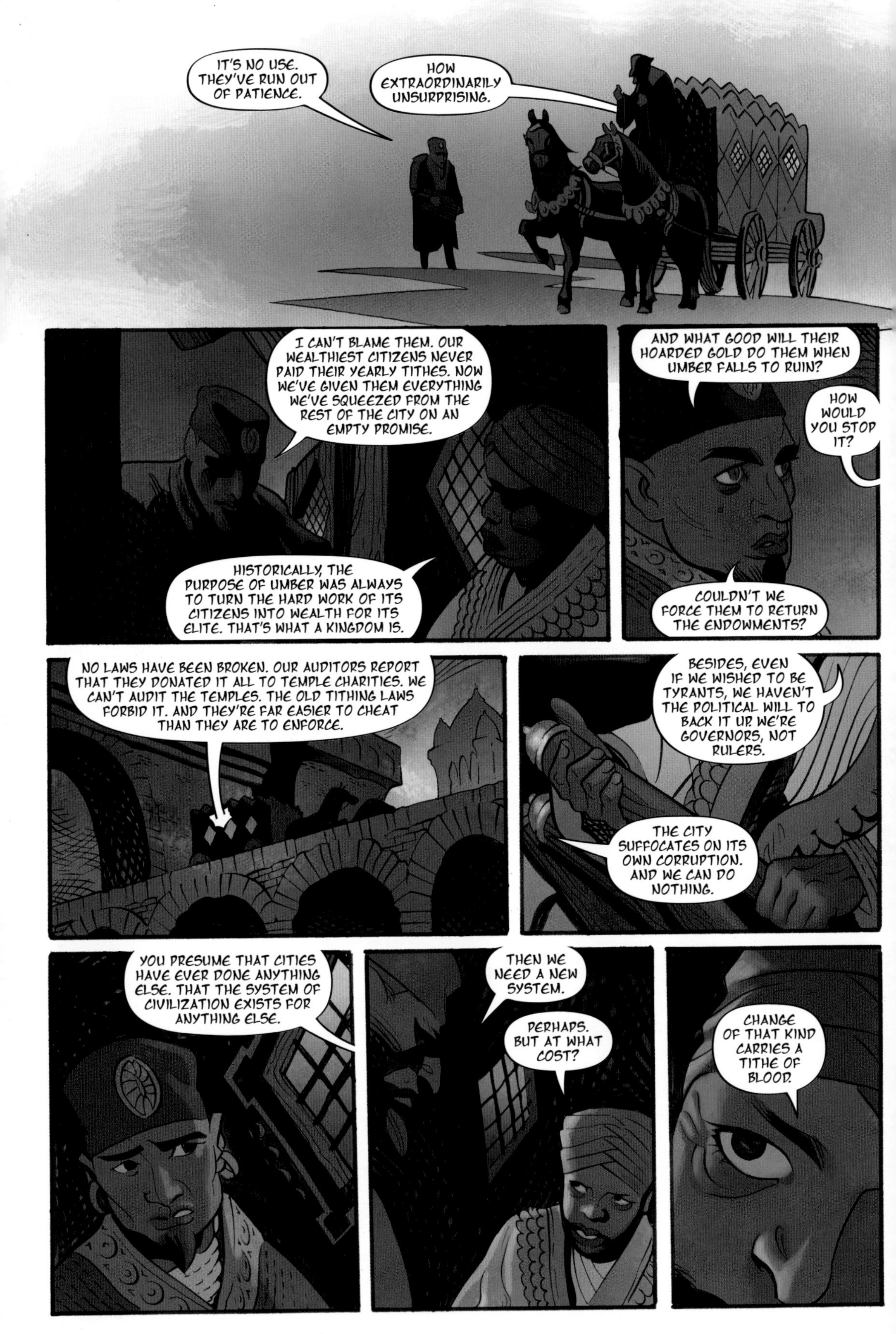
IT'S NO USE. THEY'VE RUN OUT OF PATIENCE.
HOW EXTRAORDINARILY UNSURPRISING.
I CAN'T BLAME THEM. OUR WEALTHIEST CITIZENS NEVER PAID THEIR YEARLY TITHES. NOW WE'VE GIVEN THEM EVERYTHING WE'VE SQUEEZED FROM THE REST OF THE CITY ON AN EMPTY PROMISE.
HISTORICALLY, THE PURPOSE OF UMBER WAS ALWAYS TO TURN THE HARD WORK OF ITS CITIZENS INTO WEALTH FOR ITS ELITE. THAT'S WHAT A KINGDOM IS.
AND WHAT GOOD WILL THEIR HOARDED GOLD DO THEM WHEN UMBER FALLS TO RUIN?
HOW WOULD YOU STOP IT?
COULDN'T WE FORCE THEM TO RETURN THE ENDOWMENTS?
NO LAWS HAVE BEEN BROKEN. OUR AUDITORS REPORT THAT THEY DONATED IT ALL TO TEMPLE CHARITIES. WE CAN'T AUDIT THE TEMPLES. THE OLD TITHING LAWS FORBID IT. AND THEY'RE FAR EASIER TO CHEAT THAN THEY ARE TO ENFORCE.
BESIDES, EVEN IF WE WISHED TO BE TYRANTS, WE HAVEN'T THE POLITICAL WILL TO BACK IT UP. WE'RE GOVERNORS, NOT RULERS.
THE CITY SUFFOCATES ON ITS OWN CORRUPTION. AND WE CAN DO NOTHING.
YOU PRESUME THAT CITIES HAVE EVER DONE ANYTHING ELSE. THAT THE SYSTEM OF CIVILIZATION EXISTS FOR ANYTHING ELSE.
THEN WE NEED A NEW SYSTEM.
PERHAPS. BUT AT WHAT COST?
CHANGE OF THAT KIND CARRIES A TITHE OF BLOOD.

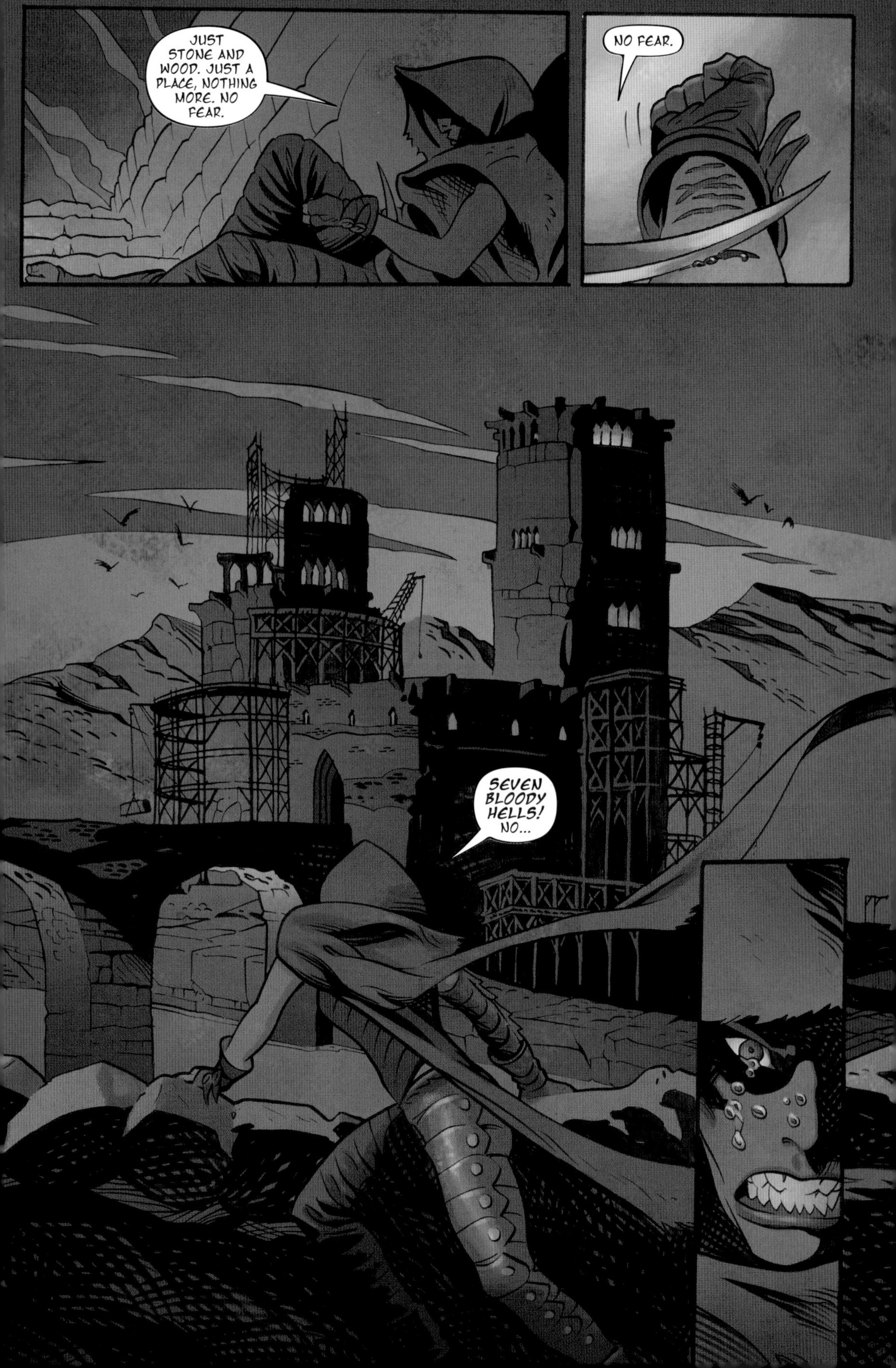
JUST STONE AND WOOD. JUST A PLACE, NOTHING MORE. NO FEAR.
NO FEAR.
SEVEN BLOODY HELLS! NO...

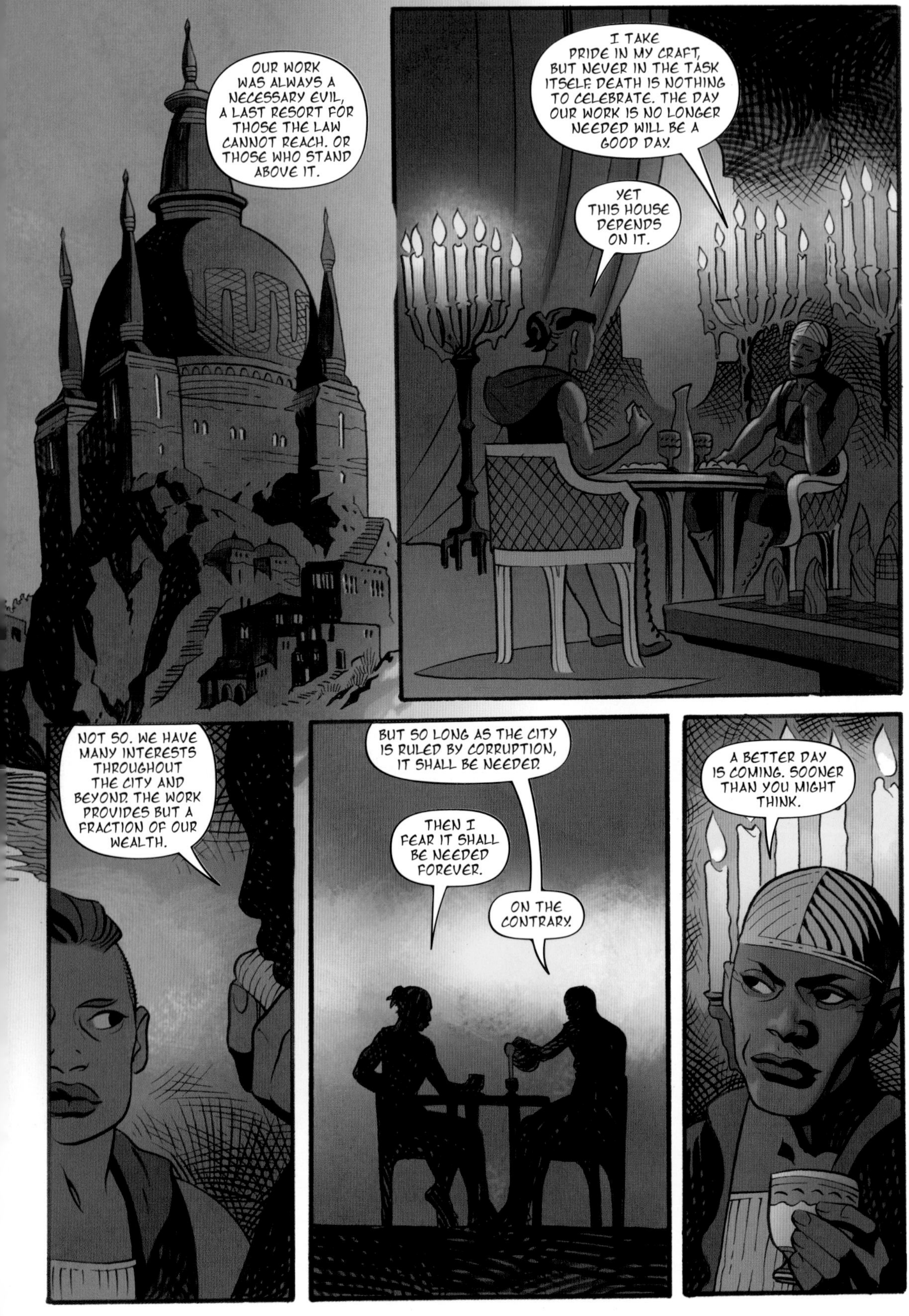
OUR WORK WAS ALWAYS A NECESSARY EVIL, A LAST RESORT FOR THOSE THE LAW CANNOT REACH. OR THOSE WHO STAND ABOVE IT.
I TAKE PRIDE IN MY CRAFT, BUT NEVER IN THE TASK ITSELF. DEATH IS NOTHING TO CELEBRATE. THE DAY OUR WORK IS NO LONGER NEEDED WILL BE A GOOD DAY.
YET THIS HOUSE DEPENDS ON IT.
NOT SO. WE HAVE MANY INTERESTS THROUGHOUT THE CITY AND BEYOND. THE WORK PROVIDES BUT A FRACTION OF OUR WEALTH.
BUT SO LONG AS THE CITY IS RULED BY CORRUPTION, IT SHALL BE NEEDED.
THEN I FEAR IT SHALL BE NEEDED FOREVER.
ON THE CONTRARY.
A BETTER DAY IS COMING. SOONER THAN YOU MIGHT THINK.

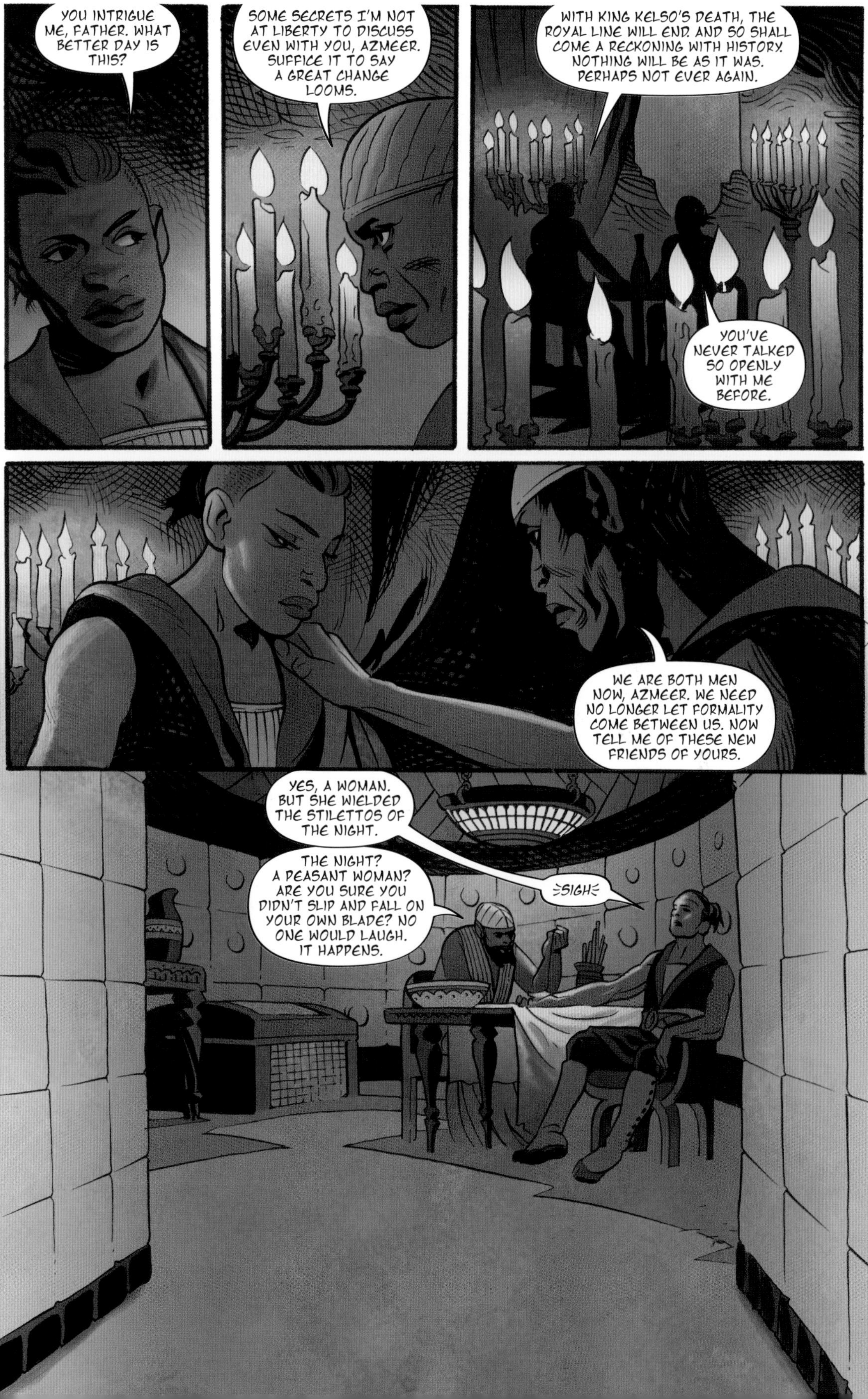
YOU INTRIGUE ME, FATHER. WHAT BETTER DAY IS THIS?
SOME SECRETS I'M NOT AT LIBERTY TO DISCUSS EVEN WITH YOU, AZMEER. SUFFICE IT TO SAY A GREAT CHANGE LOOMS.
WITH KING KELSO'S DEATH, THE ROYAL LINE WILL END. AND SO SHALL COME A RECKONING WITH HISTORY. NOTHING WILL BE AS IT WAS. PERHAPS NOT EVER AGAIN.
YOU'VE NEVER TALKED SO OPENLY WITH ME BEFORE.
WE ARE BOTH MEN NOW, AZMEER. WE NEED NO LONGER LET FORMALITY COME BETWEEN US. NOW TELL ME OF THESE NEW FRIENDS OF YOURS.
YES, A WOMAN. BUT SHE WIELDED THE STILETTOS OF THE NIGHT.
THE NIGHT? A PEASANT WOMAN? ARE YOU SURE YOU DIDN'T SLIP AND FALL ON YOUR OWN BLADE? NO ONE WOULD LAUGH. IT HAPPENS.
SIGH

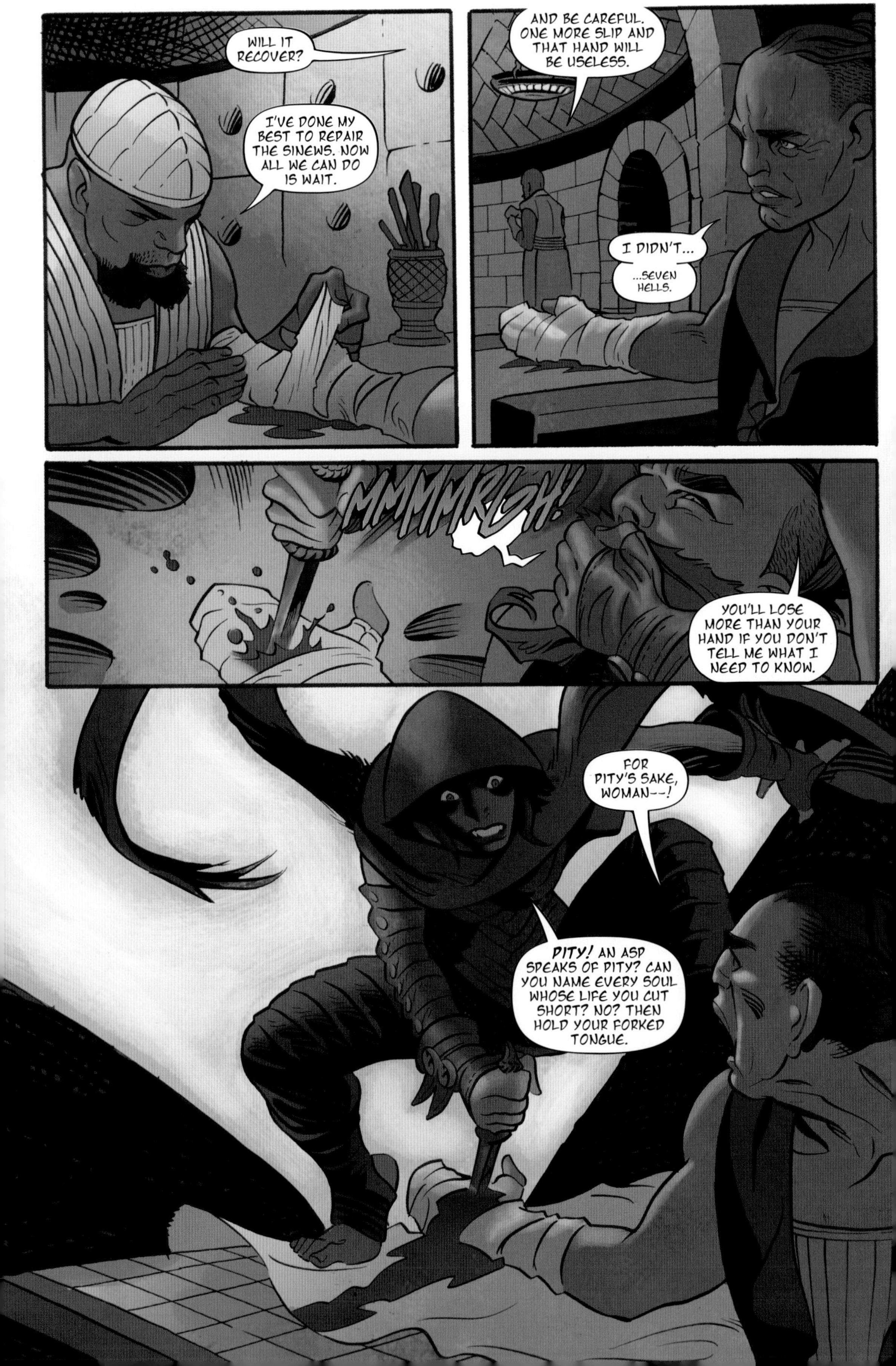
WILL IT RECOVER?
I'VE DONE MY BEST TO REPAIR THE SINEWS. NOW ALL WE CAN DO IS WAIT.
AND BE CAREFUL. ONE MORE SLIP AND THAT HAND WILL BE USELESS.
I DIDN'T...
...SEVEN HELLS.
MMMMRGH!
YOU'LL LOSE MORE THAN YOUR HAND IF YOU DON'T TELL ME WHAT I NEED TO KNOW.
FOR PITY'S SAKE, WOMAN--!
PITY! AN ASP SPEAKS OF PITY? CAN YOU NAME EVERY SOUL WHOSE LIFE YOU CUT SHORT? NO? THEN HOLD YOUR FORKED TONGUE.

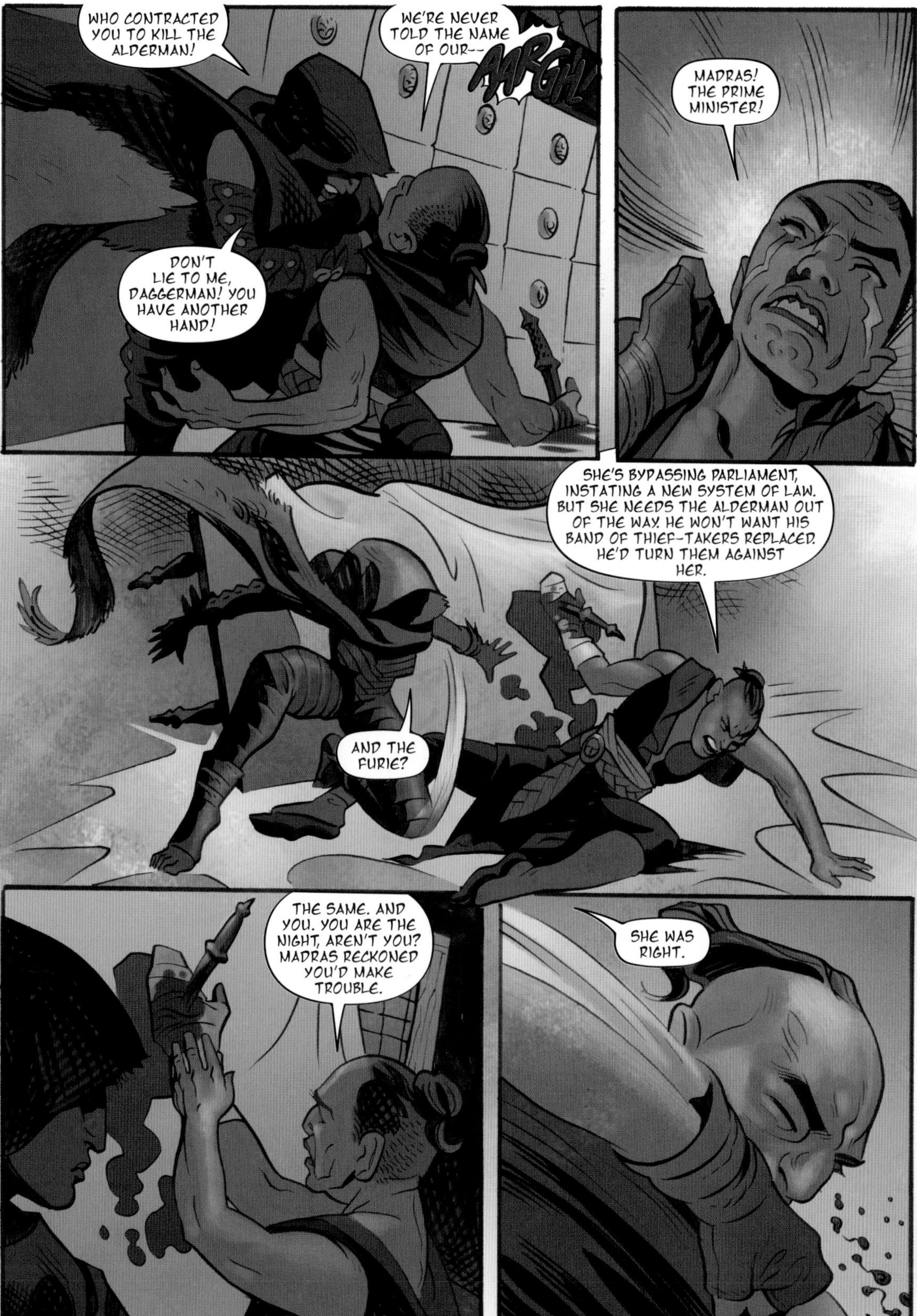
WHO CONTRACTED YOU TO KILL THE ALDERMAN!
WE'RE NEVER TOLD THE NAME OF OUR--
AARGH!
DON'T LIE TO ME, DAGGERMAN! YOU HAVE ANOTHER HAND!
MADRAS! THE PRIME MINISTER!
SHE'S BYPASSING PARLIAMENT, INSTATING A NEW SYSTEM OF LAW. BUT SHE NEEDS THE ALDERMAN OUT OF THE WAY. HE WON'T WANT HIS BAND OF THIEF-TAKERS REPLACED. HE'D TURN THEM AGAINST HER.
AND THE FURIE?
THE SAME. AND YOU. YOU ARE THE NIGHT, AREN'T YOU? MADRAS RECKONED YOU'D MAKE TROUBLE.
SHE WAS RIGHT.

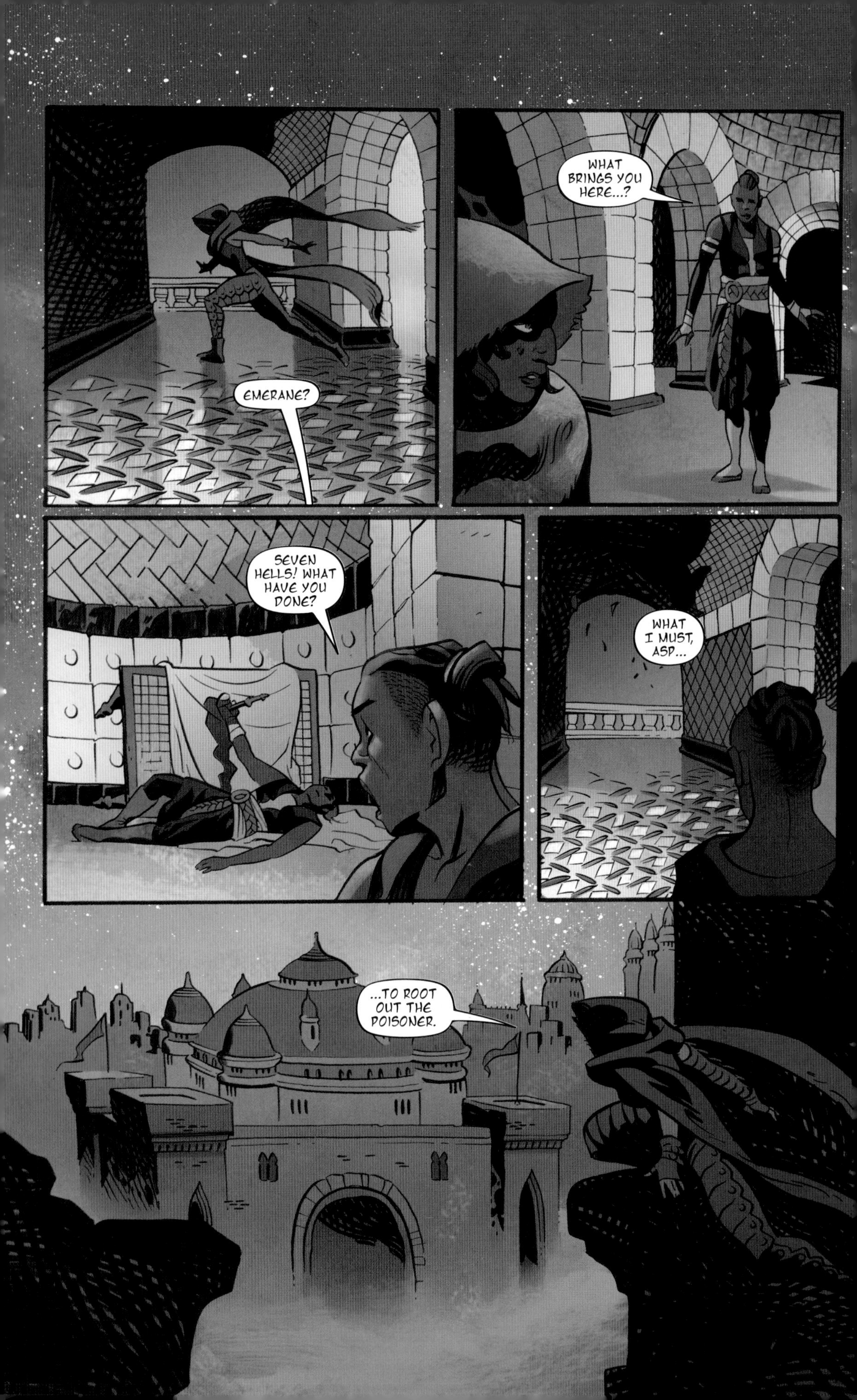
EMERANE?
WHAT BRINGS YOU HERE...?
SEVEN HELLS! WHAT HAVE YOU DONE?
WHAT I MUST, ASP...
...TO ROOT OUT THE POISONER.

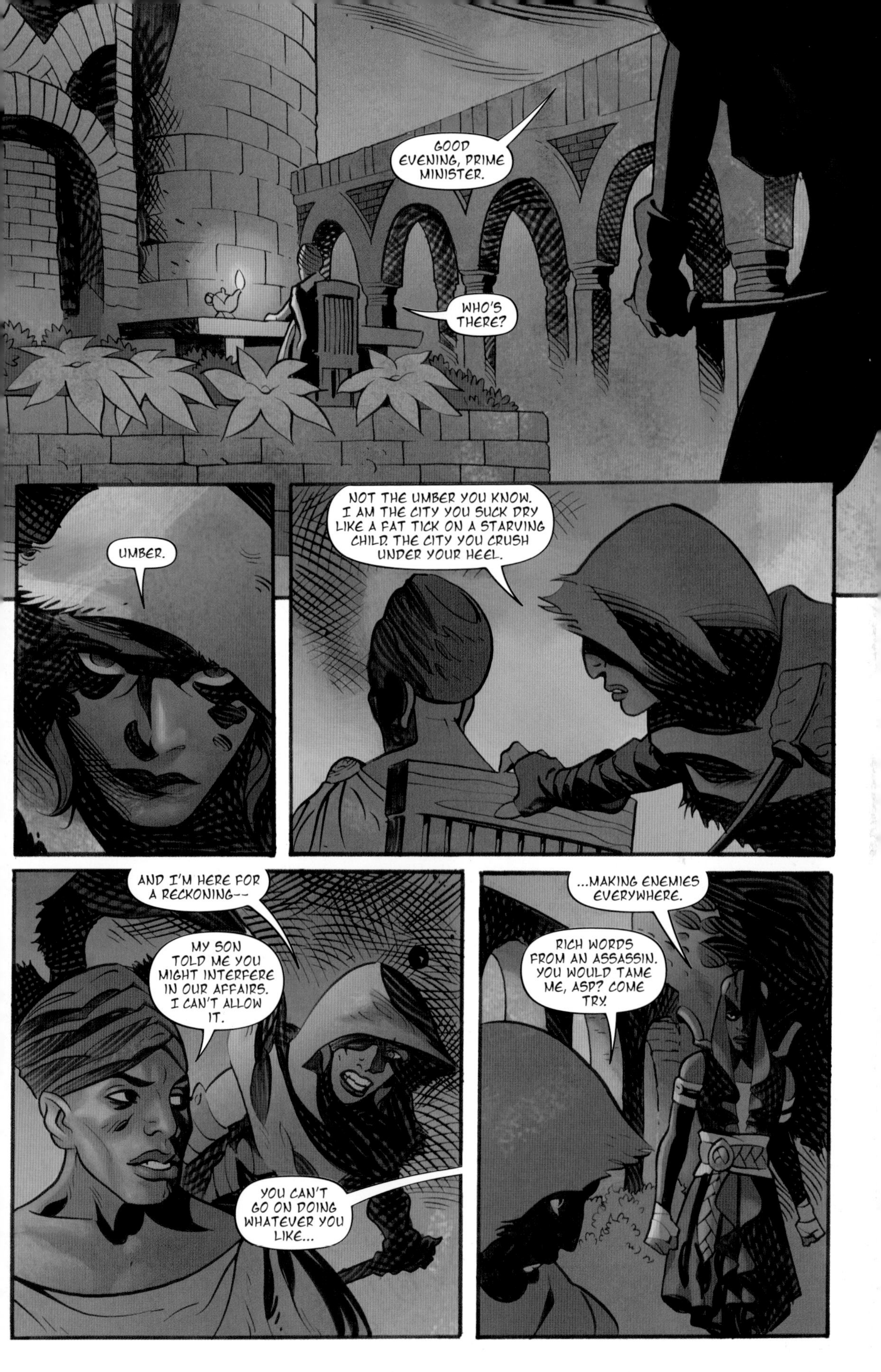
GOOD EVENING, PRIME MINISTER.
WHO'S THERE?
UMBER.
NOT THE UMBER YOU KNOW. I AM THE CITY YOU SUCK DRY LIKE A FAT TICK ON A STARVING CHILD. THE CITY YOU CRUSH UNDER YOUR HEEL.
AND I'M HERE FOR A RECKONING--
MY SON TOLD ME YOU MIGHT INTERFERE IN OUR AFFAIRS. I CAN'T ALLOW IT.
YOU CAN'T GO ON DOING WHATEVER YOU LIKE...
...MAKING ENEMIES EVERYWHERE.
RICH WORDS FROM AN ASSASSIN. YOU WOULD TAME ME, ASP? COME TRY.

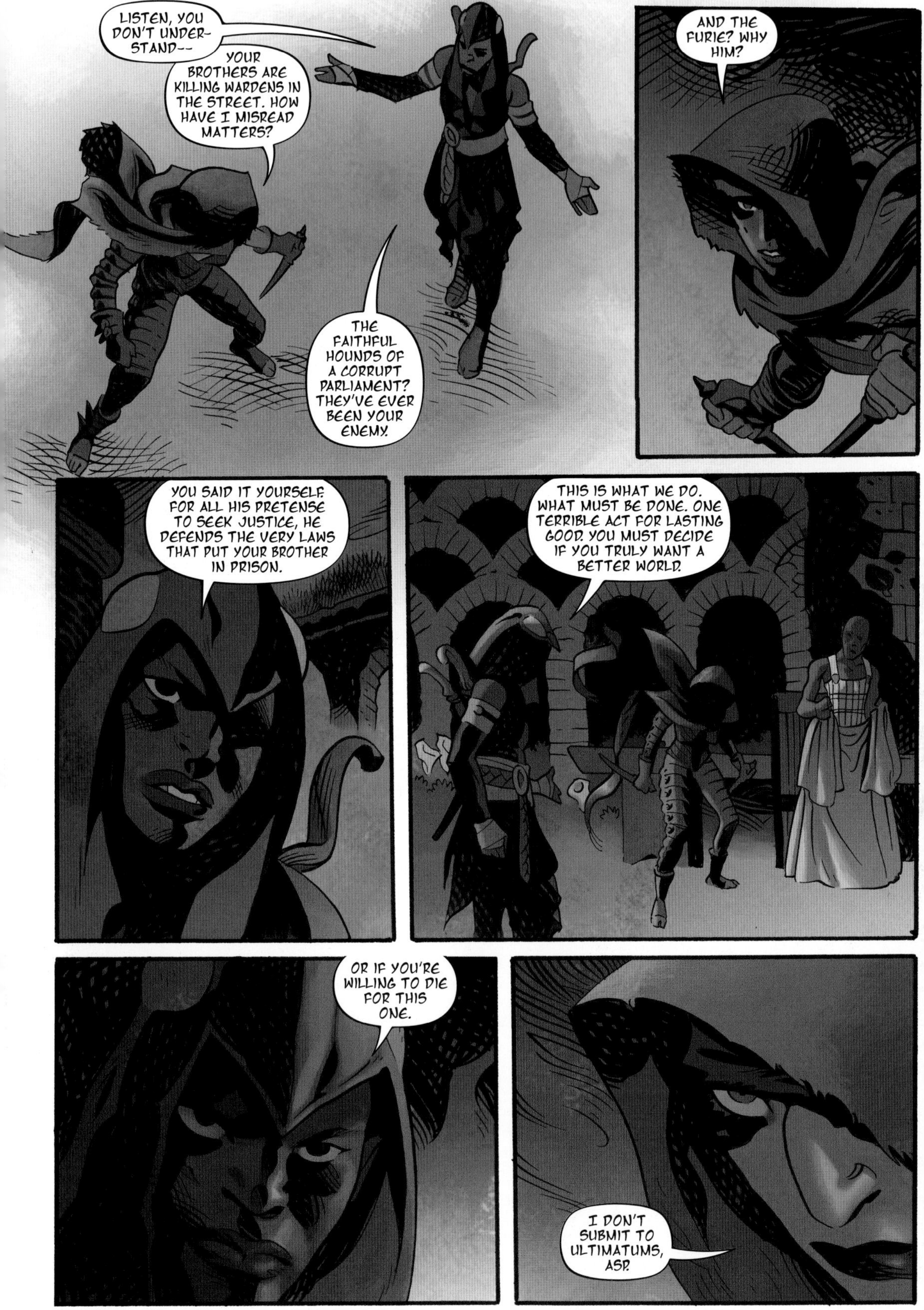
LISTEN, YOU DON'T UNDER-STAND--
YOUR BROTHERS ARE KILLING WARDENS IN THE STREET. HOW HAVE I MISREAD MATTERS?
THE FAITHFUL HOUNDS OF A CORRUPT PARLIAMENT? THEY'VE EVER BEEN YOUR ENEMY.
AND THE FURIE? WHY HIM?
YOU SAID IT YOURSELF. FOR ALL HIS PRETENSE TO SEEK JUSTICE, HE DEFENDS THE VERY LAWS THAT PUT YOUR BROTHER IN PRISON.
THIS IS WHAT WE DO. WHAT MUST BE DONE. ONE TERRIBLE ACT FOR LASTING GOOD. YOU MUST DECIDE IF YOU TRULY WANT A BETTER WORLD.
OR IF YOU'RE WILLING TO DIE FOR THIS ONE.
I DON'T SUBMIT TO ULTIMATUMS, ASP.

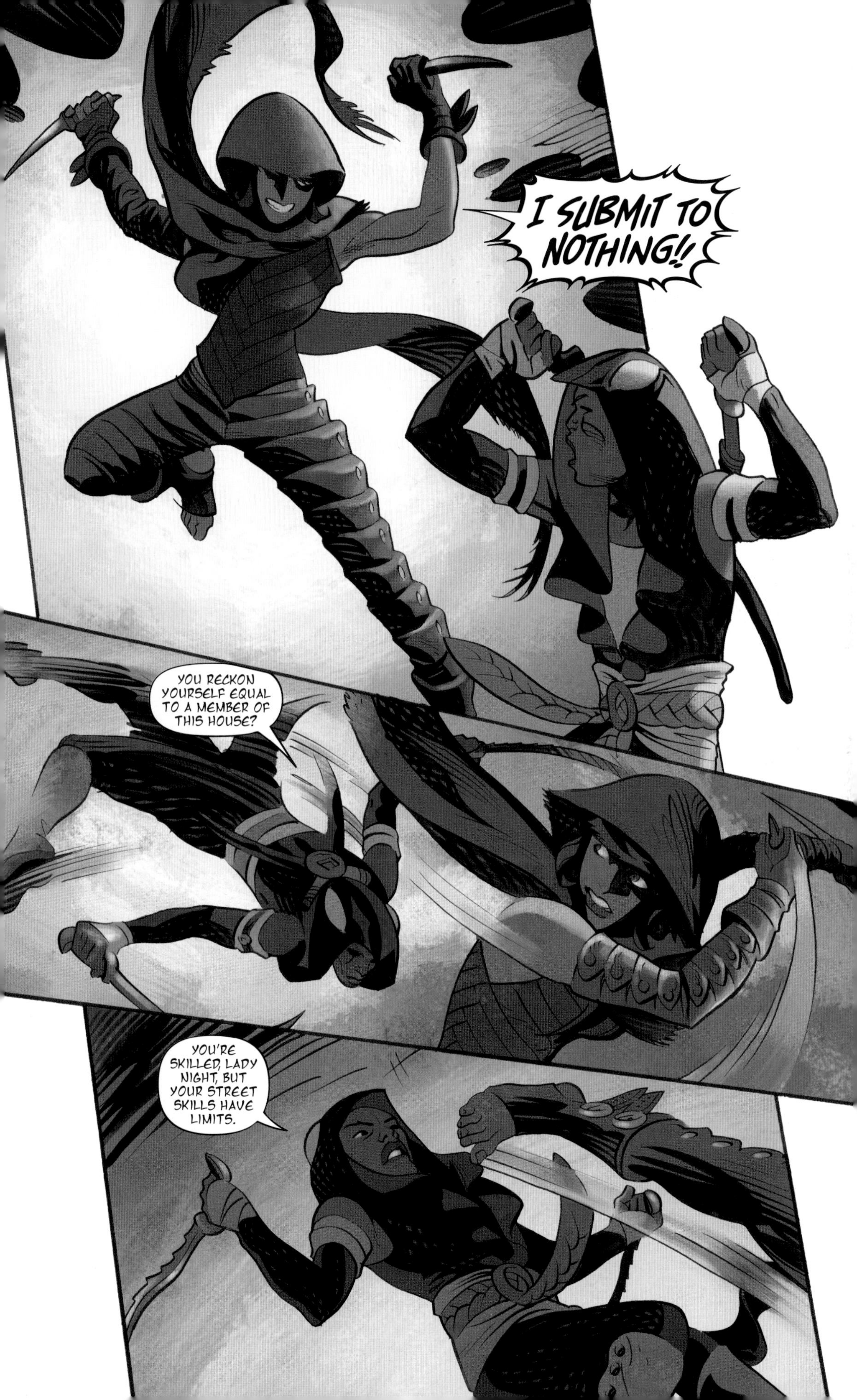
I SUBMIT TO NOTHING!!
YOU RECKON YOURSELF EQUAL TO A MEMBER OF THIS HOUSE?
YOU'RE SKILLED, LADY NIGHT, BUT YOUR STREET SKILLS HAVE LIMITS.

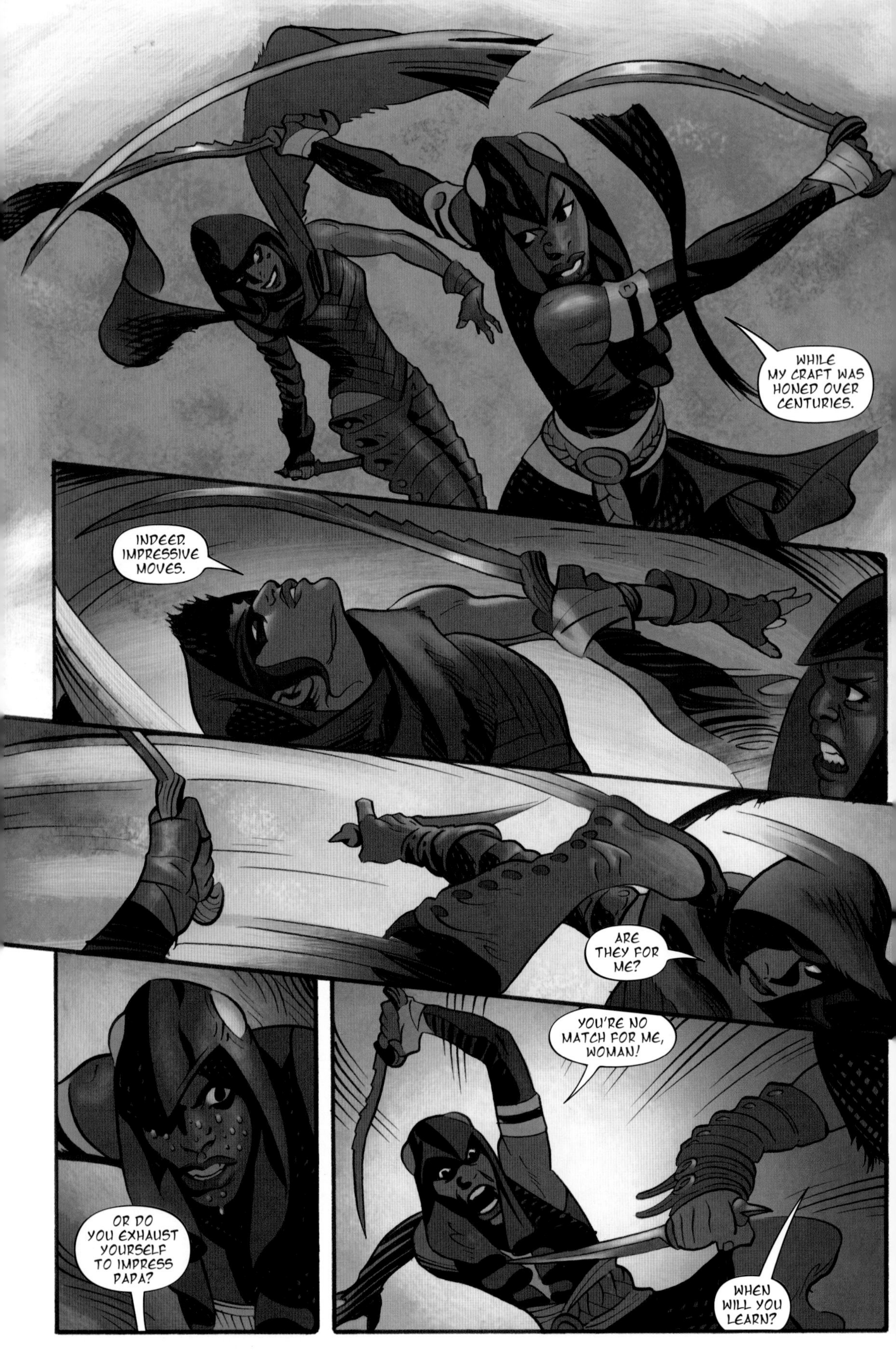
WHILE MY CRAFT WAS HONED OVER CENTURIES.
INDEED. IMPRESSIVE MOVES.
ARE THEY FOR ME?
YOU'RE NO MATCH FOR ME, WOMAN!
OR DO YOU EXHAUST YOURSELF TO IMPRESS PAPA?
WHEN WILL YOU LEARN?

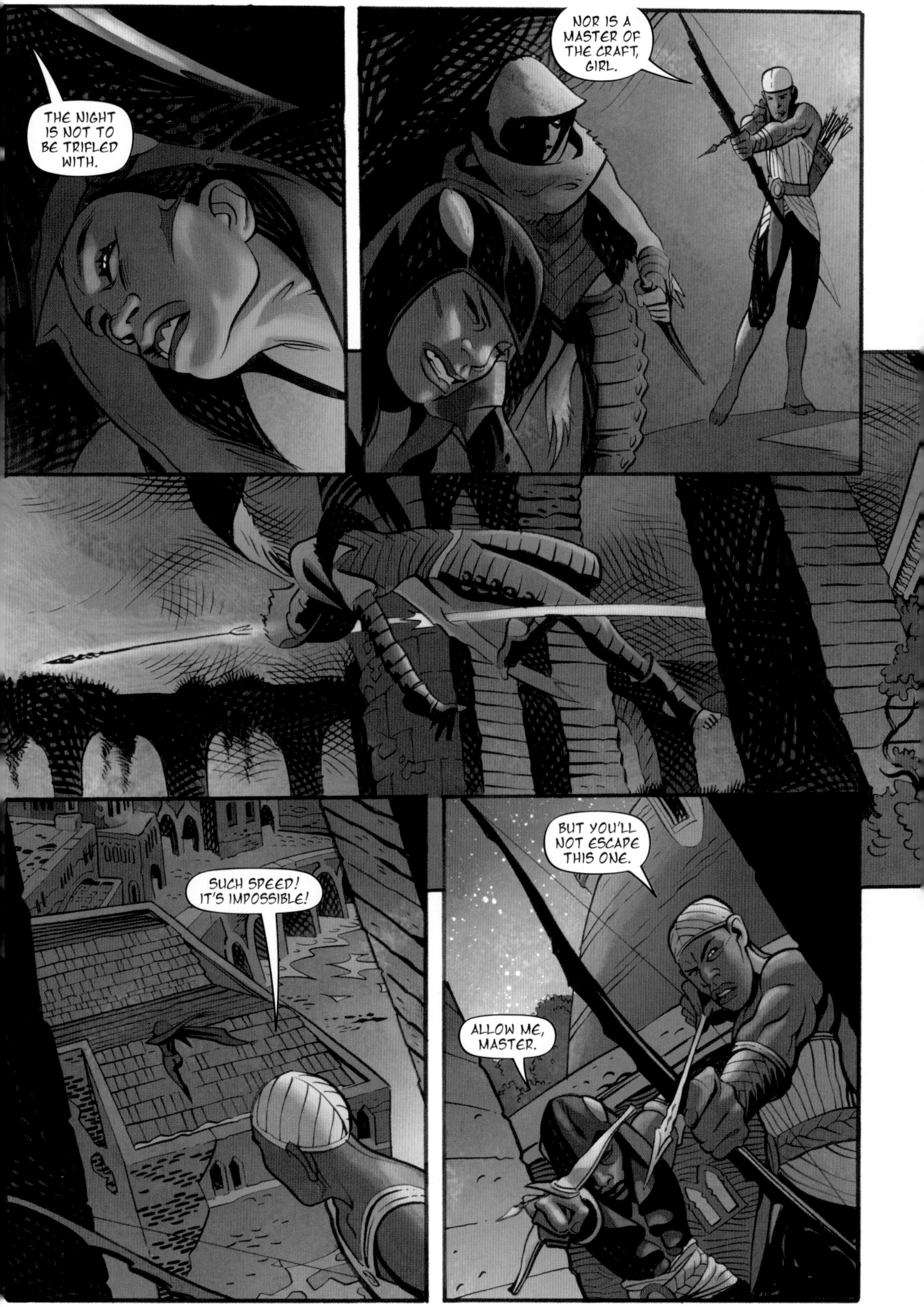
THE NIGHT IS NOT TO BE TRIFLED WITH.
NOR IS A MASTER OF THE CRAFT, GIRL.
SUCH SPEED! IT'S IMPOSSIBLE!
BUT YOU'LL NOT ESCAPE THIS ONE.
ALLOW ME, MASTER.

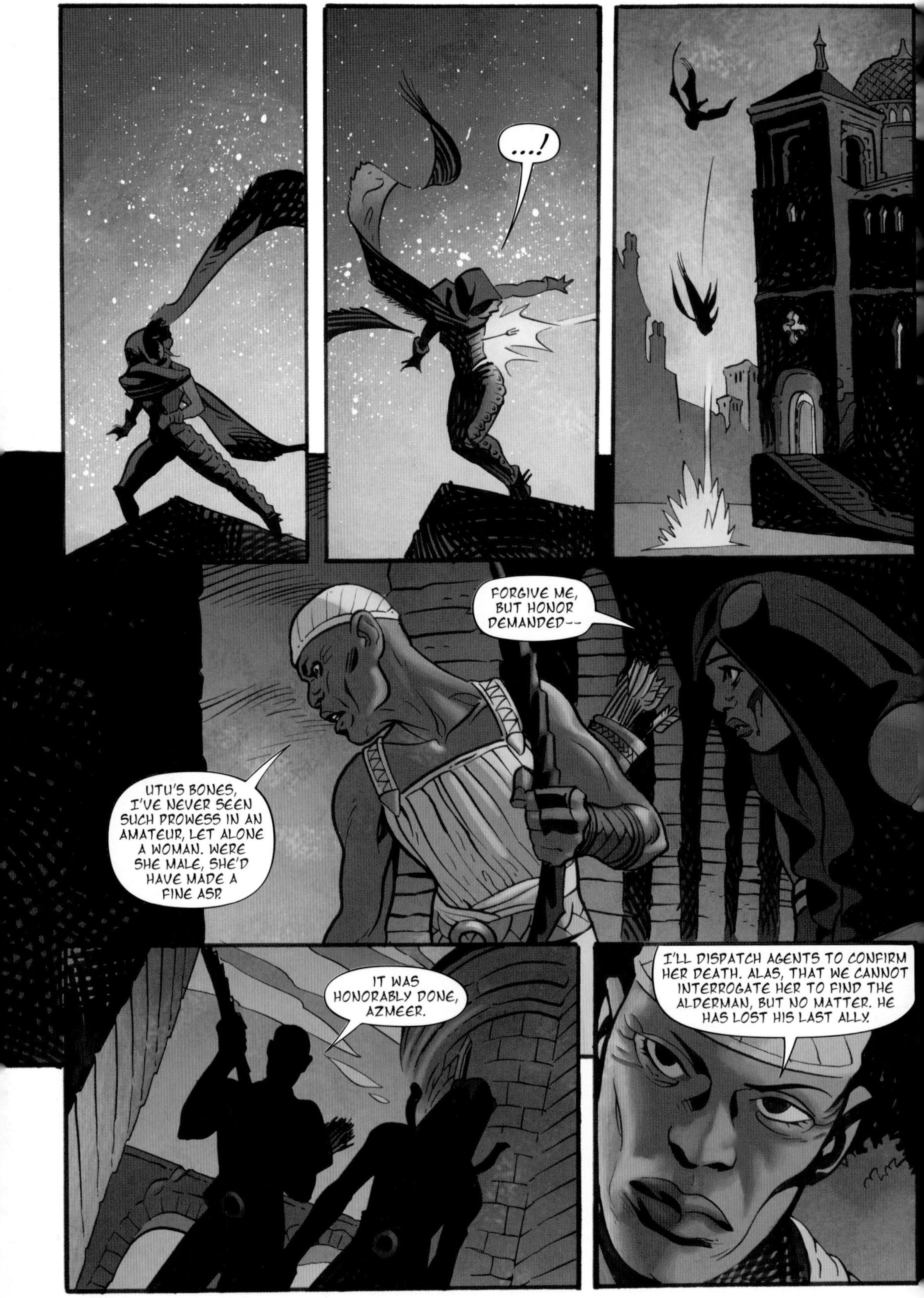
...!
FORGIVE ME, BUT HONOR DEMANDED--
UTU'S BONES, I'VE NEVER SEEN SUCH PROWESS IN AN AMATEUR, LET ALONE A WOMAN. WERE SHE MALE, SHE'D HAVE MADE A FINE ASP.
IT WAS HONORABLY DONE, AZMEER.
I'LL DISPATCH AGENTS TO CONFIRM HER DEATH. ALAS, THAT WE CANNOT INTERROGATE HER TO FIND THE ALDERMAN, BUT NO MATTER. HE HAS LOST HIS LAST ALLY.

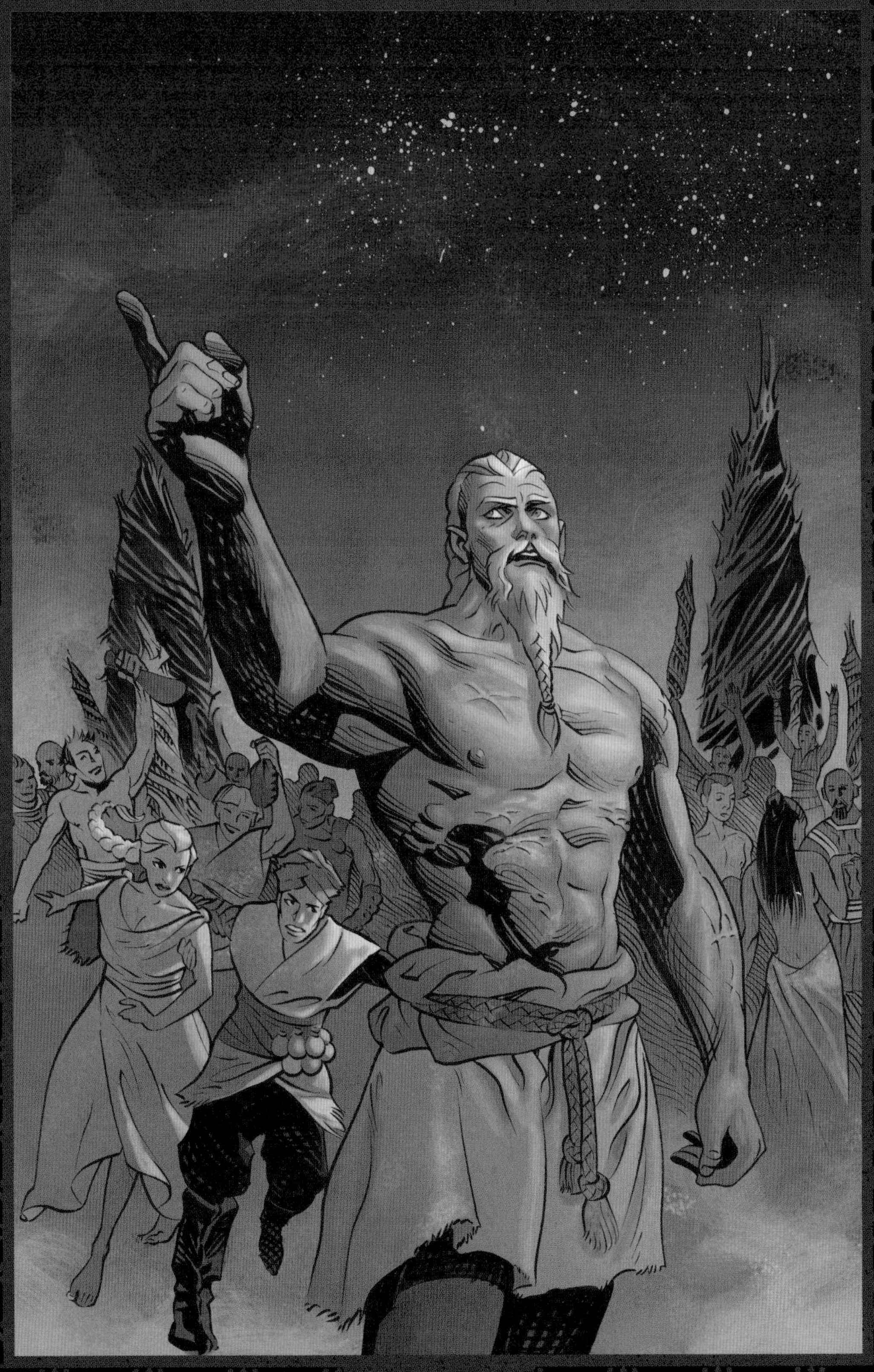

CHAPTER 3

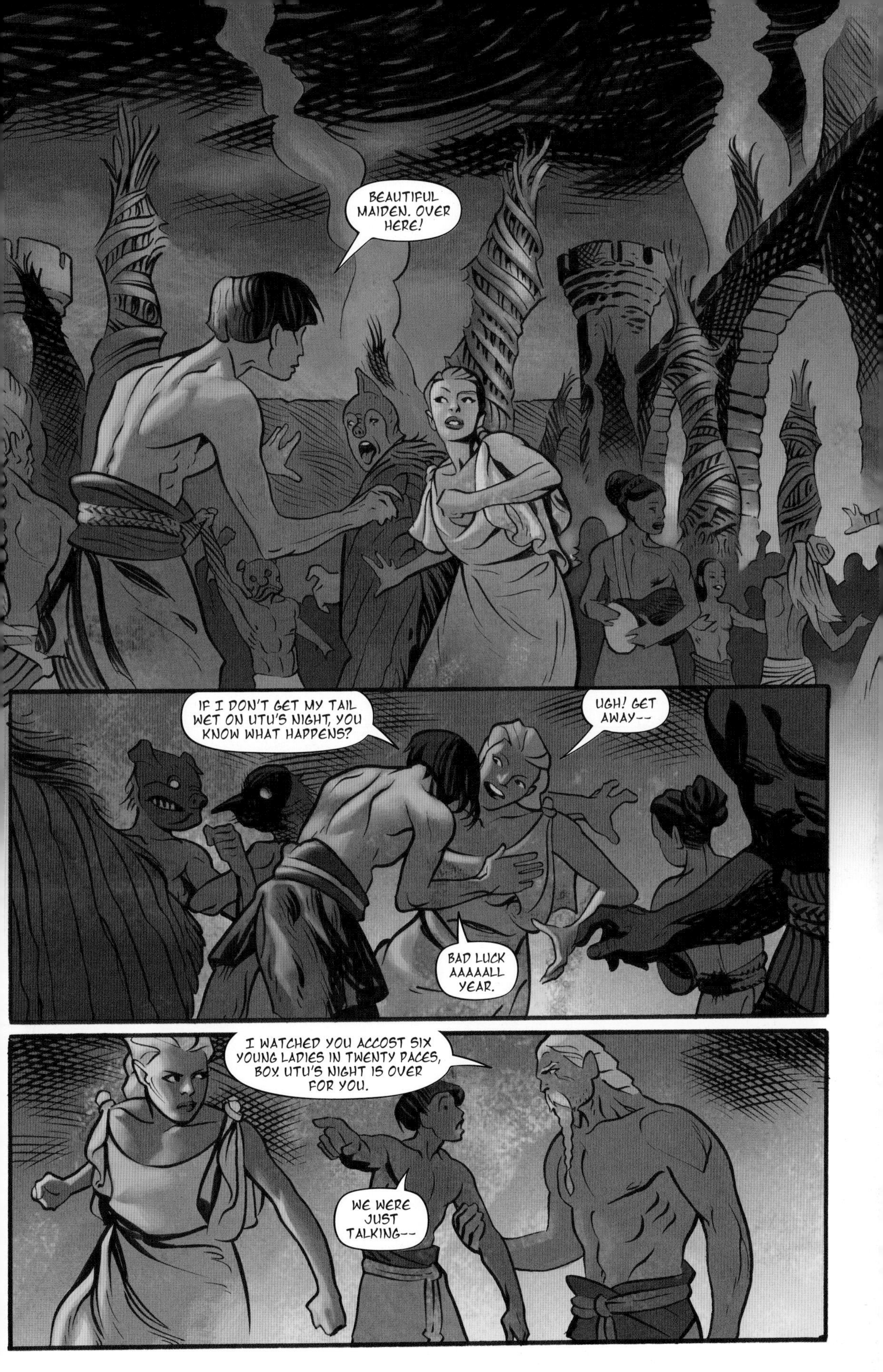
BEAUTIFUL MAIDEN. OVER HERE!
IF I DON'T GET MY TAIL WET ON UTU'S NIGHT, YOU KNOW WHAT HAPPENS?
UGH! GET AWAY--
BAD LUCK AAAAALL YEAR.
I WATCHED YOU ACCOST SIX YOUNG LADIES IN TWENTY PACES, BOY. UTU'S NIGHT IS OVER FOR YOU.
WE WERE JUST TALKING--

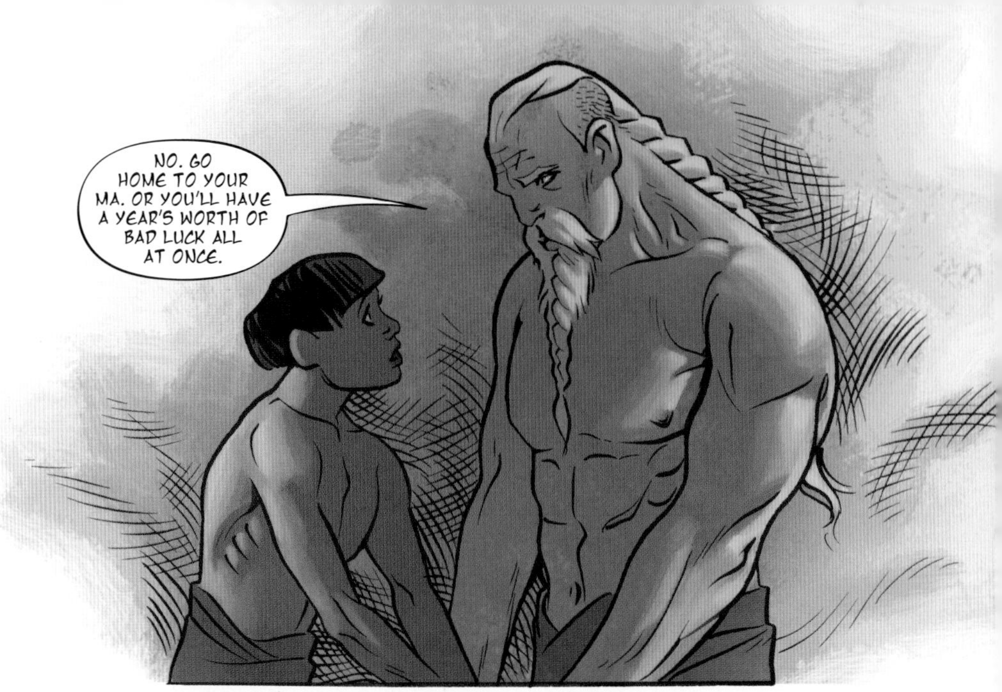
NO. GO HOME TO YOUR MA. OR YOU'LL HAVE A YEAR'S WORTH OF BAD LUCK ALL AT ONCE.

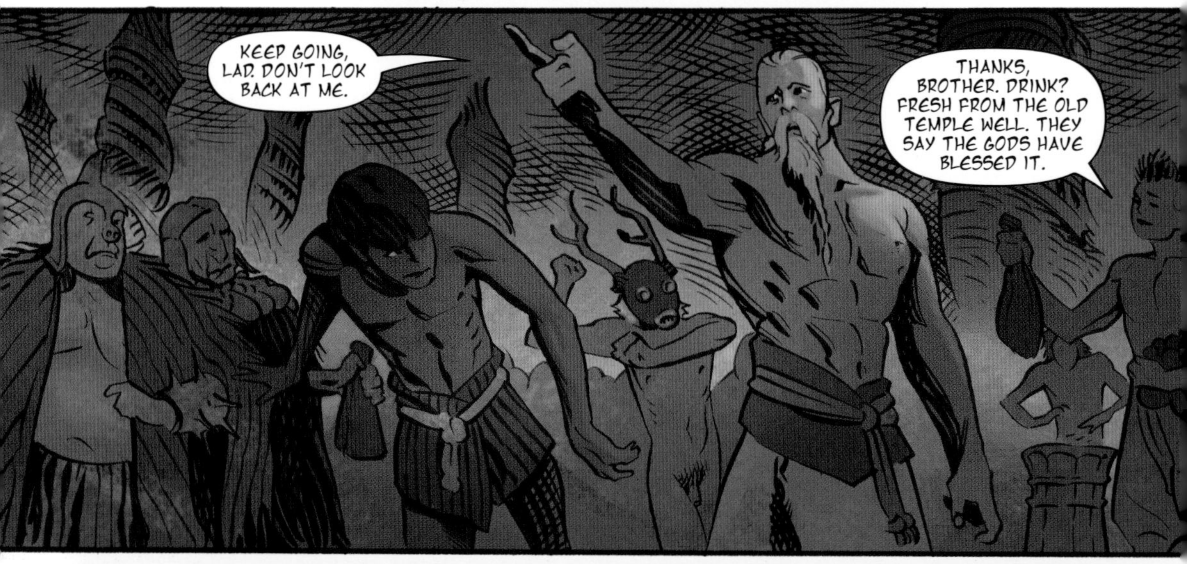
KEEP GOING, LAD. DON'T LOOK BACK AT ME.
THANKS, BROTHER. DRINK? FRESH FROM THE OLD TEMPLE WELL. THEY SAY THE GODS HAVE BLESSED IT.

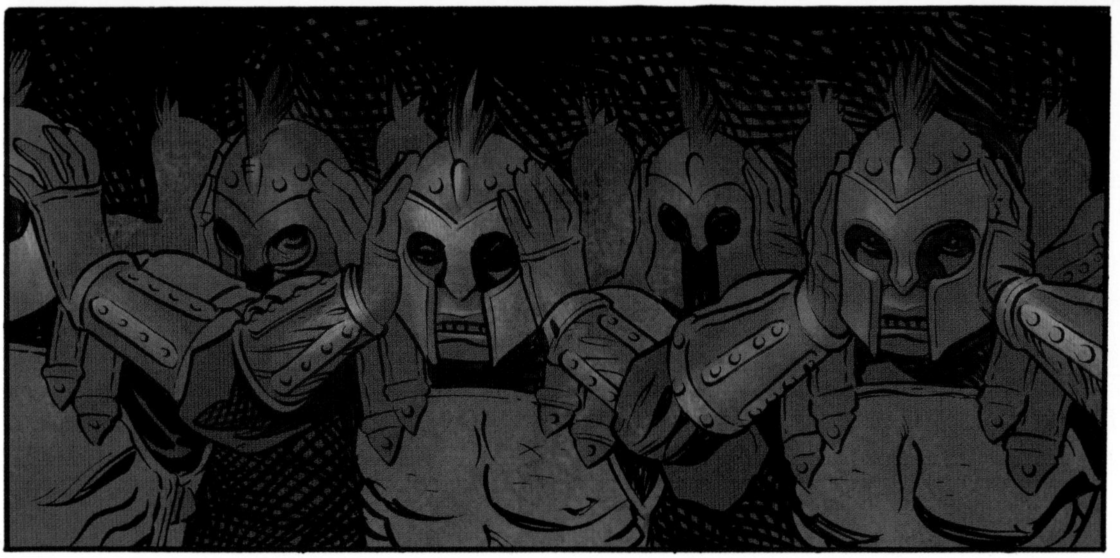

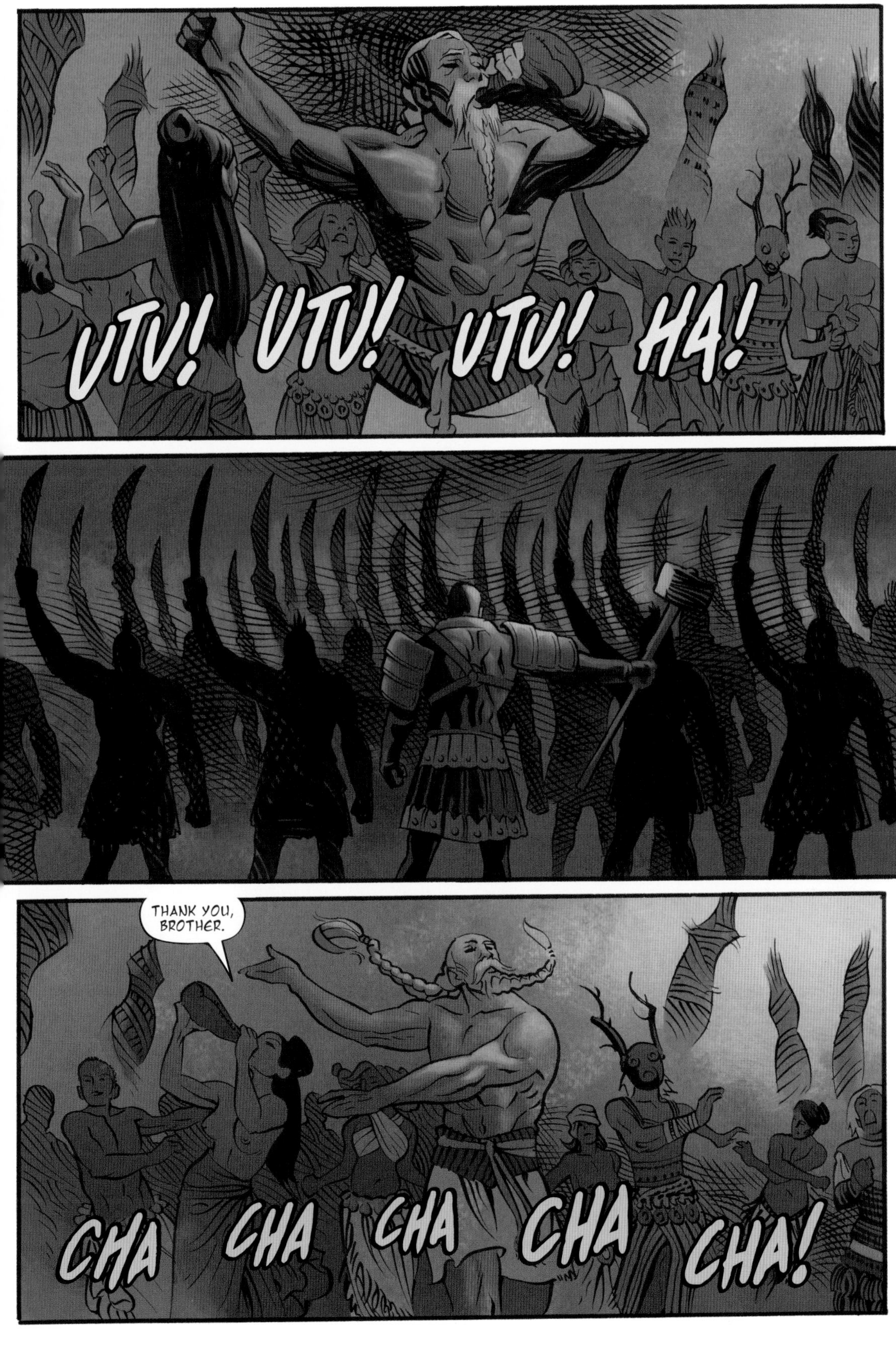
UTU! UTU! UTU! HA!
THANK YOU, BROTHER.
CHA CHA CHA CHA CHA!

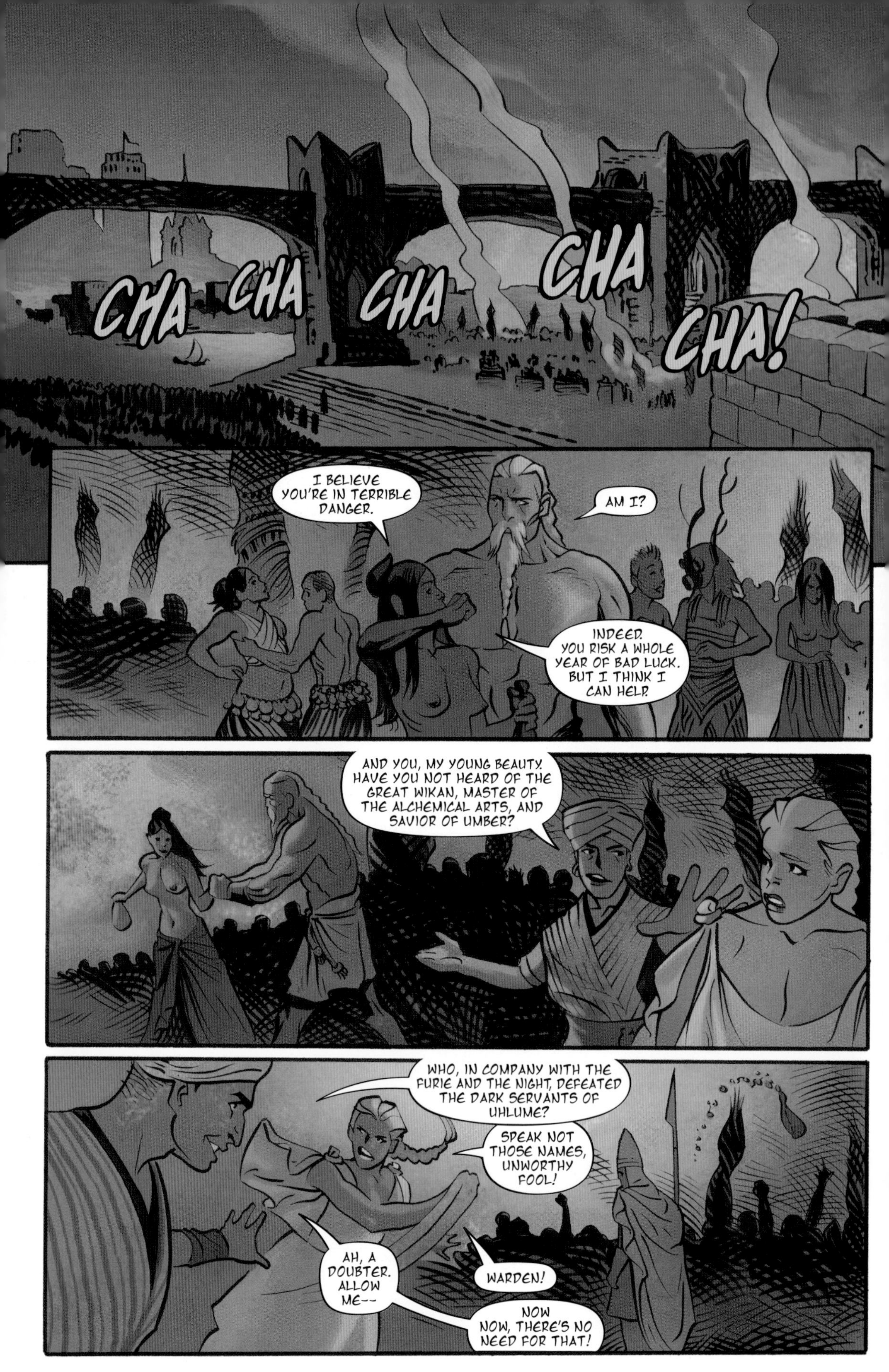

CHA CHA CHA CHA CHA!
I BELIEVE YOU'RE IN TERRIBLE DANGER.
AM I?
INDEED. YOU RISK A WHOLE YEAR OF BAD LUCK. BUT I THINK I CAN HELP.
AND YOU, MY YOUNG BEAUTY. HAVE YOU NOT HEARD OF THE GREAT WIKAN, MASTER OF THE ALCHEMICAL ARTS, AND SAVIOR OF UMBER?
WHO, IN COMPANY WITH THE FURIE AND THE NIGHT, DEFEATED THE DARK SERVANTS OF UHLUME?
SPEAK NOT THOSE NAMES, UNWORTHY FOOL!
AH, A DOUBTER. ALLOW ME--
WARDEN!
NOW NOW, THERE'S NO NEED FOR THAT!

PEOPLE OF UMBER!

WHO IN THE SEVEN HELLS ARE THEY?

I AM AMARAD, THE BLACK HAMMER, COMMANDER OF THE AMARADDAN GUARD. AS OF MIDNIGHT, BY ORDER OF PARLIAMENT, WE ARE THE CITY'S DULY DESIGNATED PEACEKEEPERS...

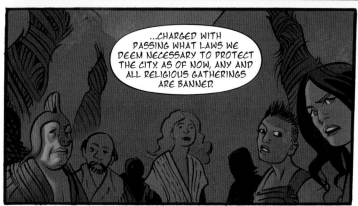

...CHARGED WITH PASSING WHAT LAWS WE DEEM NECESSARY TO PROTECT THE CITY. AS OF NOW, ANY AND ALL RELIGIOUS GATHERINGS ARE BANNED.

UTU'S NIGHT IS OVER. YOU WILL ALL DISPERSE AND RETURN TO YOUR HOMES.

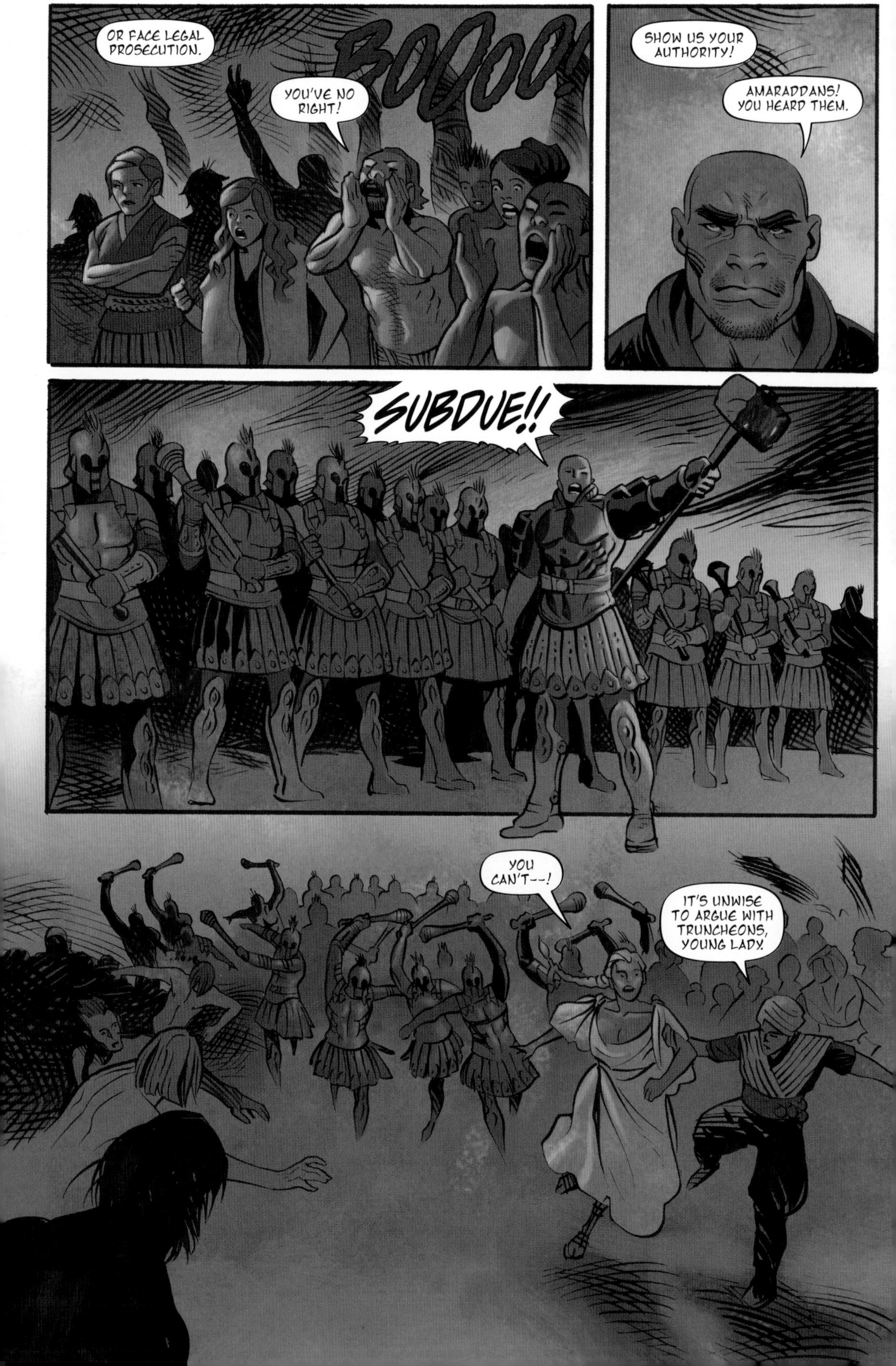
OR FACE LEGAL PROSECUTION.
BOOOOO!
YOU'VE NO RIGHT!
SHOW US YOUR AUTHORITY!
AMARADDANS! YOU HEARD THEM.
SUBDUE!!
YOU CAN'T--!
IT'S UNWISE TO ARGUE WITH TRUNCHEONS, YOUNG LADY.

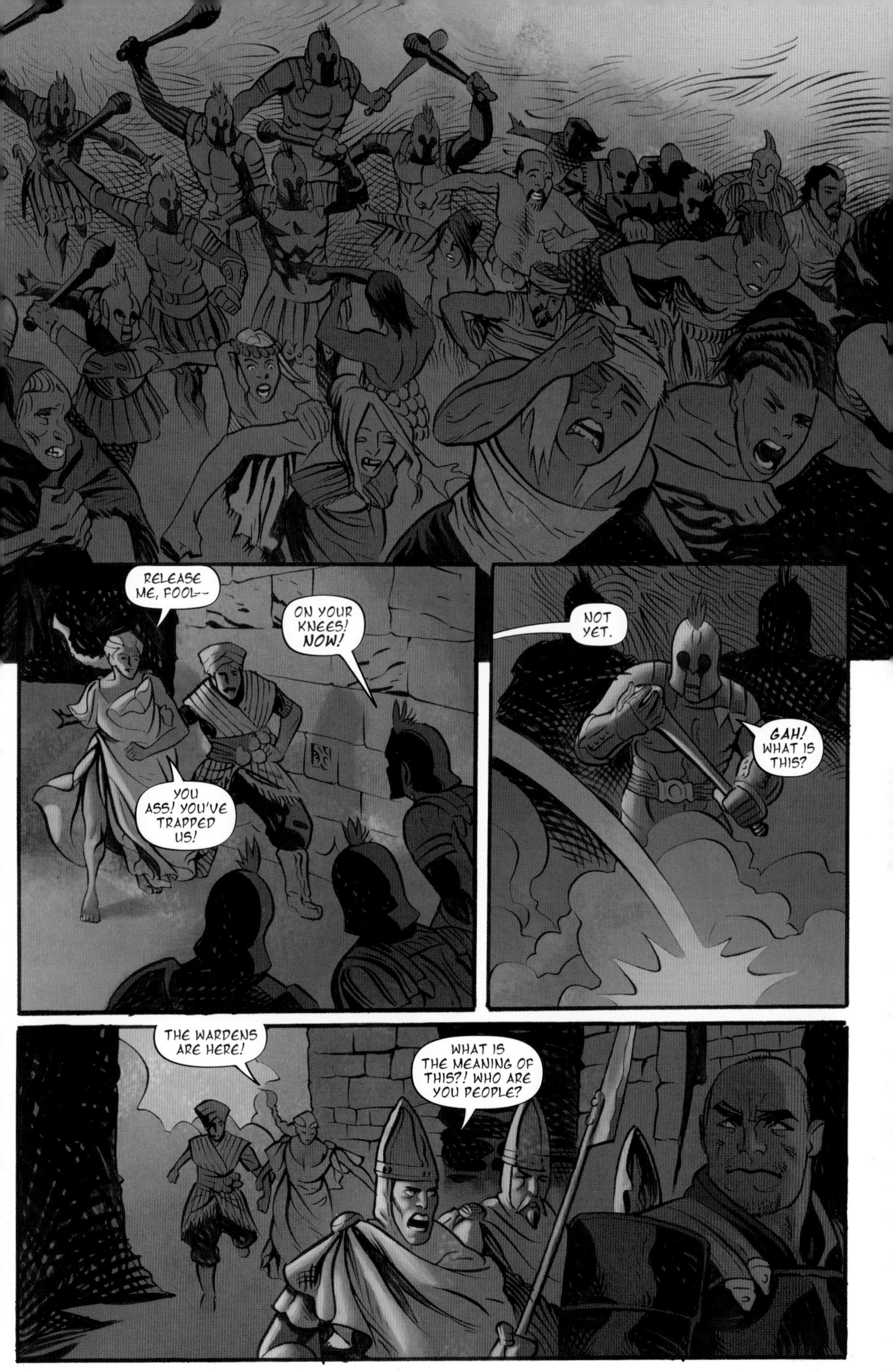
RELEASE ME, FOOL--
ON YOUR KNEES! NOW!
YOU ASS! YOU'VE TRAPPED US!
NOT YET.
GAH! WHAT IS THIS?
THE WARDENS ARE HERE!
WHAT IS THE MEANING OF THIS?! WHO ARE YOU PEOPLE?

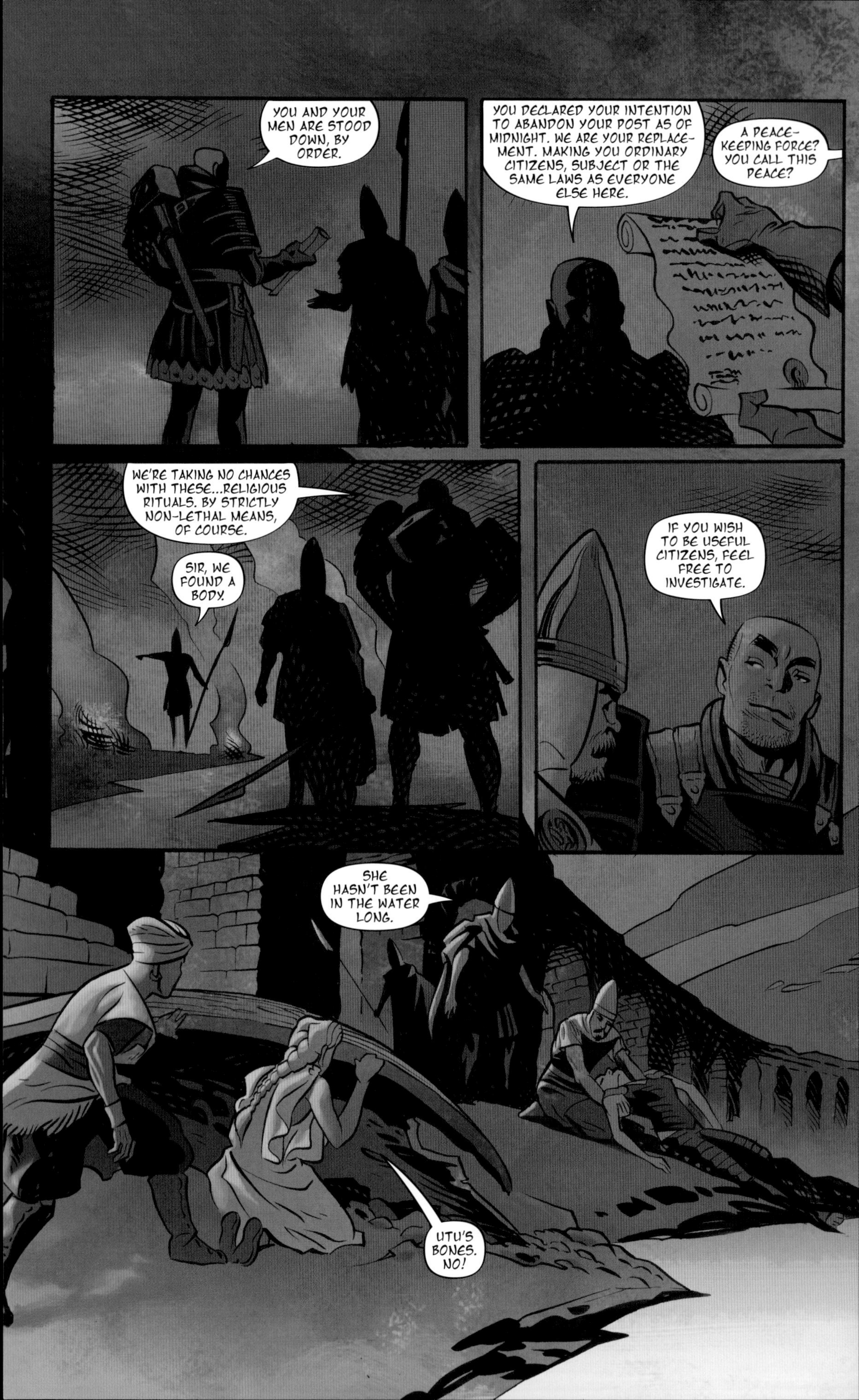
YOU AND YOUR MEN ARE STOOD DOWN, BY ORDER.
YOU DECLARED YOUR INTENTION TO ABANDON YOUR POST AS OF MIDNIGHT. WE ARE YOUR REPLACEMENT. MAKING YOU ORDINARY CITIZENS, SUBJECT OR THE SAME LAWS AS EVERYONE ELSE HERE.
A PEACE-KEEPING FORCE? YOU CALL THIS PEACE?
WE'RE TAKING NO CHANCES WITH THESE...RELIGIOUS RITUALS. BY STRICTLY NON-LETHAL MEANS, OF COURSE.
SIR, WE FOUND A BODY.
IF YOU WISH TO BE USEFUL CITIZENS, FEEL FREE TO INVESTIGATE.
SHE HASN'T BEEN IN THE WATER LONG.
UTU'S BONES. NO!

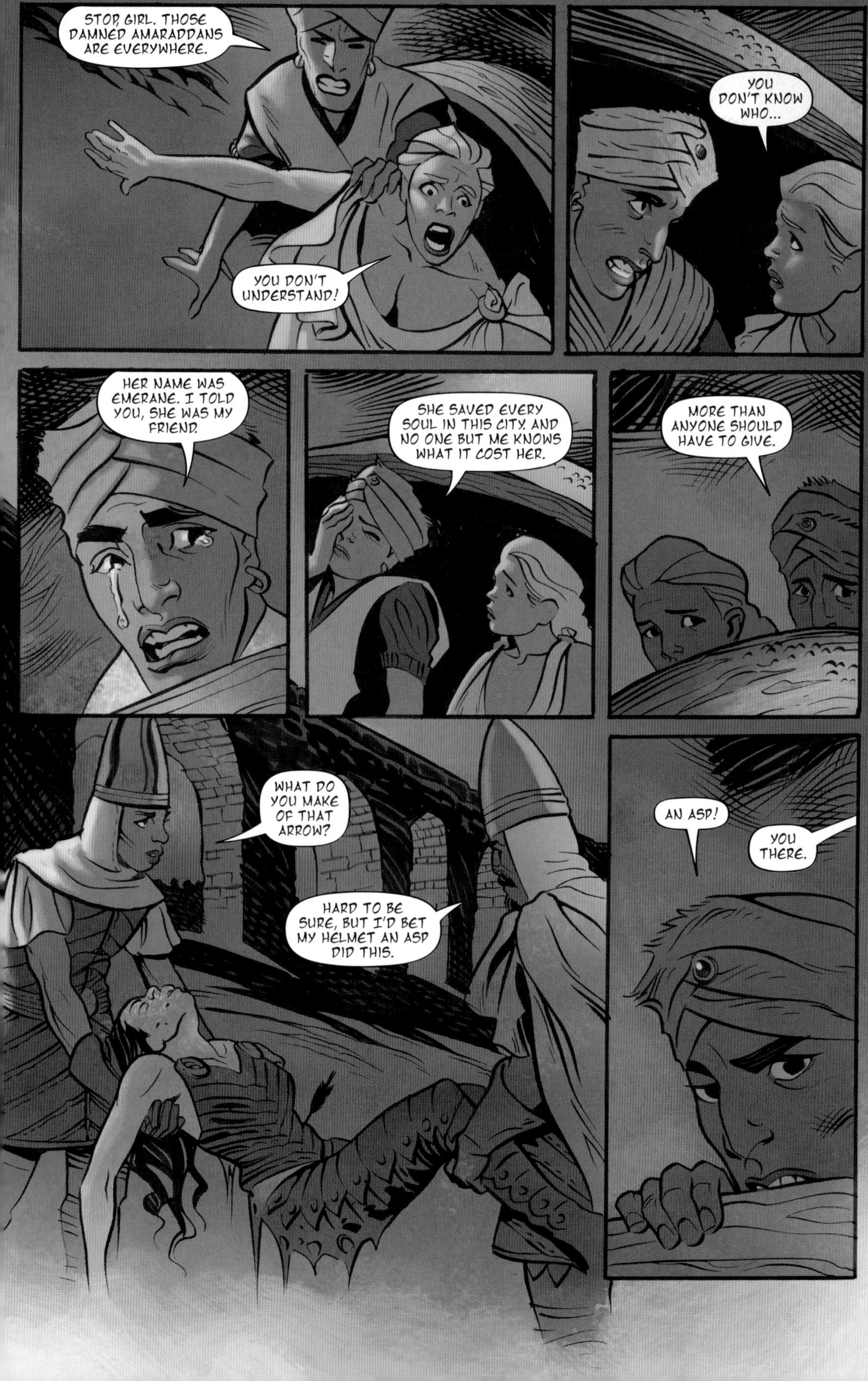
STOP, GIRL. THOSE DAMNED AMARADDANS ARE EVERYWHERE.
YOU DON'T UNDERSTAND!
YOU DON'T KNOW WHO...
HER NAME WAS EMERANE. I TOLD YOU, SHE WAS MY FRIEND.
SHE SAVED EVERY SOUL IN THIS CITY. AND NO ONE BUT ME KNOWS WHAT IT COST HER.
MORE THAN ANYONE SHOULD HAVE TO GIVE.
WHAT DO YOU MAKE OF THAT ARROW?
HARD TO BE SURE, BUT I'D BET MY HELMET AN ASP DID THIS.
AN ASP!
YOU THERE.

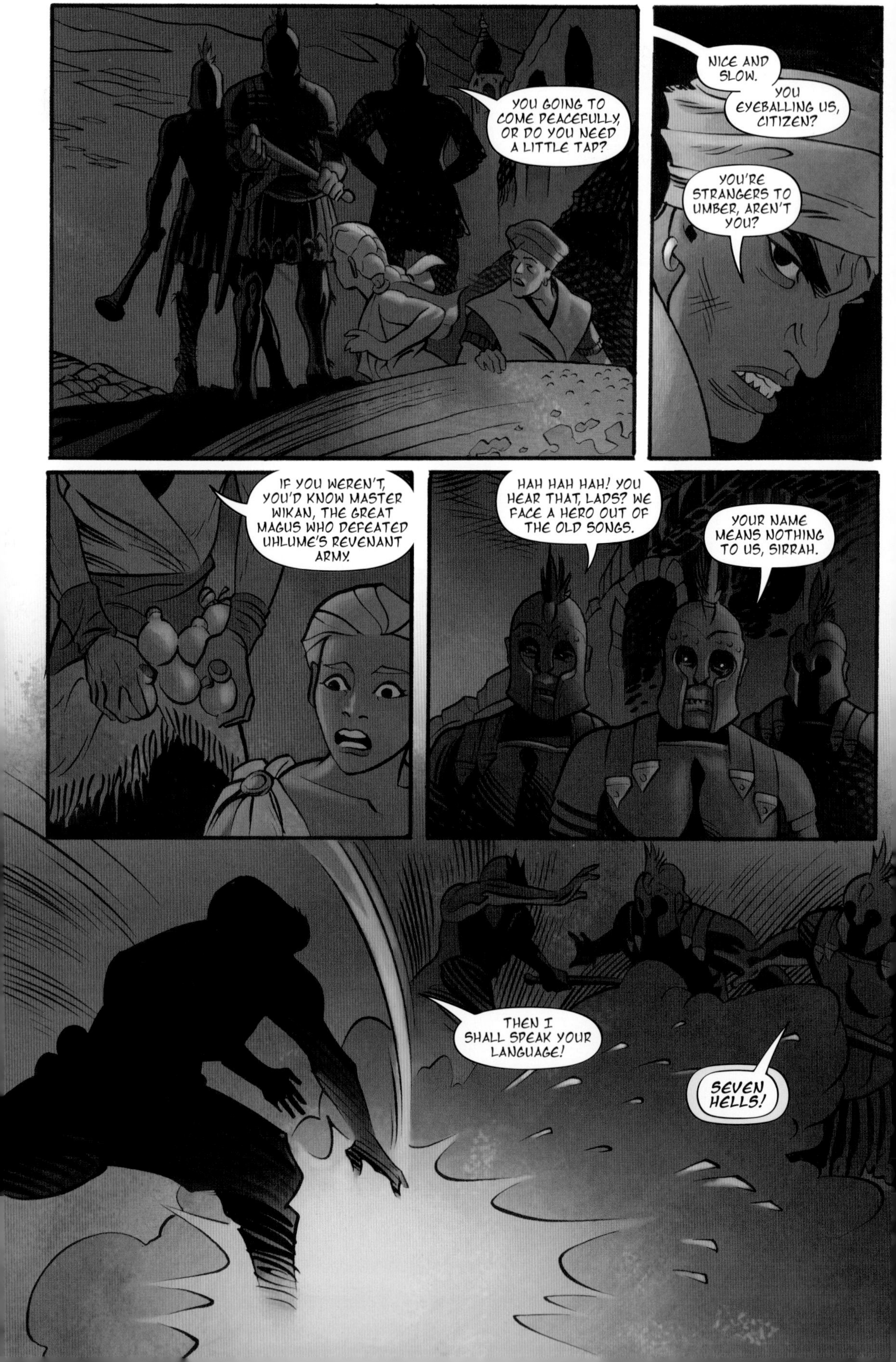
YOU GOING TO COME PEACEFULLY, OR DO YOU NEED A LITTLE TAP?
NICE AND SLOW.
YOU EYEBALLING US, CITIZEN?
YOU'RE STRANGERS TO UMBER, AREN'T YOU?
IF YOU WEREN'T, YOU'D KNOW MASTER WIKAN, THE GREAT MAGUS WHO DEFEATED UHLUME'S REVENANT ARMY.
HAH HAH HAH! YOU HEAR THAT, LADS? WE FACE A HERO OUT OF THE OLD SONGS.
YOUR NAME MEANS NOTHING TO US, SIRRAH.
THEN I SHALL SPEAK YOUR LANGUAGE!
SEVEN HELLS!

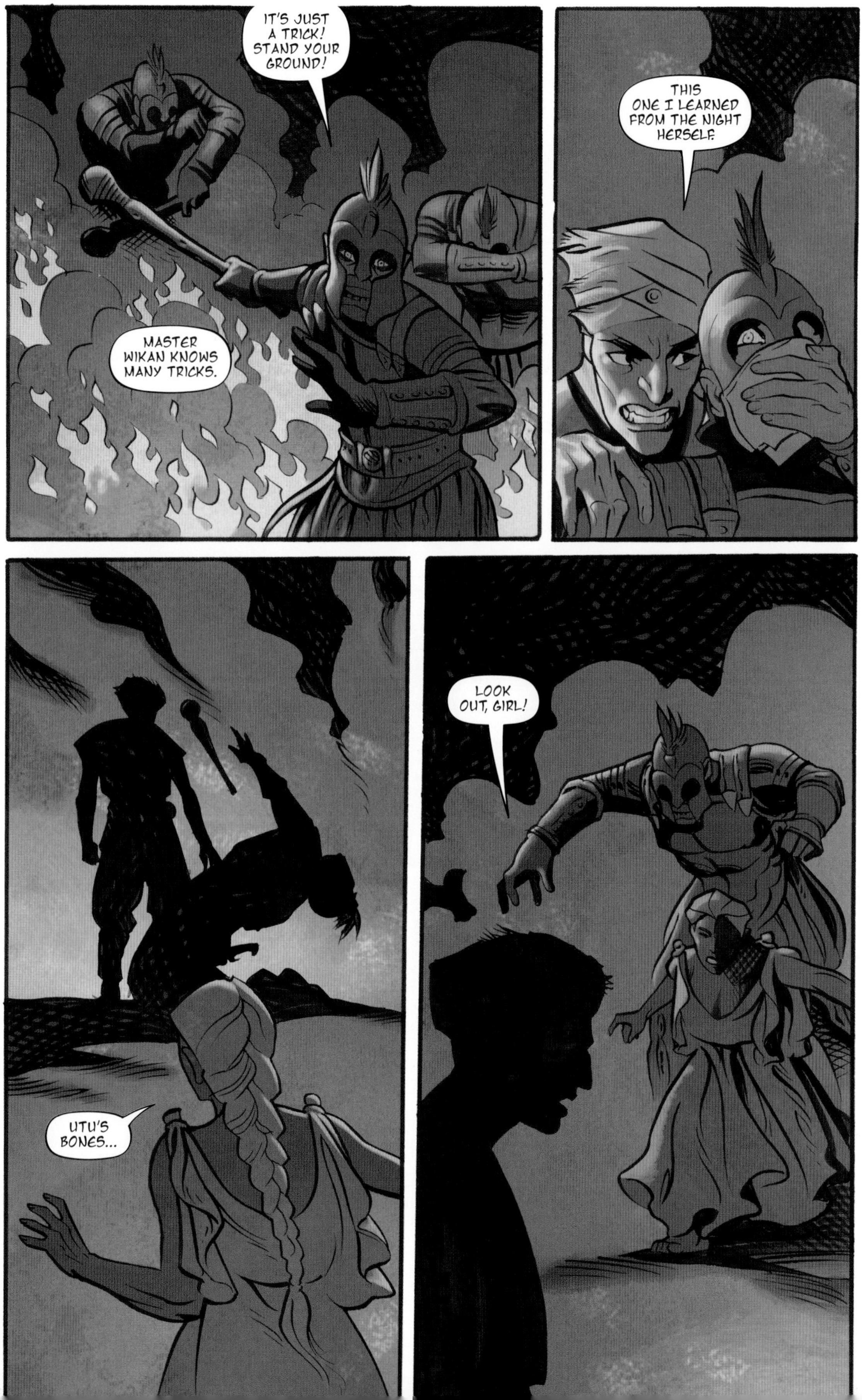
IT'S JUST A TRICK! STAND YOUR GROUND!
MASTER WIKAN KNOWS MANY TRICKS.
THIS ONE I LEARNED FROM THE NIGHT HERSELF.
UTU'S BONES...
LOOK OUT, GIRL!

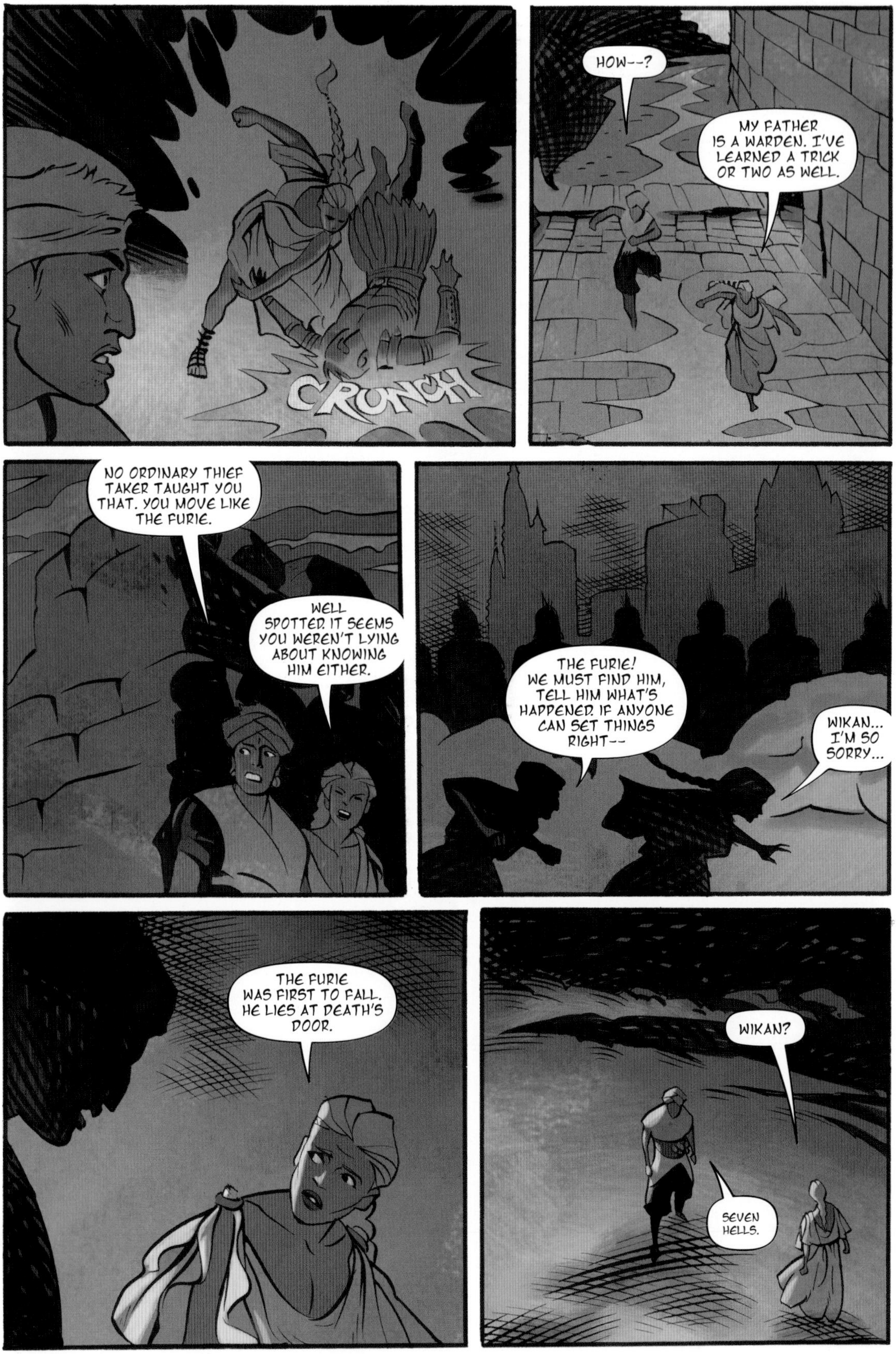
CRUNCH
HOW--?
MY FATHER IS A WARDEN. I'VE LEARNED A TRICK OR TWO AS WELL.
NO ORDINARY THIEF TAKER TAUGHT YOU THAT. YOU MOVE LIKE THE FURIE.
WELL SPOTTED. IT SEEMS YOU WEREN'T LYING ABOUT KNOWING HIM EITHER.
THE FURIE! WE MUST FIND HIM, TELL HIM WHAT'S HAPPENED. IF ANYONE CAN SET THINGS RIGHT--
WIKAN... I'M SO SORRY...
THE FURIE WAS FIRST TO FALL. HE LIES AT DEATH'S DOOR.
WIKAN?
SEVEN HELLS.

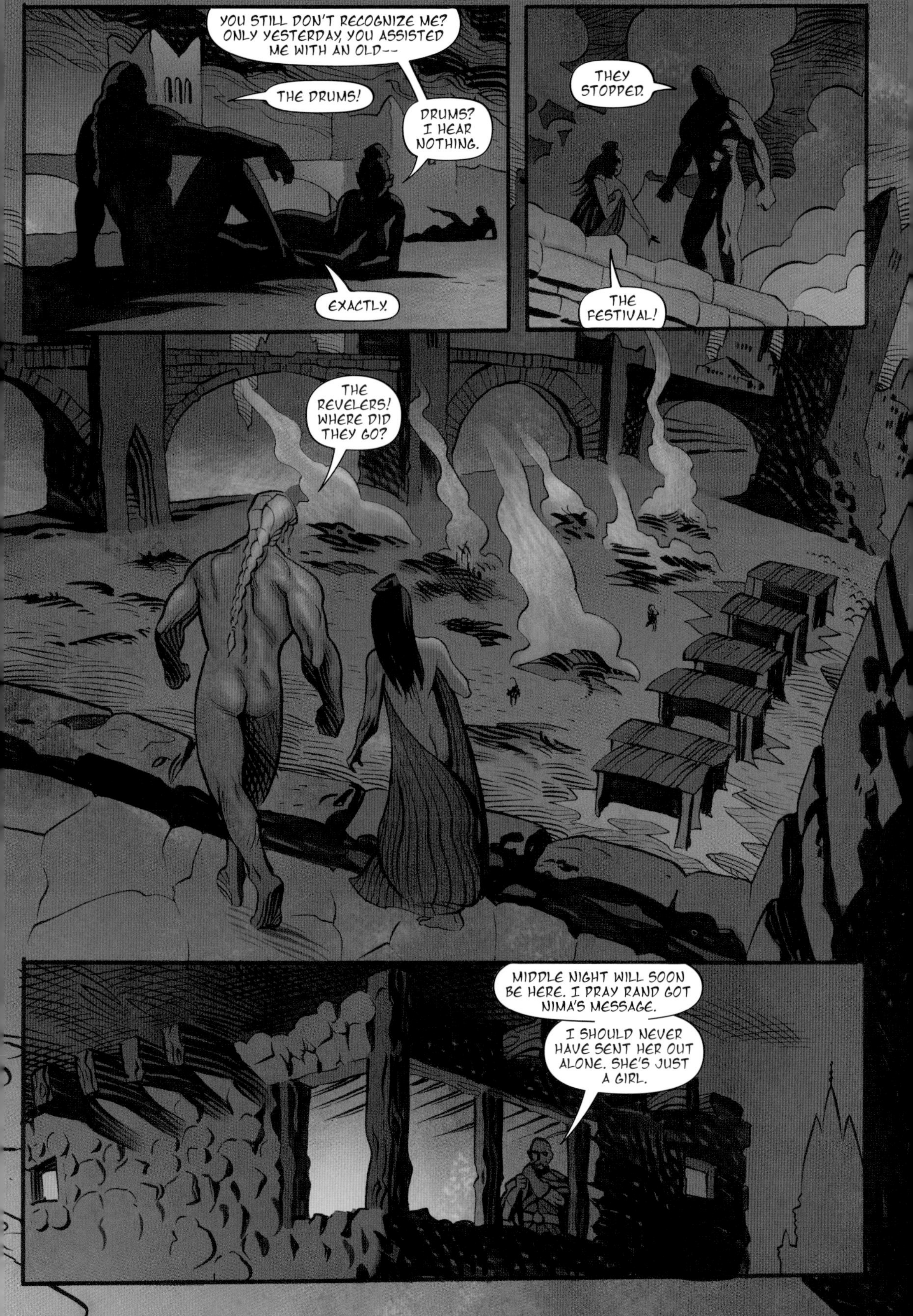
YOU STILL DON'T RECOGNIZE ME? ONLY YESTERDAY, YOU ASSISTED ME WITH AN OLD--
THE DRUMS!
DRUMS? I HEAR NOTHING.
EXACTLY.
THEY STOPPED.
THE FESTIVAL!
THE REVELERS! WHERE DID THEY GO?
MIDDLE NIGHT WILL SOON BE HERE. I PRAY RAND GOT NIMA'S MESSAGE.
I SHOULD NEVER HAVE SENT HER OUT ALONE. SHE'S JUST A GIRL.

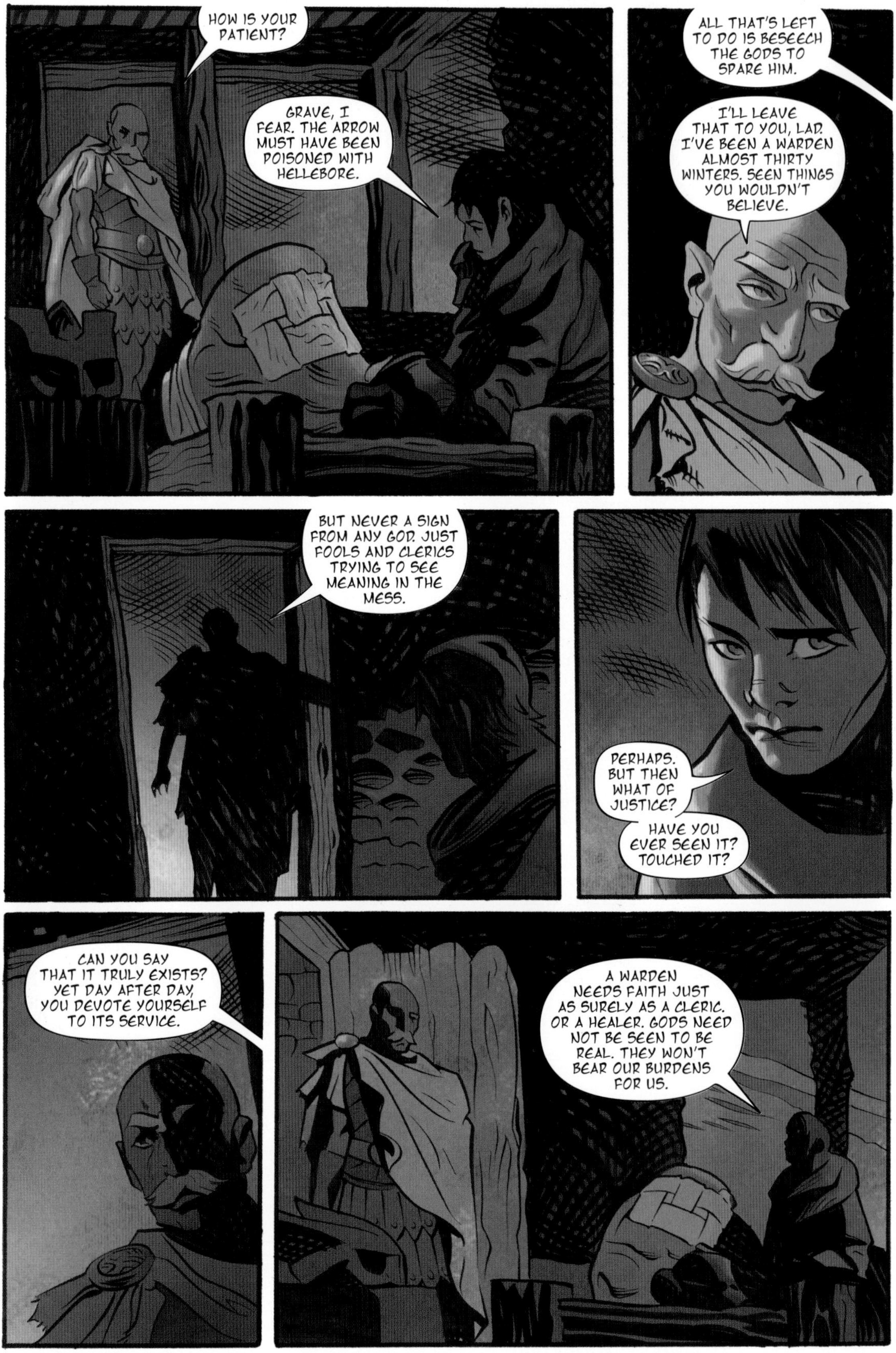
HOW IS YOUR PATIENT?
GRAVE, I FEAR. THE ARROW MUST HAVE BEEN POISONED WITH HELLEBORE.
ALL THAT'S LEFT TO DO IS BESEECH THE GODS TO SPARE HIM.
I'LL LEAVE THAT TO YOU, LAD. I'VE BEEN A WARDEN ALMOST THIRTY WINTERS. SEEN THINGS YOU WOULDN'T BELIEVE.
BUT NEVER A SIGN FROM ANY GOD. JUST FOOLS AND CLERICS TRYING TO SEE MEANING IN THE MESS.
PERHAPS. BUT THEN WHAT OF JUSTICE?
HAVE YOU EVER SEEN IT? TOUCHED IT?
CAN YOU SAY THAT IT TRULY EXISTS? YET DAY AFTER DAY, YOU DEVOTE YOURSELF TO ITS SERVICE.
A WARDEN NEEDS FAITH JUST AS SURELY AS A CLERIC. OR A HEALER. GODS NEED NOT BE SEEN TO BE REAL. THEY WON'T BEAR OUR BURDENS FOR US.

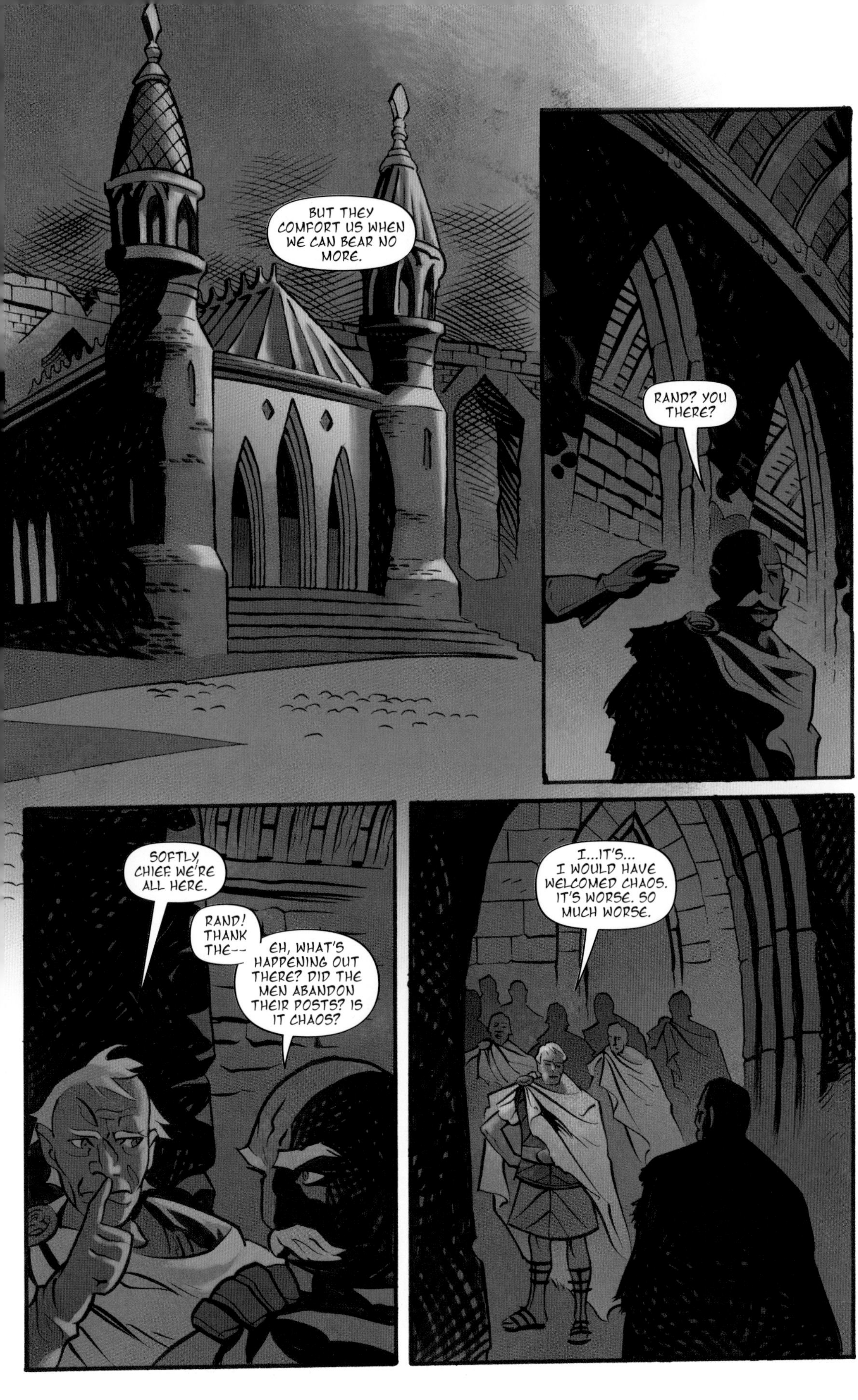
BUT THEY COMFORT US WHEN WE CAN BEAR NO MORE.
RAND? YOU THERE?
SOFTLY, CHIEF. WE'RE ALL HERE.
RAND! THANK THE--
EH, WHAT'S HAPPENING OUT THERE? DID THE MEN ABANDON THEIR POSTS? IS IT CHAOS?
I...IT'S... I WOULD HAVE WELCOMED CHAOS. IT'S WORSE. SO MUCH WORSE.

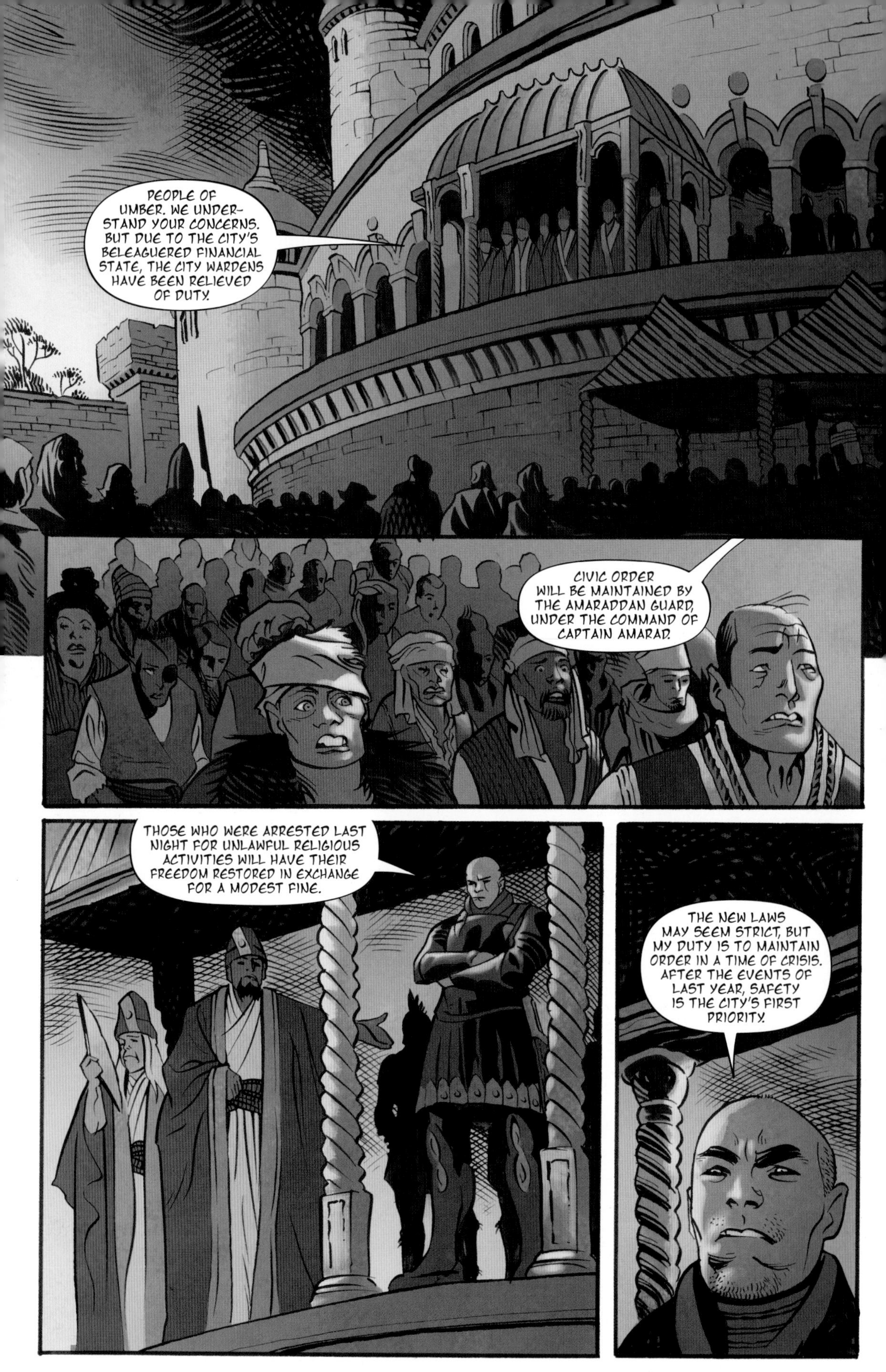
PEOPLE OF UMBER. WE UNDERSTAND YOUR CONCERNS. BUT DUE TO THE CITY'S BELEAGUERED FINANCIAL STATE, THE CITY WARDENS HAVE BEEN RELIEVED OF DUTY.
CIVIC ORDER WILL BE MAINTAINED BY THE AMARADDAN GUARD, UNDER THE COMMAND OF CAPTAIN AMARAD.
THOSE WHO WERE ARRESTED LAST NIGHT FOR UNLAWFUL RELIGIOUS ACTIVITIES WILL HAVE THEIR FREEDOM RESTORED IN EXCHANGE FOR A MODEST FINE.
THE NEW LAWS MAY SEEM STRICT, BUT MY DUTY IS TO MAINTAIN ORDER IN A TIME OF CRISIS. AFTER THE EVENTS OF LAST YEAR, SAFETY IS THE CITY'S FIRST PRIORITY.

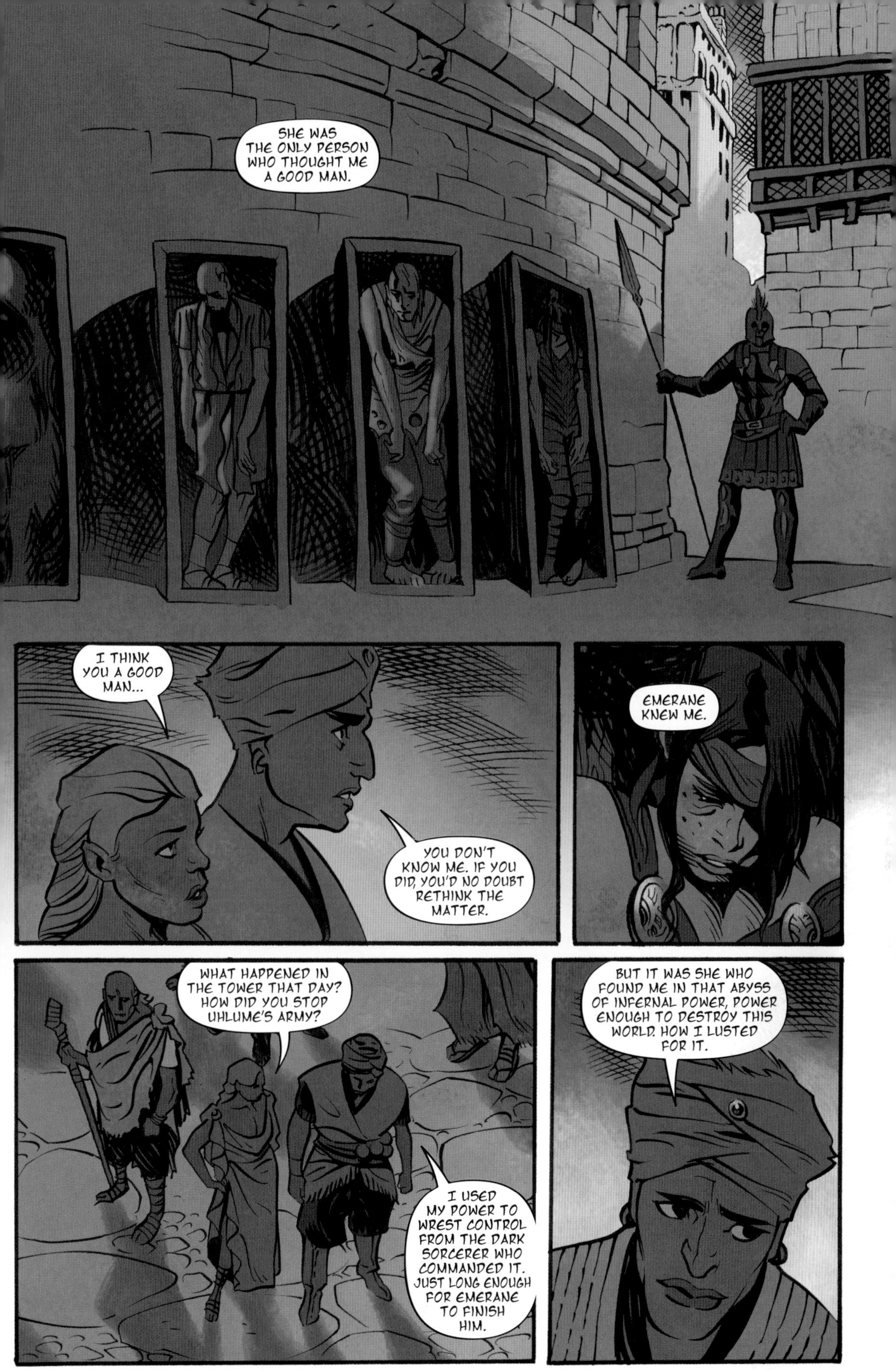
SHE WAS THE ONLY PERSON WHO THOUGHT ME A GOOD MAN.
I THINK YOU A GOOD MAN...
YOU DON'T KNOW ME. IF YOU DID, YOU'D NO DOUBT RETHINK THE MATTER.
EMERANE KNEW ME.
WHAT HAPPENED IN THE TOWER THAT DAY? HOW DID YOU STOP UHLUME'S ARMY?
I USED MY POWER TO WREST CONTROL FROM THE DARK SORCERER WHO COMMANDED IT. JUST LONG ENOUGH FOR EMERANE TO FINISH HIM.
BUT IT WAS SHE WHO FOUND ME IN THAT ABYSS OF INFERNAL POWER, POWER ENOUGH TO DESTROY THIS WORLD. HOW I LUSTED FOR IT.

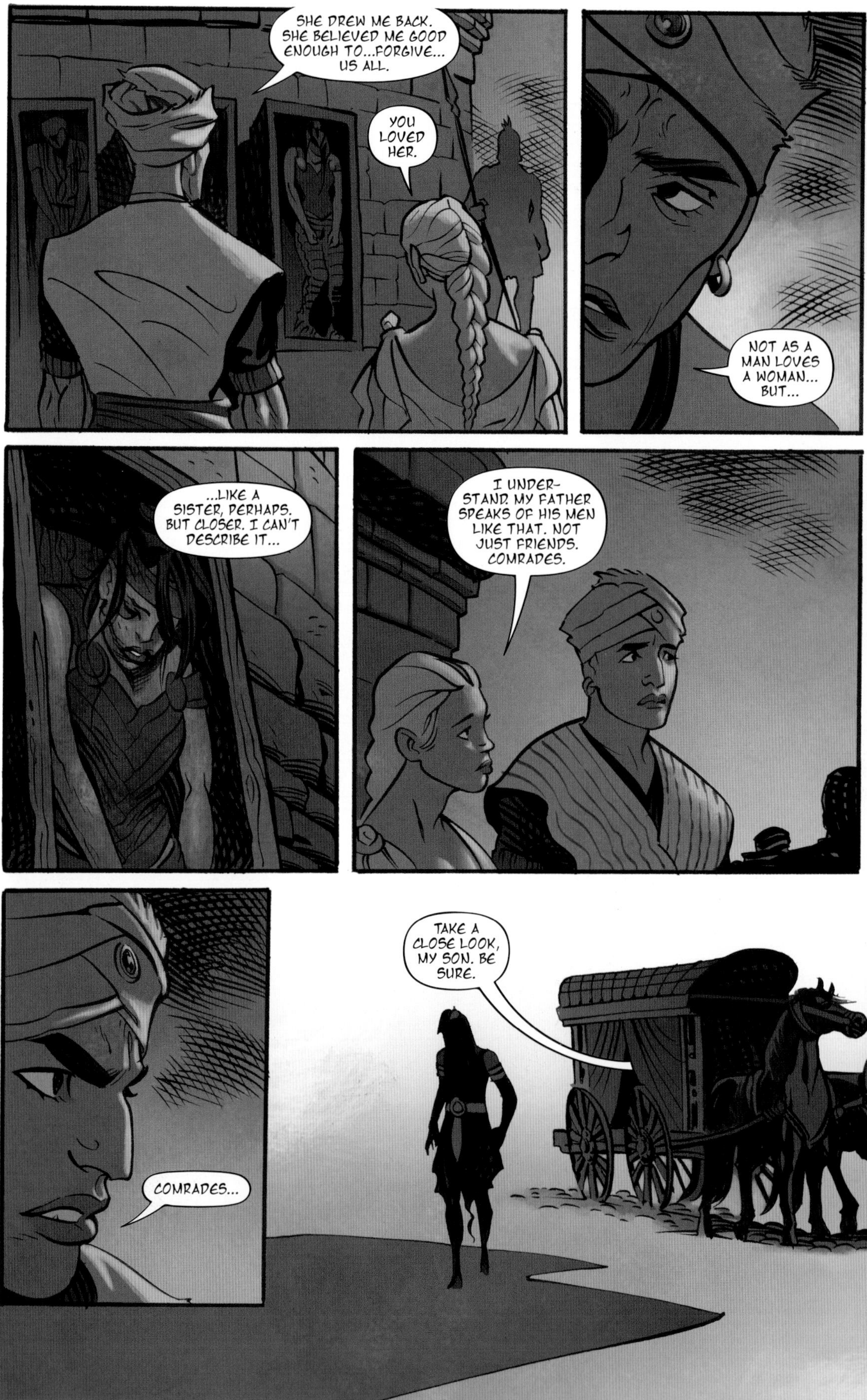
SHE DREW ME BACK. SHE BELIEVED ME GOOD ENOUGH TO...FORGIVE... US ALL.
YOU LOVED HER.
NOT AS A MAN LOVES A WOMAN... BUT...
...LIKE A SISTER, PERHAPS. BUT CLOSER. I CAN'T DESCRIBE IT...
I UNDER-STAND. MY FATHER SPEAKS OF HIS MEN LIKE THAT. NOT JUST FRIENDS. COMRADES.
COMRADES...
TAKE A CLOSE LOOK, MY SON. BE SURE.

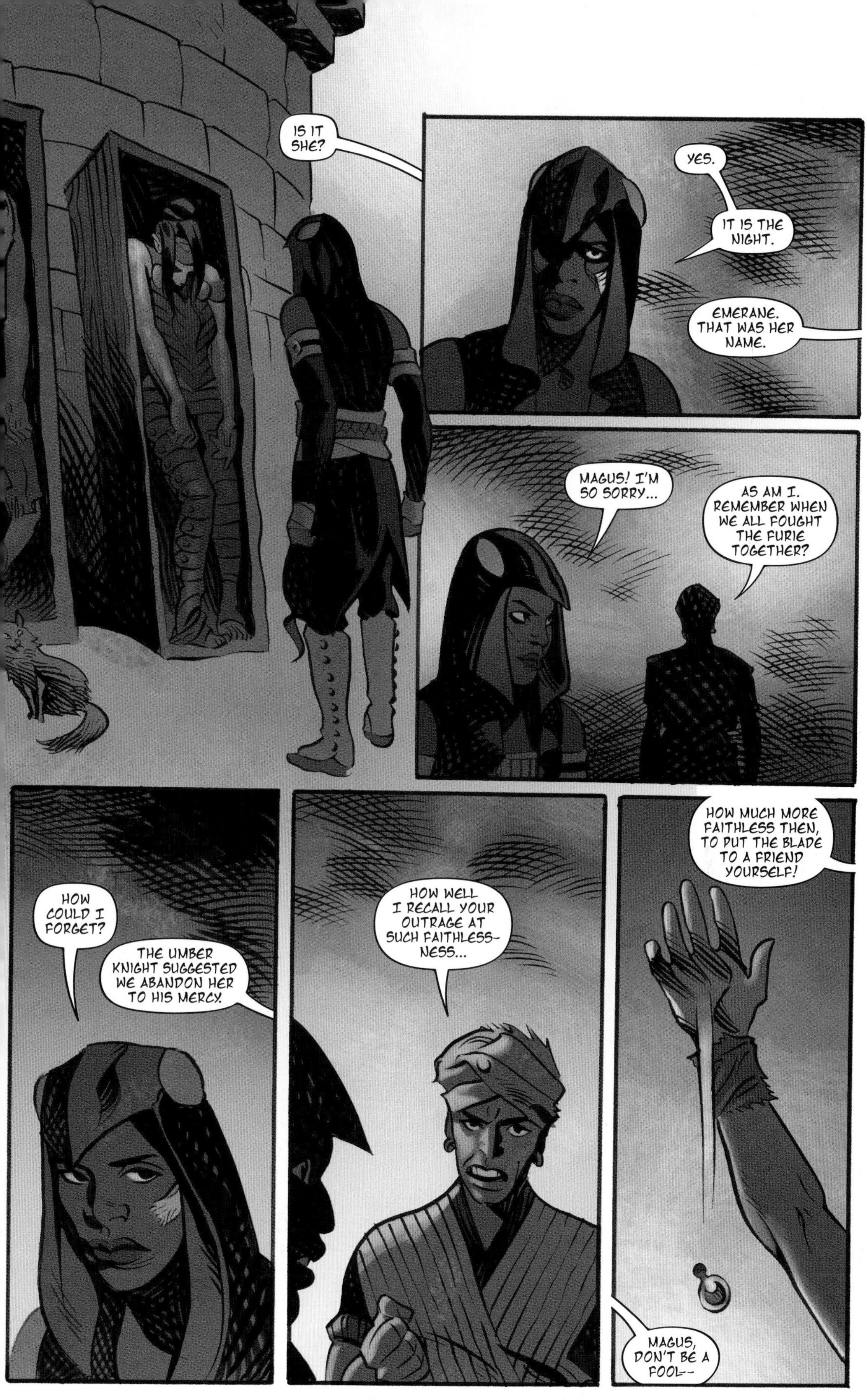
IS IT SHE?
YES.
IT IS THE NIGHT.
EMERANE. THAT WAS HER NAME.
MAGUS! I'M SO SORRY...
AS AM I. REMEMBER WHEN WE ALL FOUGHT THE FURIE TOGETHER?
HOW COULD I FORGET?
THE UMBER KNIGHT SUGGESTED WE ABANDON HER TO HIS MERCY.
HOW WELL I RECALL YOUR OUTRAGE AT SUCH FAITHLESS-NESS...
HOW MUCH MORE FAITHLESS THEN, TO PUT THE BLADE TO A FRIEND YOURSELF!
MAGUS, DON'T BE A FOOL--

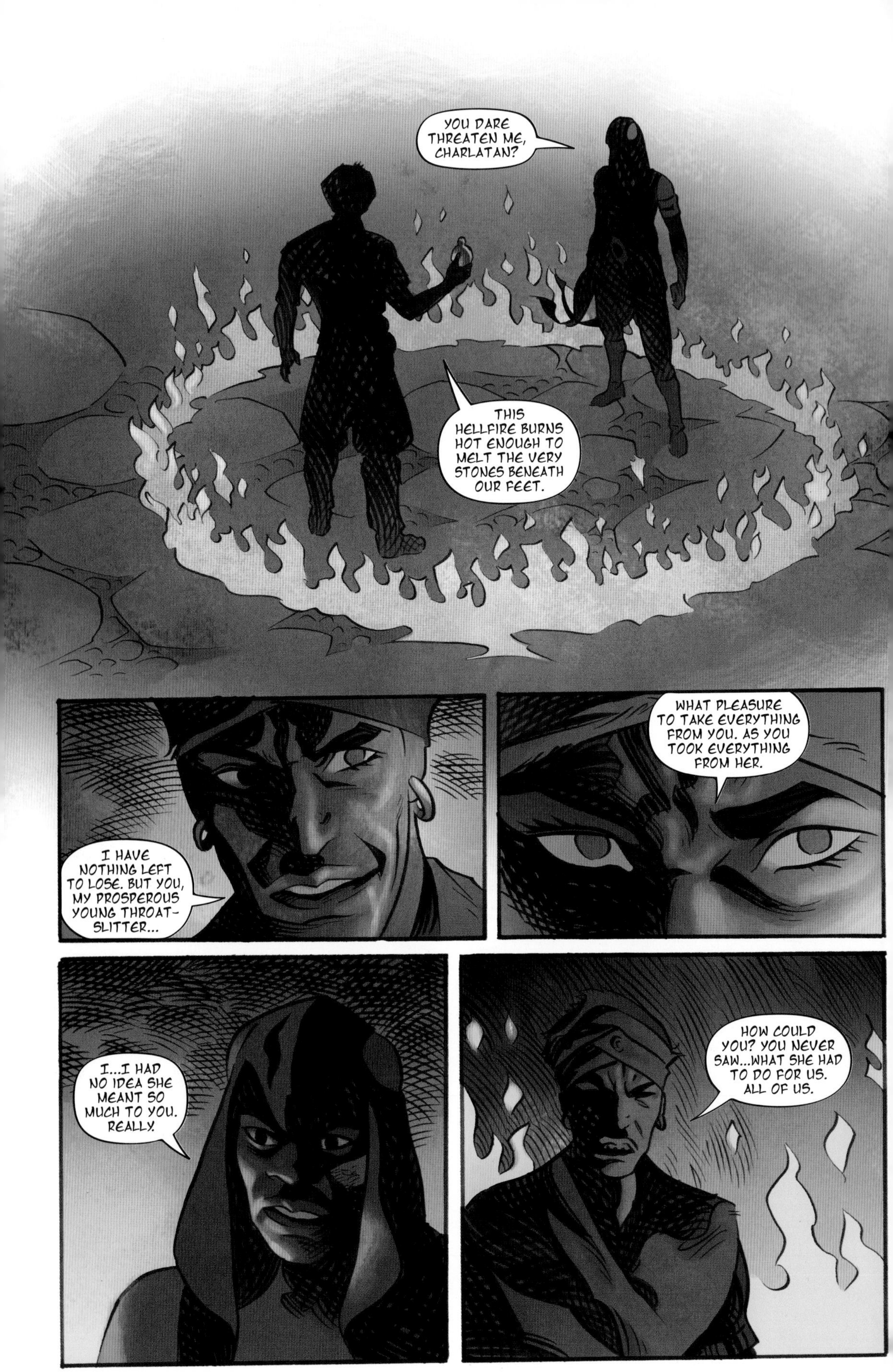
YOU DARE THREATEN ME, CHARLATAN?
THIS HELLFIRE BURNS HOT ENOUGH TO MELT THE VERY STONES BENEATH OUR FEET.
I HAVE NOTHING LEFT TO LOSE. BUT YOU, MY PROSPEROUS YOUNG THROAT-SLITTER...
WHAT PLEASURE TO TAKE EVERYTHING FROM YOU. AS YOU TOOK EVERYTHING FROM HER.
I...I HAD NO IDEA SHE MEANT SO MUCH TO YOU. REALLY.
HOW COULD YOU? YOU NEVER SAW...WHAT SHE HAD TO DO FOR US. ALL OF US.

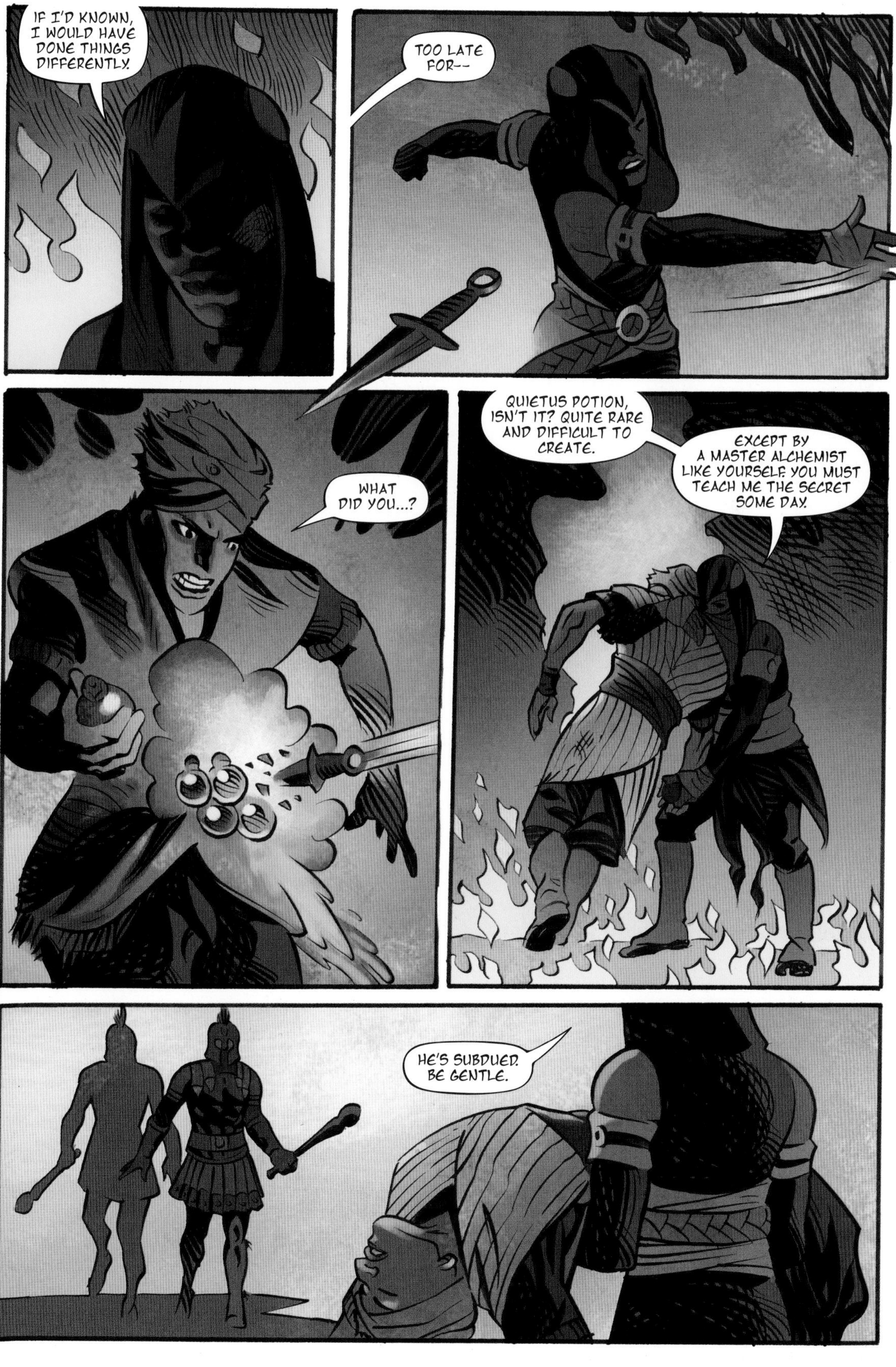
IF I'D KNOWN, I WOULD HAVE DONE THINGS DIFFERENTLY.
TOO LATE FOR--
WHAT DID YOU...?
QUIETUS POTION, ISN'T IT? QUITE RARE AND DIFFICULT TO CREATE.
EXCEPT BY A MASTER ALCHEMIST LIKE YOURSELF. YOU MUST TEACH ME THE SECRET SOME DAY.
HE'S SUBDUED. BE GENTLE.

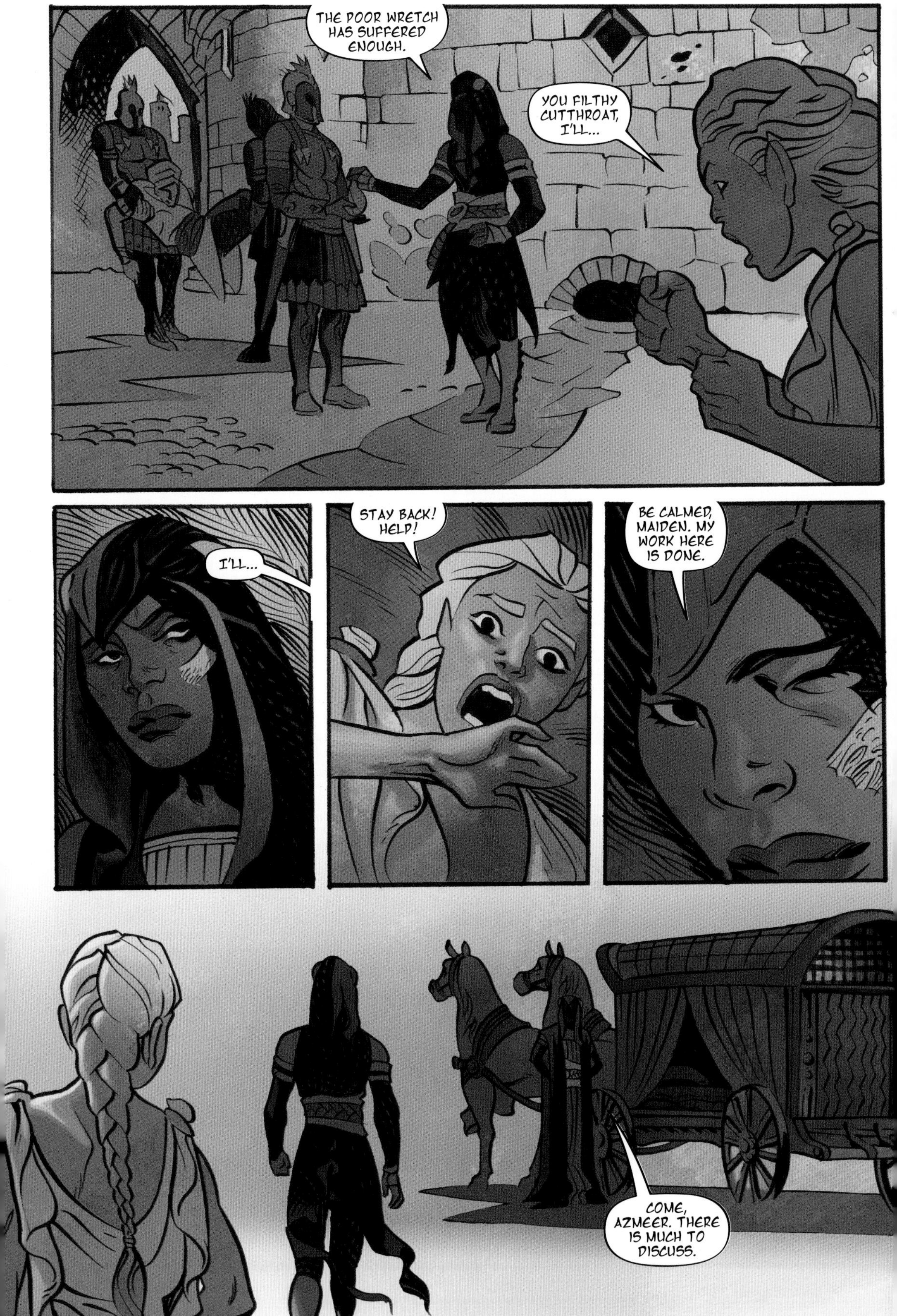
THE POOR WRETCH HAS SUFFERED ENOUGH.
YOU FILTHY CUTTHROAT, I'LL...
I'LL...
STAY BACK! HELP!
BE CALMED, MAIDEN. MY WORK HERE IS DONE.
COME, AZMEER. THERE IS MUCH TO DISCUSS.

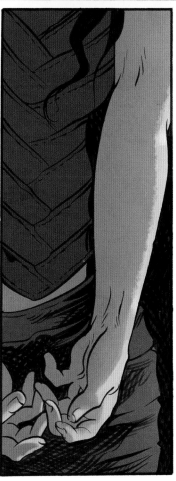

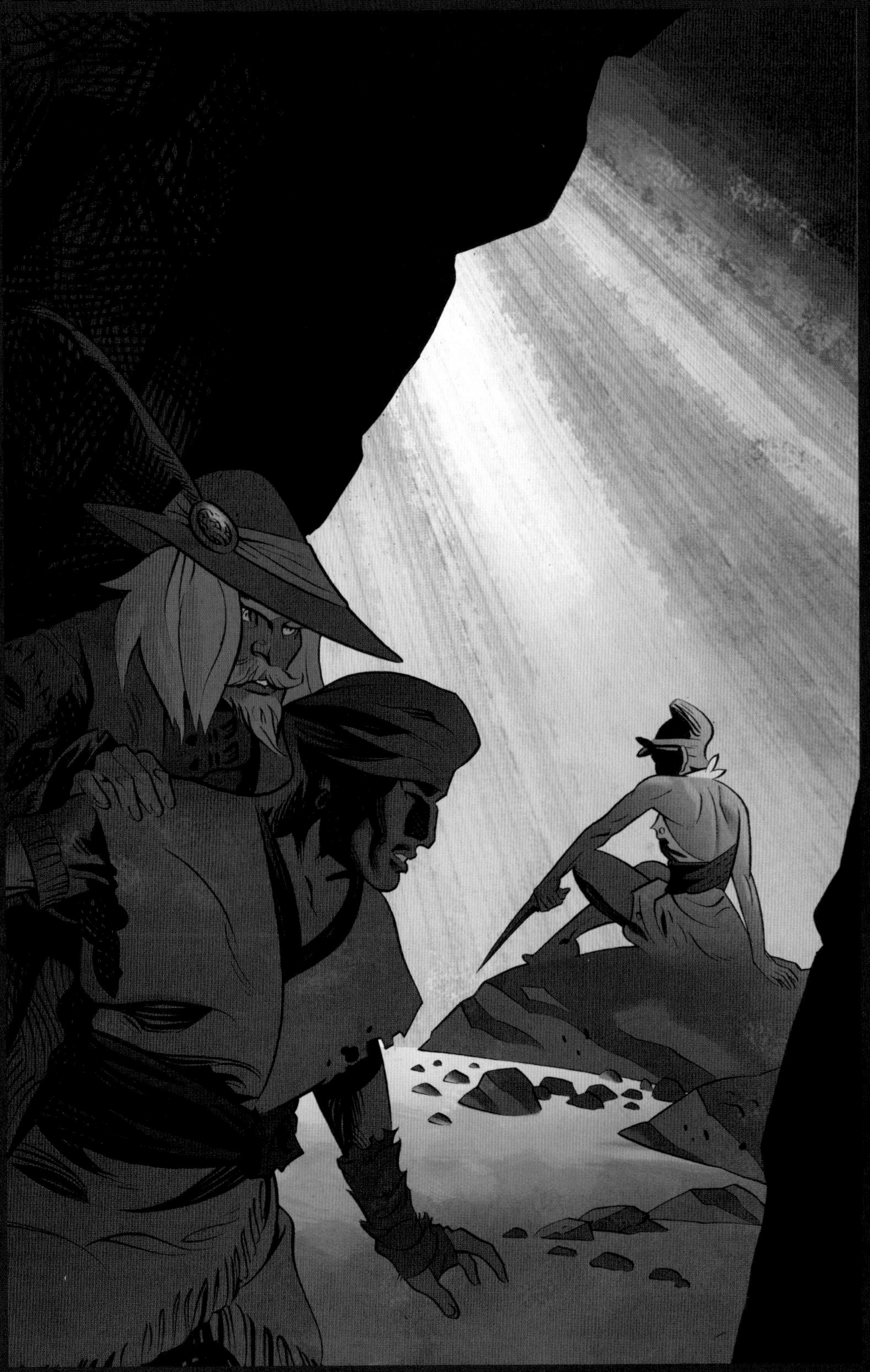

CHAPTER 4

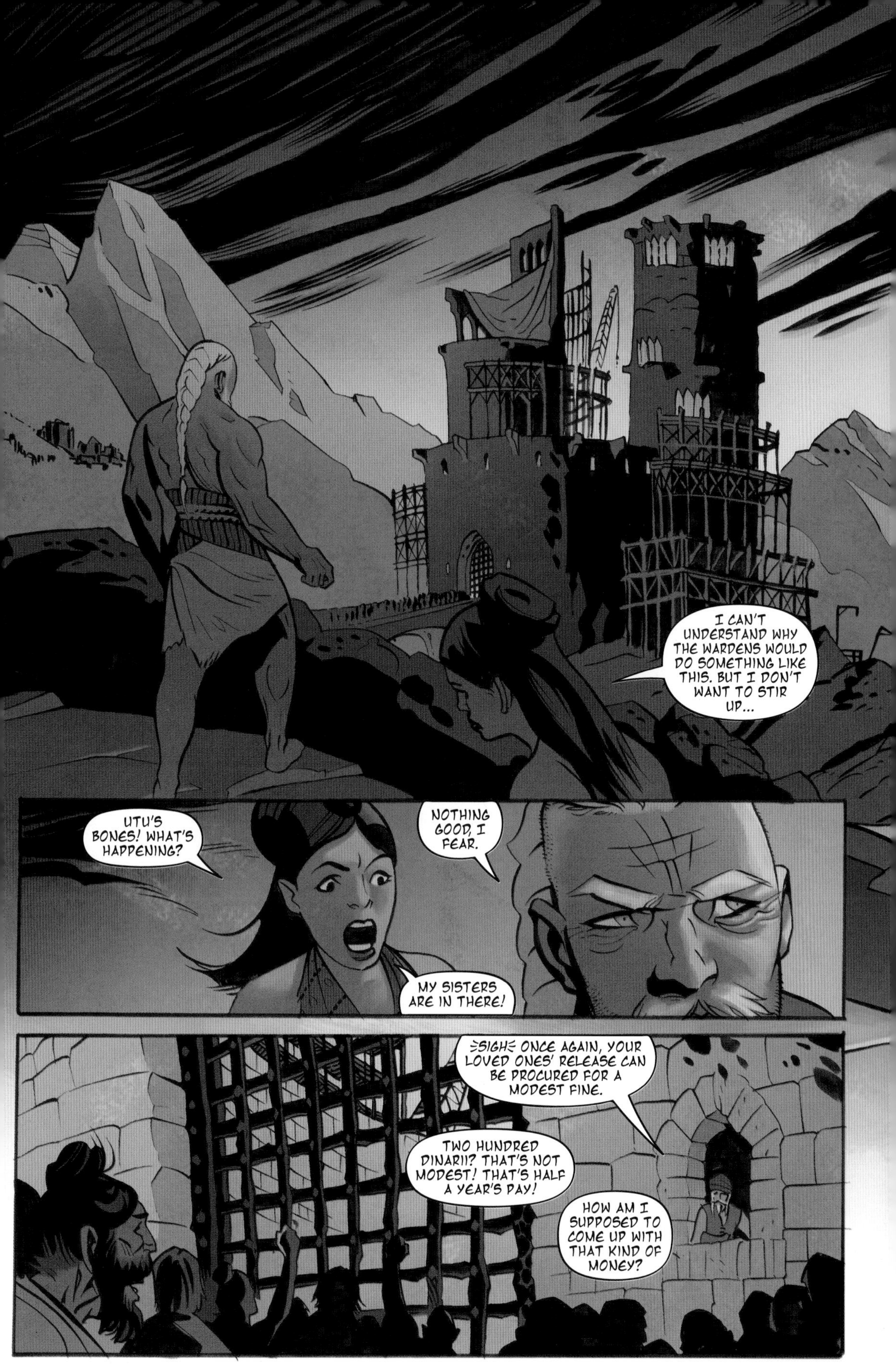
I CAN'T UNDERSTAND WHY THE WARDENS WOULD DO SOMETHING LIKE THIS. BUT I DON'T WANT TO STIR UP...
UTU'S BONES! WHAT'S HAPPENING?
NOTHING GOOD, I FEAR.
MY SISTERS ARE IN THERE!
≡SIGH≡ ONCE AGAIN, YOUR LOVED ONES' RELEASE CAN BE PROCURED FOR A MODEST FINE.
TWO HUNDRED DINARII? THAT'S NOT MODEST! THAT'S HALF A YEAR'S PAY!
HOW AM I SUPPOSED TO COME UP WITH THAT KIND OF MONEY?

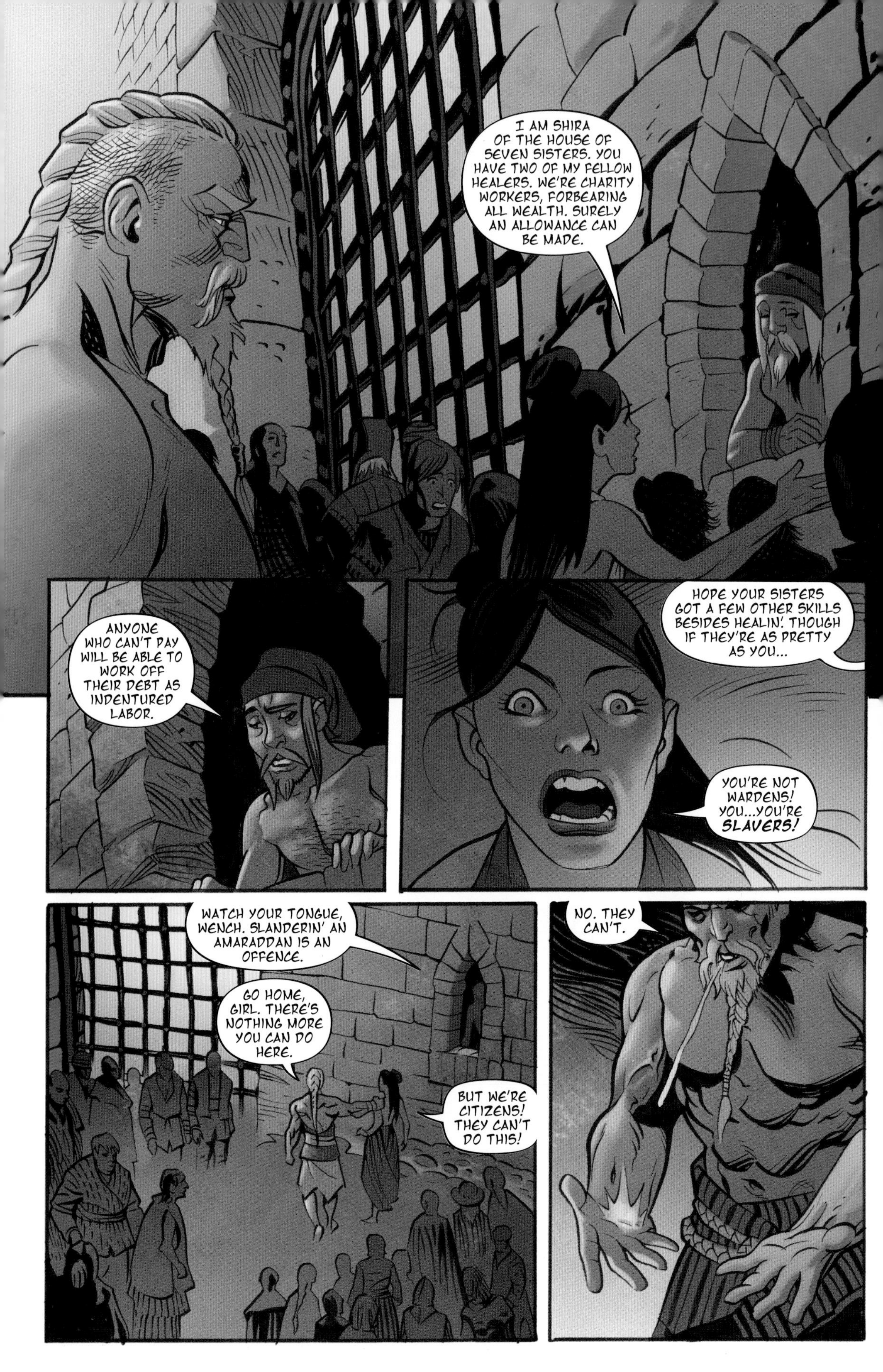
I AM SHIRA OF THE HOUSE OF SEVEN SISTERS. YOU HAVE TWO OF MY FELLOW HEALERS. WE'RE CHARITY WORKERS, FORBEARING ALL WEALTH. SURELY AN ALLOWANCE CAN BE MADE.
ANYONE WHO CAN'T PAY WILL BE ABLE TO WORK OFF THEIR DEBT AS INDENTURED LABOR.
HOPE YOUR SISTERS GOT A FEW OTHER SKILLS BESIDES HEALIN'. THOUGH IF THEY'RE AS PRETTY AS YOU...
YOU'RE NOT WARDENS! YOU...YOU'RE SLAVERS!
WATCH YOUR TONGUE, WENCH. SLANDERIN' AN AMARADDAN IS AN OFFENCE.
GO HOME, GIRL. THERE'S NOTHING MORE YOU CAN DO HERE.
BUT WE'RE CITIZENS! THEY CAN'T DO THIS!
NO. THEY CAN'T.

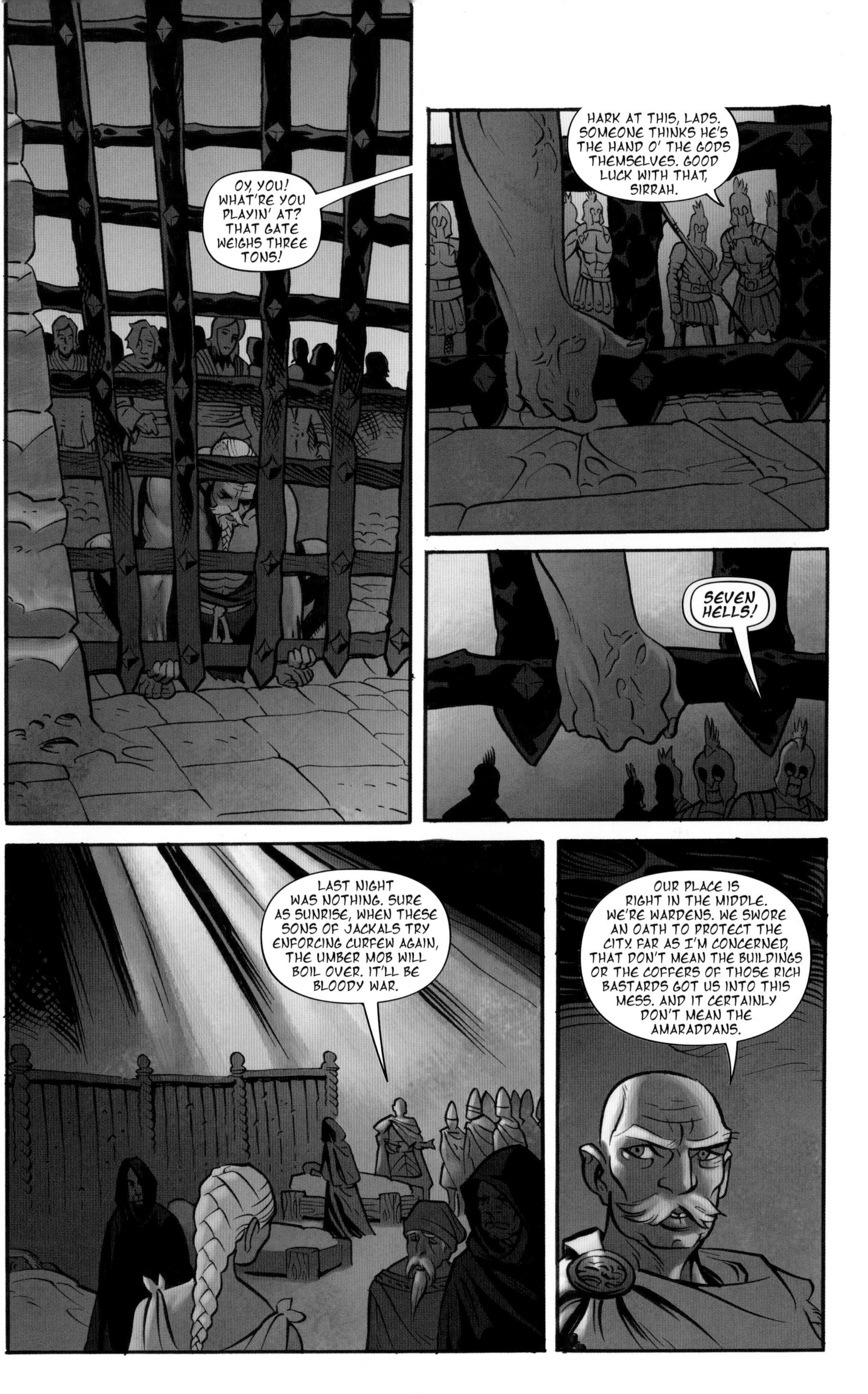
OY, YOU! WHAT'RE YOU PLAYIN' AT? THAT GATE WEIGHS THREE TONS!
HARK AT THIS, LADS. SOMEONE THINKS HE'S THE HAND O' THE GODS THEMSELVES. GOOD LUCK WITH THAT, SIRRAH.
SEVEN HELLS!
LAST NIGHT WAS NOTHING. SURE AS SUNRISE, WHEN THESE SONS OF JACKALS TRY ENFORCING CURFEW AGAIN, THE UMBER MOB WILL BOIL OVER. IT'LL BE BLOODY WAR.
OUR PLACE IS RIGHT IN THE MIDDLE. WE'RE WARDENS. WE SWORE AN OATH TO PROTECT THE CITY. FAR AS I'M CONCERNED, THAT DON'T MEAN THE BUILDINGS OR THE COFFERS OF THOSE RICH BASTARDS GOT US INTO THIS MESS. AND IT CERTAINLY DON'T MEAN THE AMARADDANS.

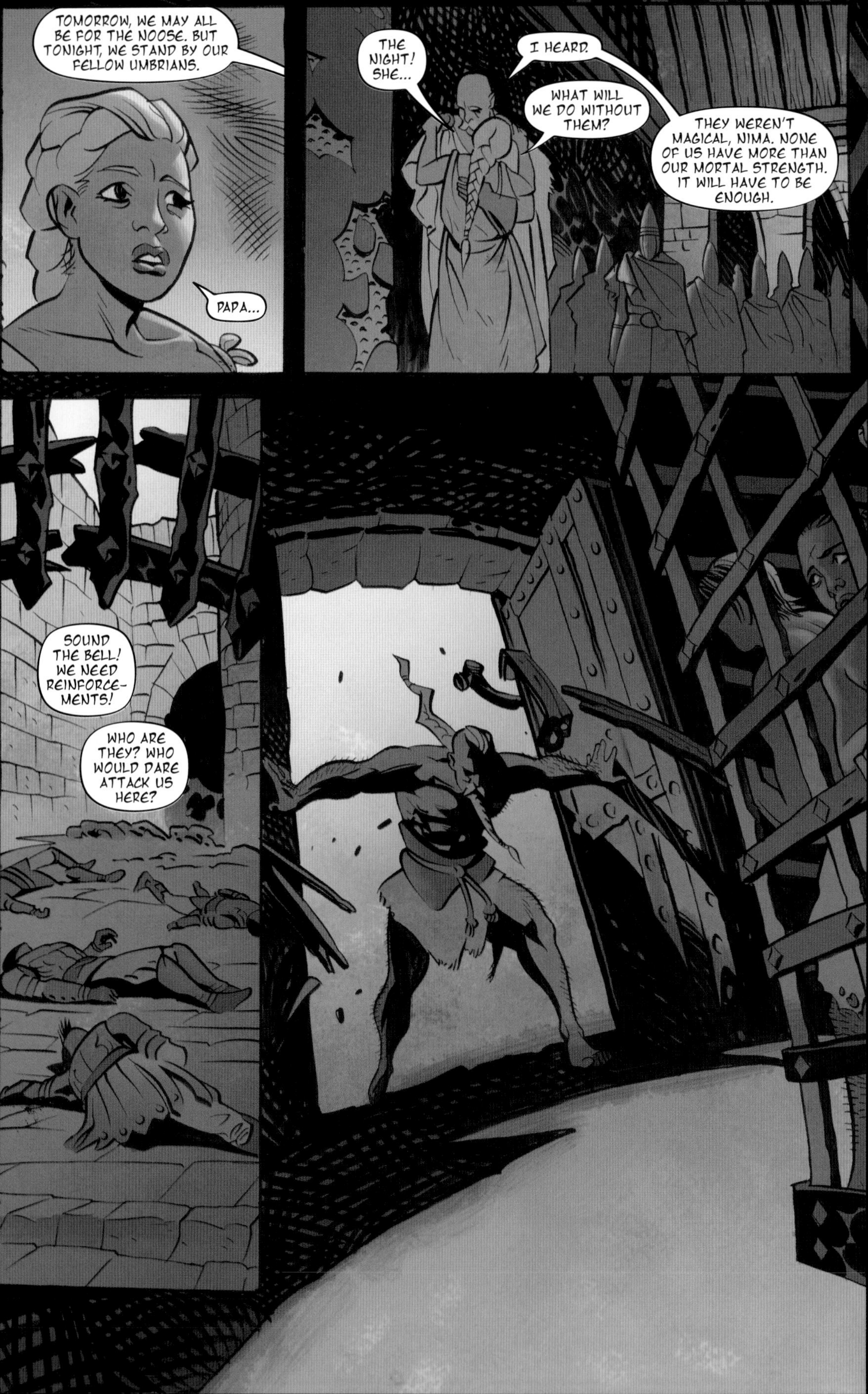
TOMORROW, WE MAY ALL BE FOR THE NOOSE. BUT TONIGHT, WE STAND BY OUR FELLOW UMBRIANS.
PAPA...
THE NIGHT! SHE...
I HEARD.
WHAT WILL WE DO WITHOUT THEM?
THEY WEREN'T MAGICAL, NIMA. NONE OF US HAVE MORE THAN OUR MORTAL STRENGTH. IT WILL HAVE TO BE ENOUGH.
SOUND THE BELL! WE NEED REINFORCE-MENTS!
WHO ARE THEY? WHO WOULD DARE ATTACK US HERE?

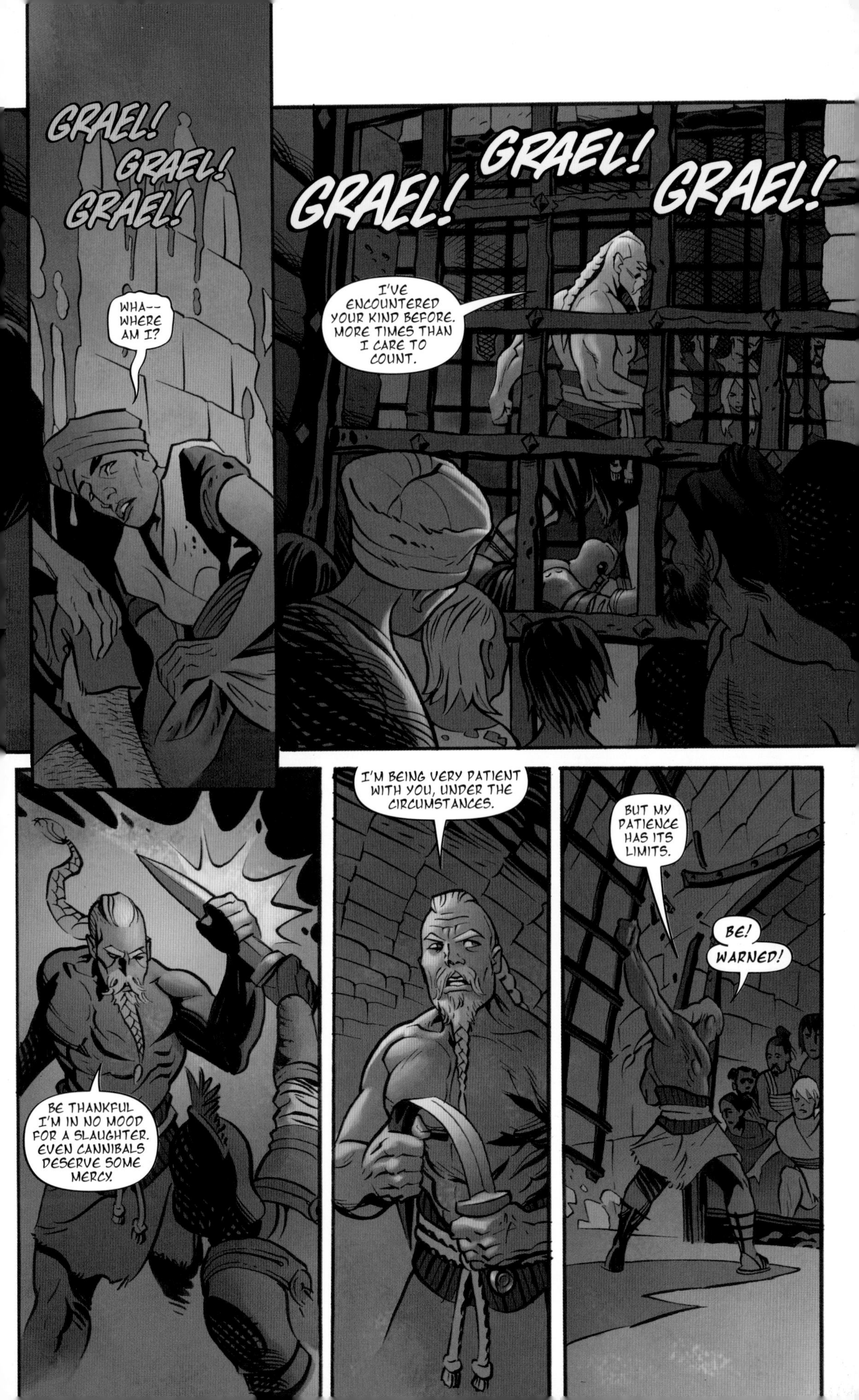
GRAEL! GRAEL! GRAEL!
WHA-- WHERE AM I?
GRAEL! GRAEL! GRAEL!
I'VE ENCOUNTERED YOUR KIND BEFORE. MORE TIMES THAN I CARE TO COUNT.
BE THANKFUL I'M IN NO MOOD FOR A SLAUGHTER. EVEN CANNIBALS DESERVE SOME MERCY.
I'M BEING VERY PATIENT WITH YOU, UNDER THE CIRCUMSTANCES.
BUT MY PATIENCE HAS ITS LIMITS.
BE! WARNED!

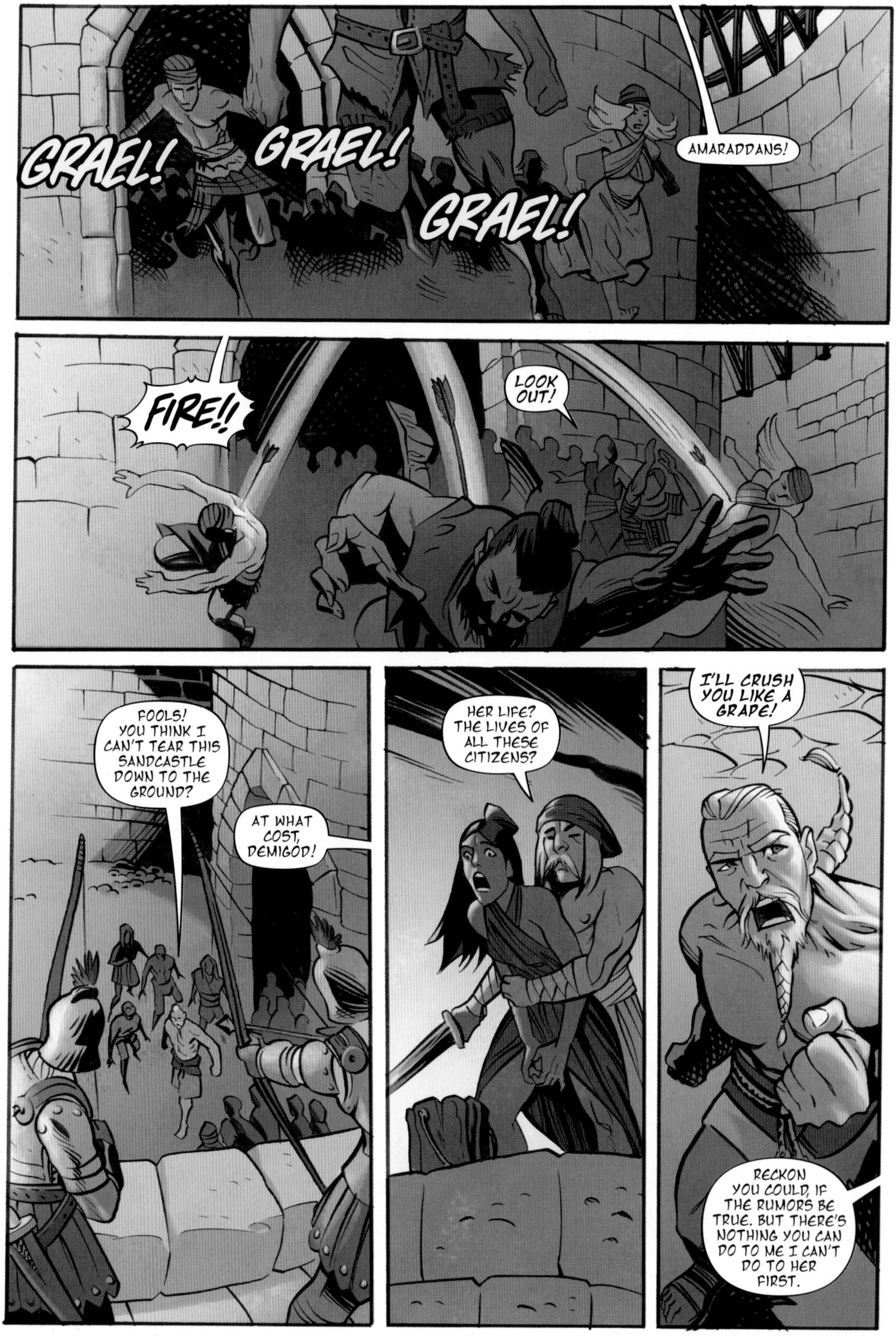
GRAEL!
GRAEL!
GRAEL!
AMARADDANS!
FIRE!!
LOOK OUT!
FOOLS! YOU THINK I CAN'T TEAR THIS SANDCASTLE DOWN TO THE GROUND?
AT WHAT COST, DEMIGOD!
HER LIFE? THE LIVES OF ALL THESE CITIZENS?
I'LL CRUSH YOU LIKE A GRAPE!
RECKON YOU COULD, IF THE RUMORS BE TRUE. BUT THERE'S NOTHING YOU CAN DO TO ME I CAN'T DO TO HER FIRST.

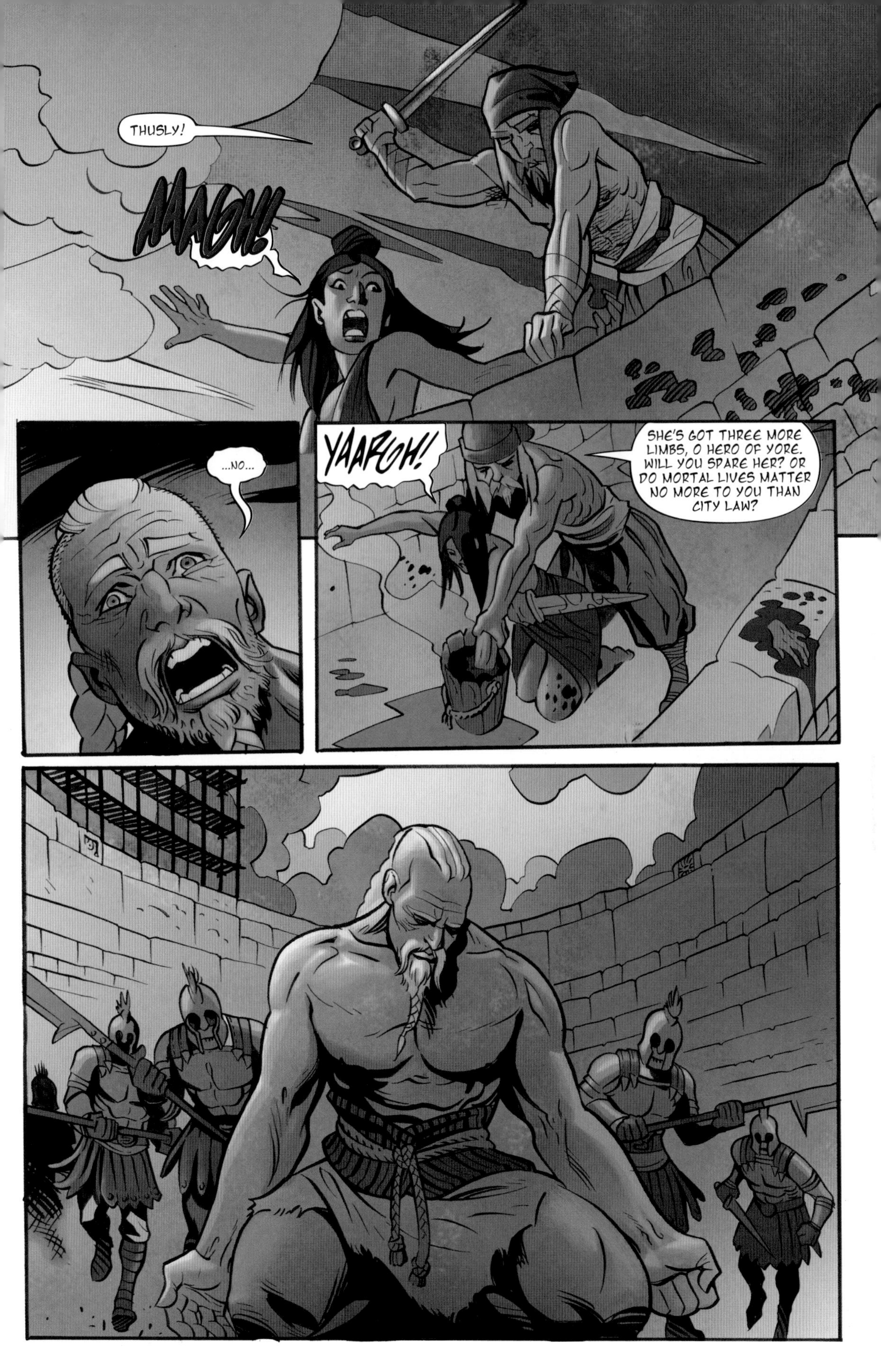
THUSLY!
AAAAGH!
...NO...
YAAROH!
SHE'S GOT THREE MORE LIMBS, O HERO OF YORE. WILL YOU SPARE HER? OR DO MORTAL LIVES MATTER NO MORE TO YOU THAN CITY LAW?

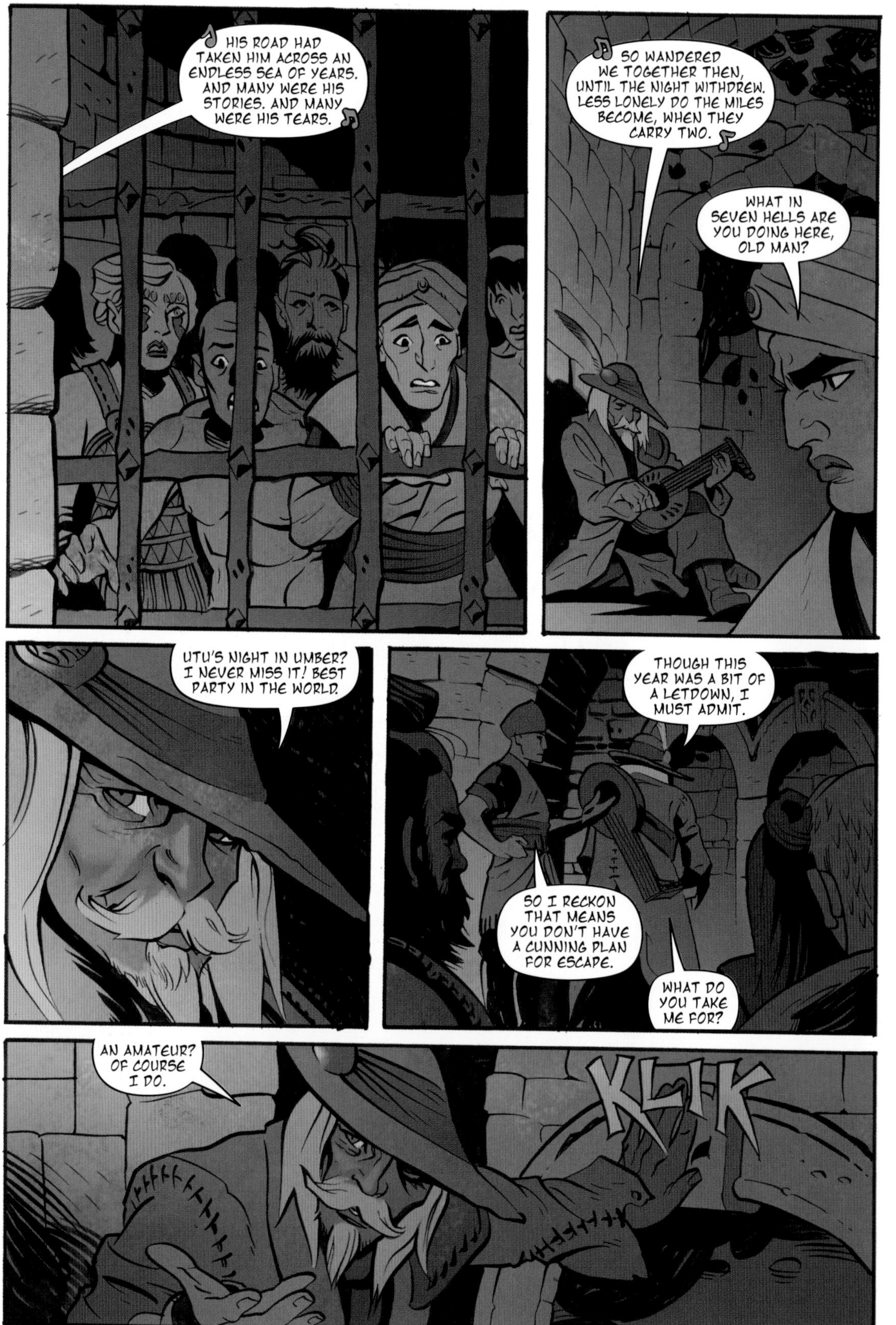

HIS ROAD HAD TAKEN HIM ACROSS AN ENDLESS SEA OF YEARS. AND MANY WERE HIS STORIES. AND MANY WERE HIS TEARS.
SO WANDERED WE TOGETHER THEN, UNTIL THE NIGHT WITHDREW. LESS LONELY DO THE MILES BECOME, WHEN THEY CARRY TWO.
WHAT IN SEVEN HELLS ARE YOU DOING HERE, OLD MAN?
UTU'S NIGHT IN UMBER? I NEVER MISS IT! BEST PARTY IN THE WORLD.
THOUGH THIS YEAR WAS A BIT OF A LETDOWN, I MUST ADMIT.
SO I RECKON THAT MEANS YOU DON'T HAVE A CUNNING PLAN FOR ESCAPE.
WHAT DO YOU TAKE ME FOR?
AN AMATEUR? OF COURSE I DO.
KLIK

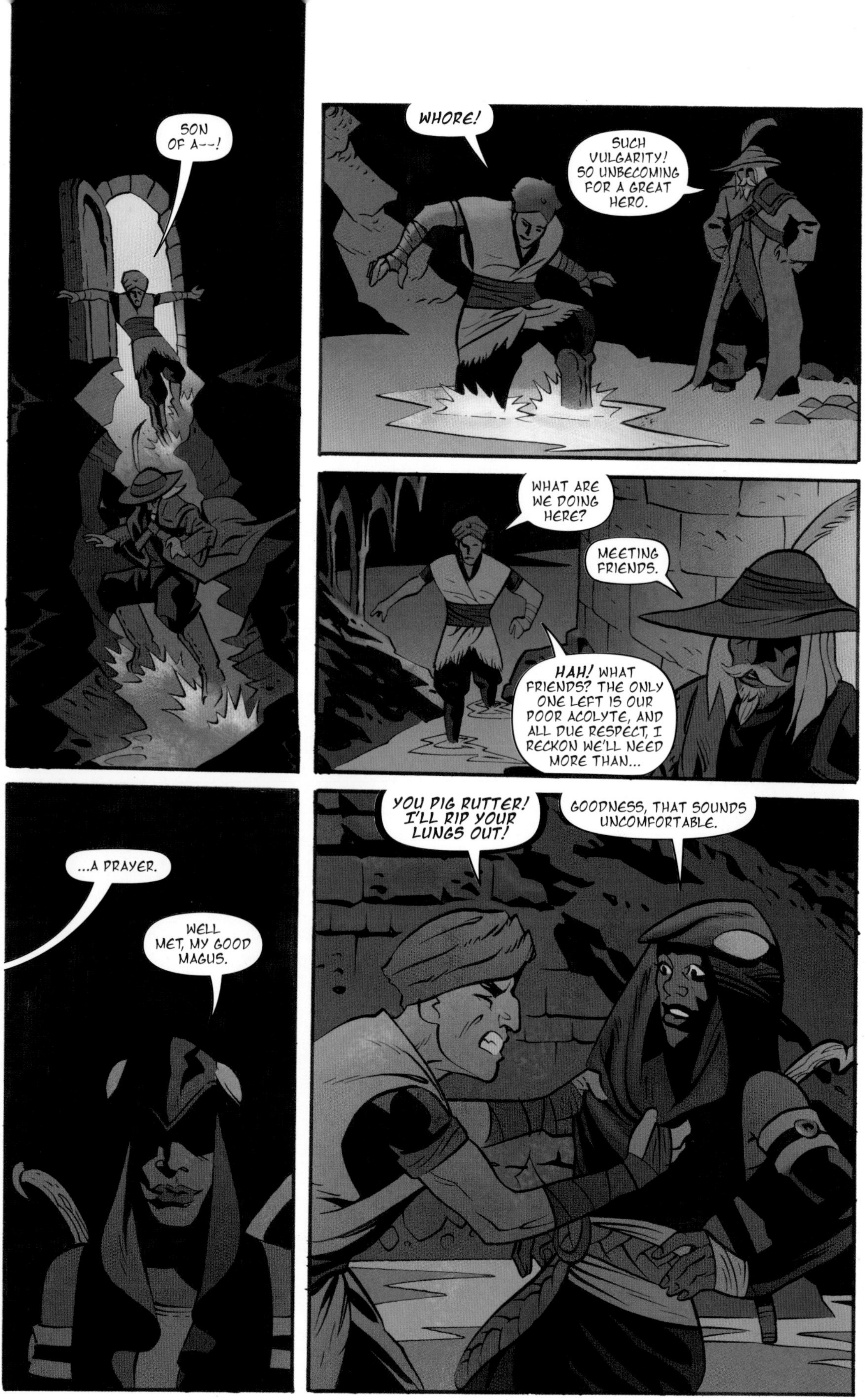
SON OF A--!
WHORE!
SUCH VULGARITY! SO UNBECOMING FOR A GREAT HERO.
WHAT ARE WE DOING HERE?
MEETING FRIENDS.
HAH! WHAT FRIENDS? THE ONLY ONE LEFT IS OUR POOR ACOLYTE, AND ALL DUE RESPECT, I RECKON WE'LL NEED MORE THAN...
...A PRAYER.
WELL MET, MY GOOD MAGUS.
YOU PIG RUTTER! I'LL RIP YOUR LUNGS OUT!
GOODNESS, THAT SOUNDS UNCOMFORTABLE.

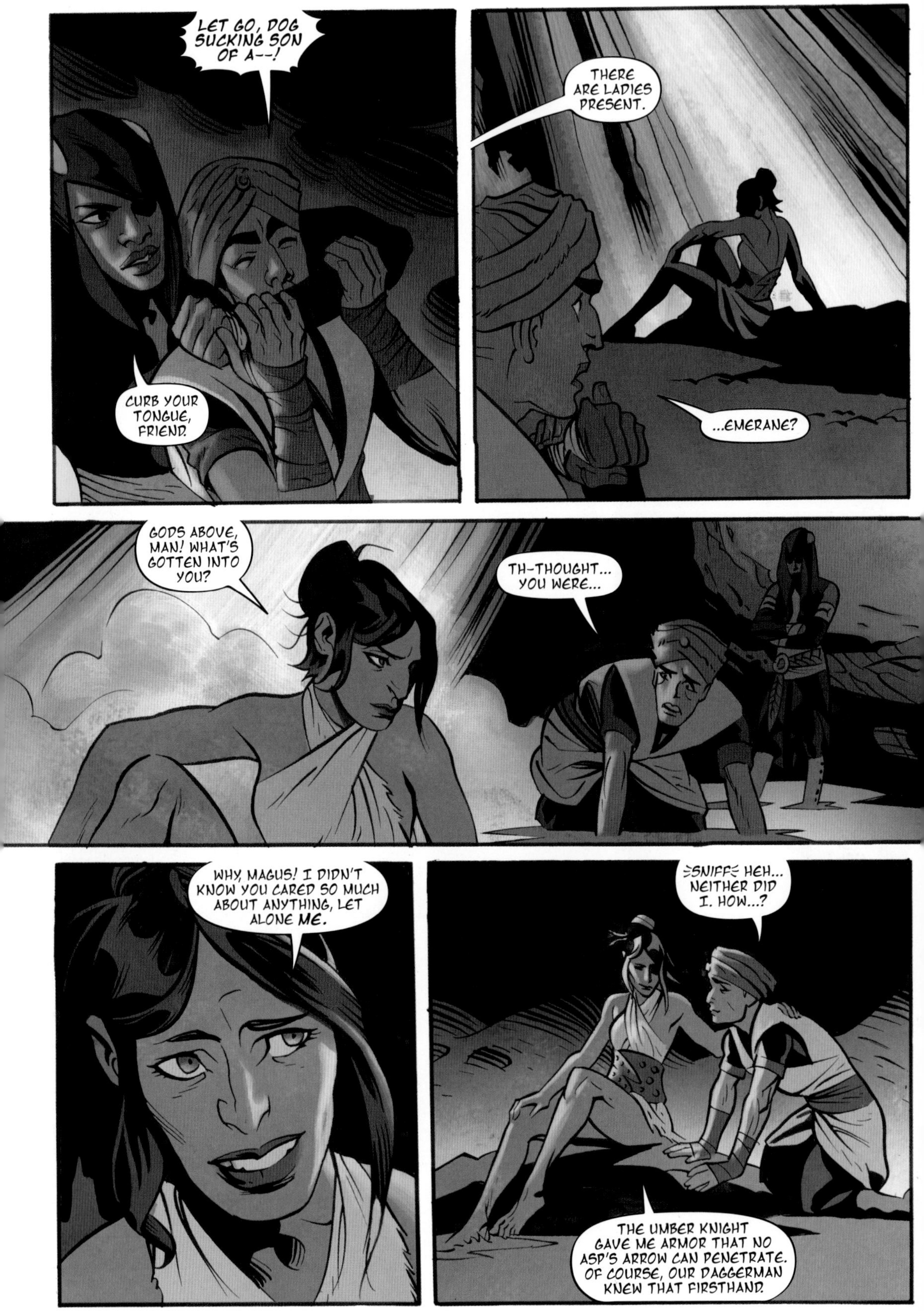
LET GO, DOG SUCKING SON OF A--!
CURB YOUR TONGUE, FRIEND.
THERE ARE LADIES PRESENT.
...EMERANE?
GODS ABOVE, MAN! WHAT'S GOTTEN INTO YOU?
TH-THOUGHT... YOU WERE...
WHY, MAGUS! I DIDN'T KNOW YOU CARED SO MUCH ABOUT ANYTHING, LET ALONE **ME**.
SNIFF HEH... NEITHER DID I. HOW...?
THE UMBER KNIGHT GAVE ME ARMOR THAT NO ASP'S ARROW CAN PENETRATE. OF COURSE, OUR DAGGERMAN KNEW THAT FIRSTHAND.

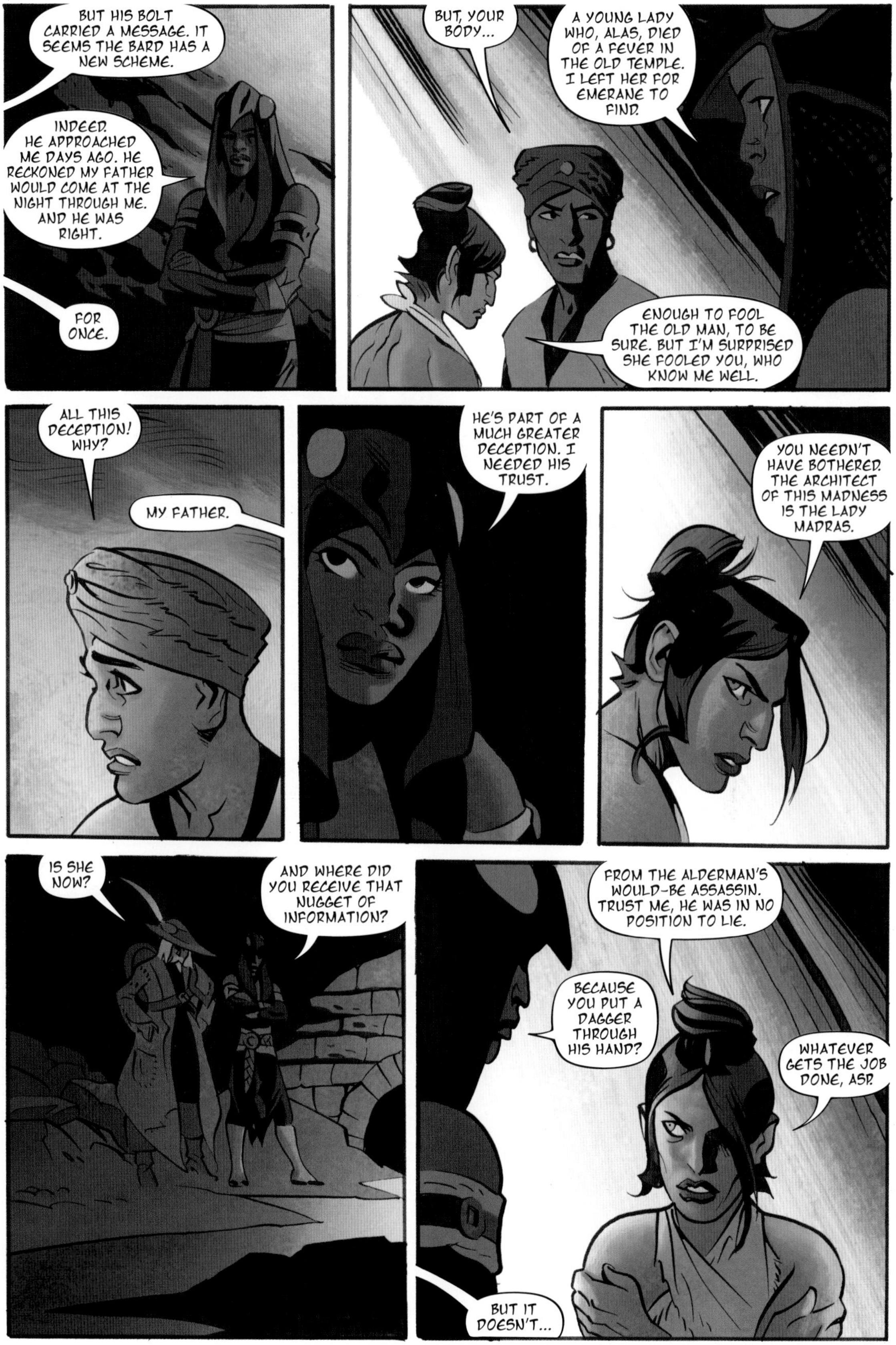
BUT HIS BOLT CARRIED A MESSAGE. IT SEEMS THE BARD HAS A NEW SCHEME.
INDEED. HE APPROACHED ME DAYS AGO. HE RECKONED MY FATHER WOULD COME AT THE NIGHT THROUGH ME. AND HE WAS RIGHT.
FOR ONCE.
BUT, YOUR BODY...
A YOUNG LADY WHO, ALAS, DIED OF A FEVER IN THE OLD TEMPLE. I LEFT HER FOR EMERANE TO FIND.
ENOUGH TO FOOL THE OLD MAN, TO BE SURE. BUT I'M SURPRISED SHE FOOLED YOU, WHO KNOW ME WELL.
ALL THIS DECEPTION! WHY?
MY FATHER.
HE'S PART OF A MUCH GREATER DECEPTION. I NEEDED HIS TRUST.
YOU NEEDN'T HAVE BOTHERED. THE ARCHITECT OF THIS MADNESS IS THE LADY MADRAS.
IS SHE NOW?
AND WHERE DID YOU RECEIVE THAT NUGGET OF INFORMATION?
FROM THE ALDERMAN'S WOULD-BE ASSASSIN. TRUST ME, HE WAS IN NO POSITION TO LIE.
BECAUSE YOU PUT A DAGGER THROUGH HIS HAND?
WHATEVER GETS THE JOB DONE, ASP.
BUT IT DOESN'T...

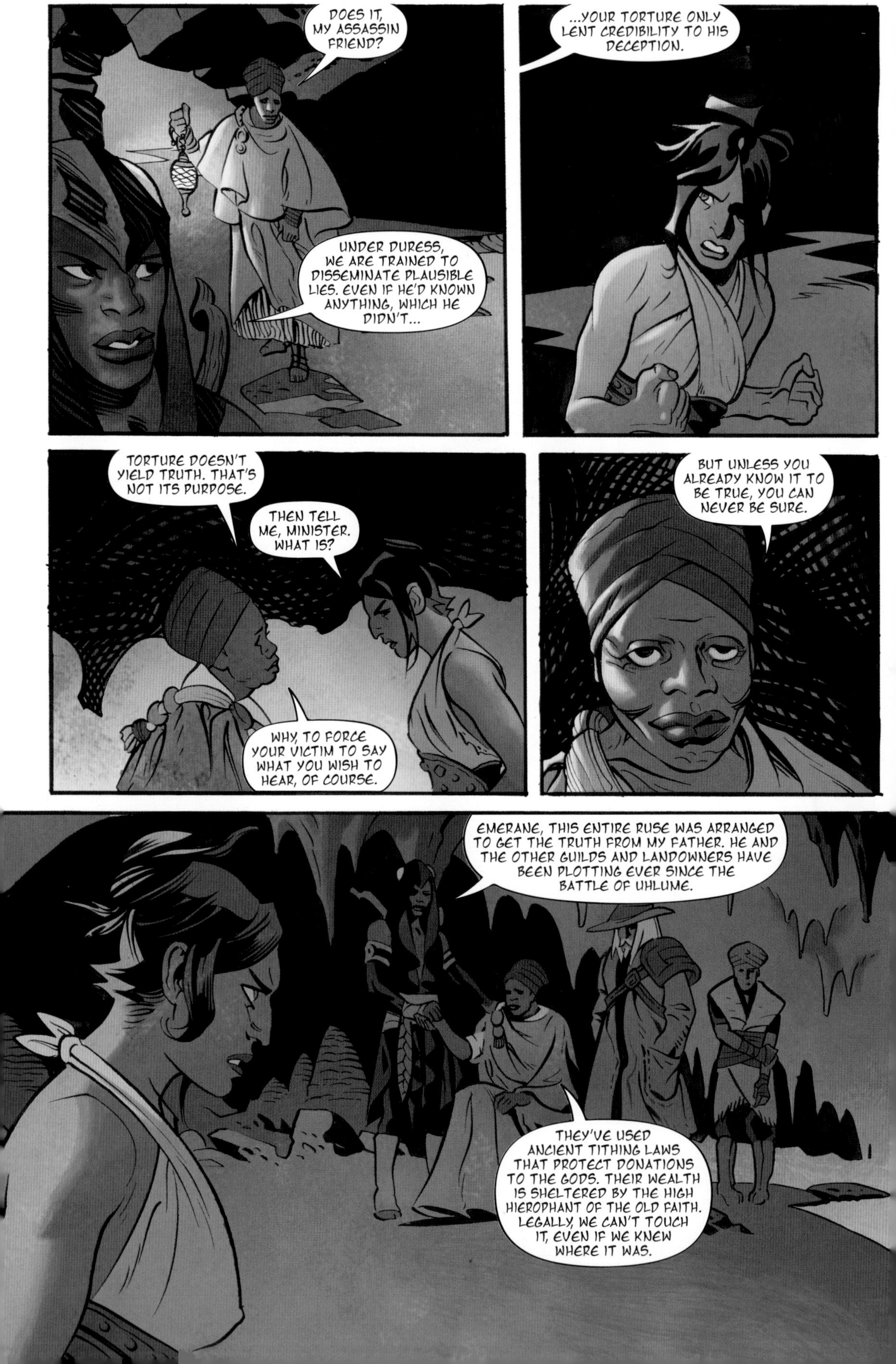
DOES IT, MY ASSASSIN FRIEND?
UNDER DURESS, WE ARE TRAINED TO DISSEMINATE PLAUSIBLE LIES. EVEN IF HE'D KNOWN ANYTHING, WHICH HE DIDN'T...
...YOUR TORTURE ONLY LENT CREDIBILITY TO HIS DECEPTION.
TORTURE DOESN'T YIELD TRUTH. THAT'S NOT ITS PURPOSE.
THEN TELL ME, MINISTER. WHAT IS?
WHY, TO FORCE YOUR VICTIM TO SAY WHAT YOU WISH TO HEAR, OF COURSE.
BUT UNLESS YOU ALREADY KNOW IT TO BE TRUE, YOU CAN NEVER BE SURE.
EMERANE, THIS ENTIRE RUSE WAS ARRANGED TO GET THE TRUTH FROM MY FATHER. HE AND THE OTHER GUILDS AND LANDOWNERS HAVE BEEN PLOTTING EVER SINCE THE BATTLE OF UHLUME.
THEY'VE USED ANCIENT TITHING LAWS THAT PROTECT DONATIONS TO THE GODS. THEIR WEALTH IS SHELTERED BY THE HIGH HIEROPHANT OF THE OLD FAITH. LEGALLY, WE CAN'T TOUCH IT, EVEN IF WE KNEW WHERE IT WAS.

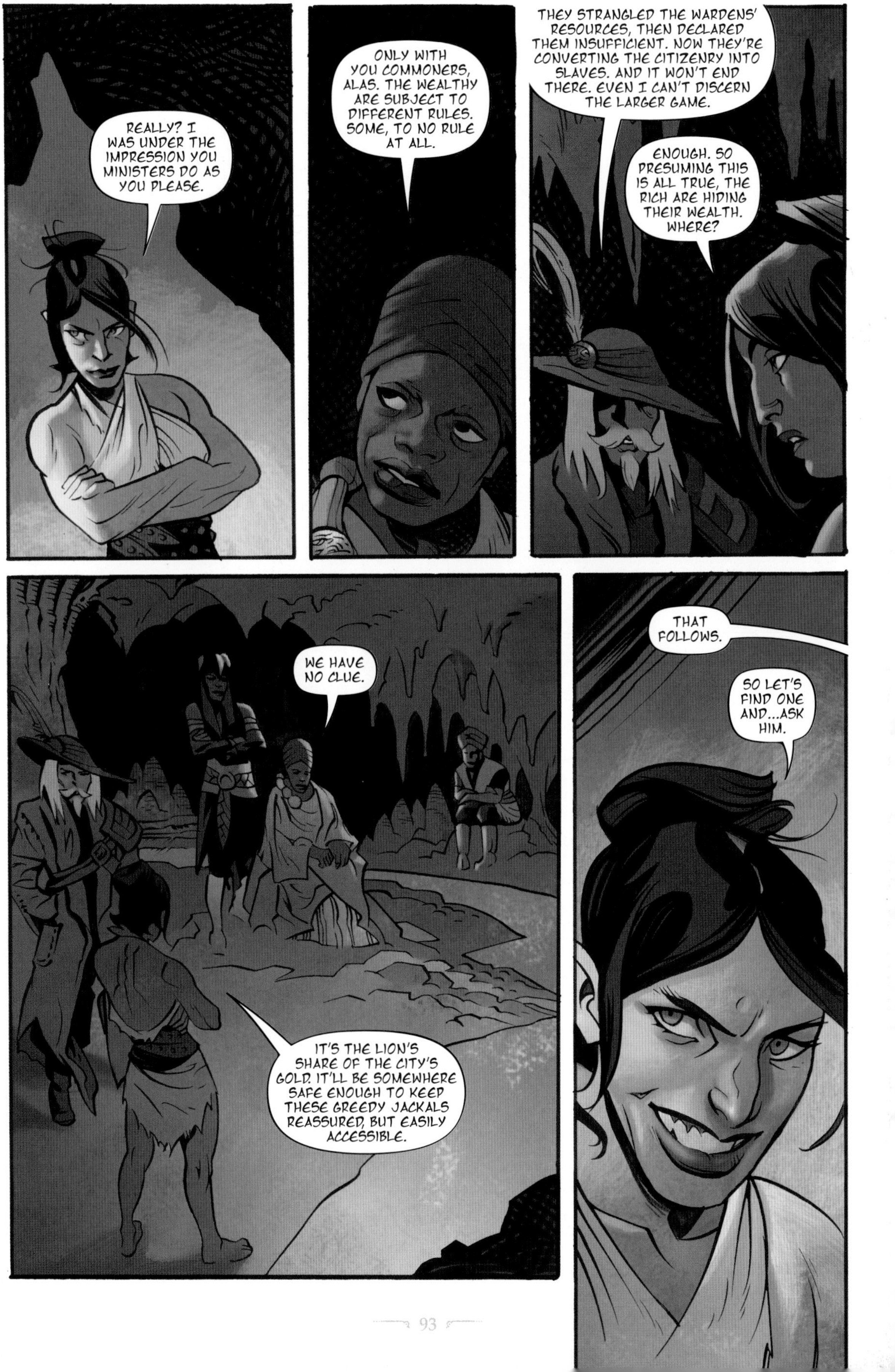
REALLY? I WAS UNDER THE IMPRESSION YOU MINISTERS DO AS YOU PLEASE.
ONLY WITH YOU COMMONERS, ALAS. THE WEALTHY ARE SUBJECT TO DIFFERENT RULES. SOME, TO NO RULE AT ALL.
THEY STRANGLED THE WARDENS' RESOURCES, THEN DECLARED THEM INSUFFICIENT. NOW THEY'RE CONVERTING THE CITIZENRY INTO SLAVES. AND IT WON'T END THERE. EVEN I CAN'T DISCERN THE LARGER GAME.
ENOUGH. SO PRESUMING THIS IS ALL TRUE, THE RICH ARE HIDING THEIR WEALTH. WHERE?
WE HAVE NO CLUE.
IT'S THE LION'S SHARE OF THE CITY'S GOLD. IT'LL BE SOMEWHERE SAFE ENOUGH TO KEEP THESE GREEDY JACKALS REASSURED, BUT EASILY ACCESSIBLE.
THAT FOLLOWS.
SO LET'S FIND ONE AND...ASK HIM.

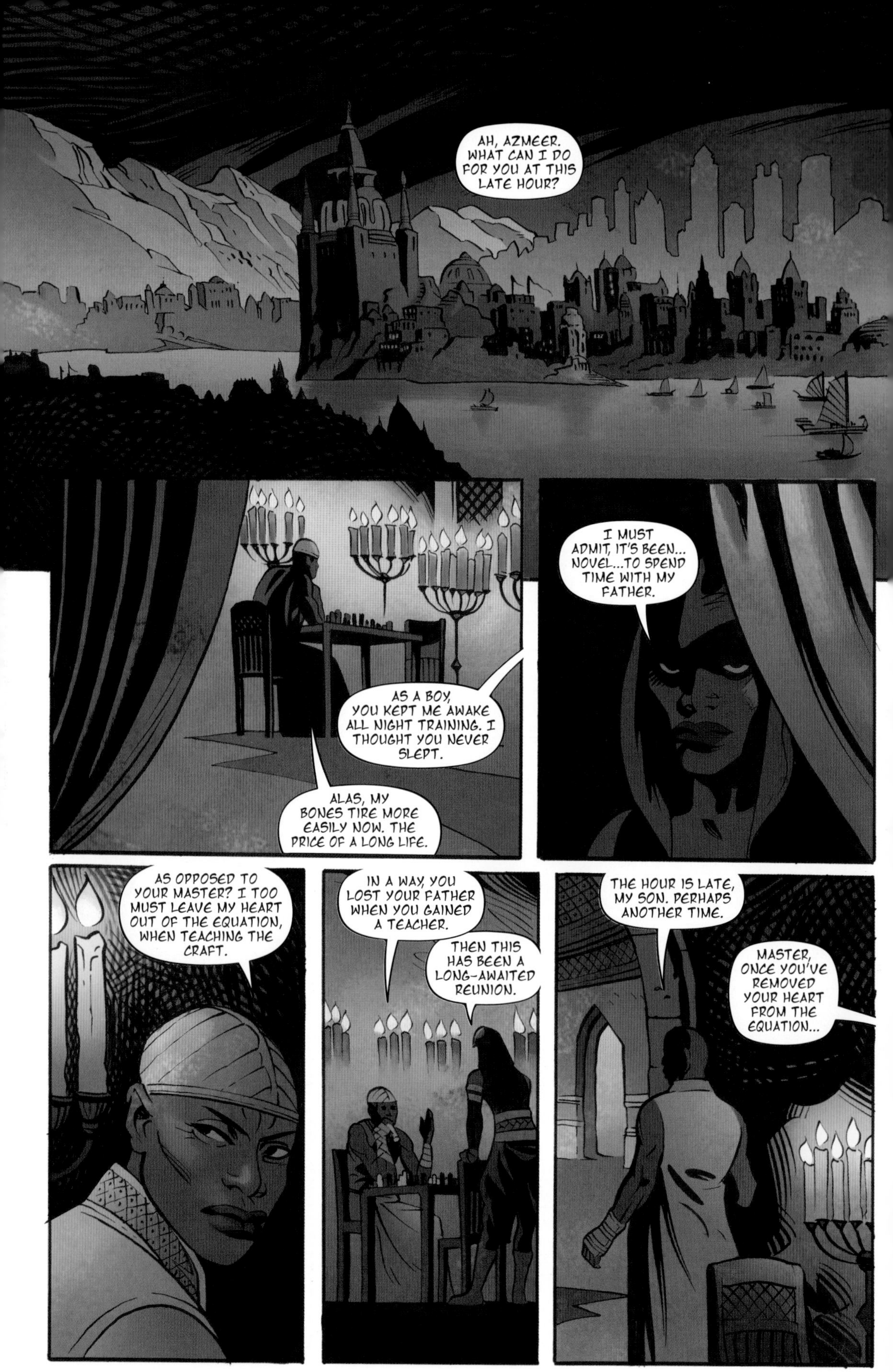
AH, AZMEER. WHAT CAN I DO FOR YOU AT THIS LATE HOUR?
I MUST ADMIT, IT'S BEEN... NOVEL...TO SPEND TIME WITH MY FATHER.
AS A BOY, YOU KEPT ME AWAKE ALL NIGHT TRAINING. I THOUGHT YOU NEVER SLEPT.
ALAS, MY BONES TIRE MORE EASILY NOW. THE PRICE OF A LONG LIFE.
AS OPPOSED TO YOUR MASTER? I TOO MUST LEAVE MY HEART OUT OF THE EQUATION, WHEN TEACHING THE CRAFT.
IN A WAY, YOU LOST YOUR FATHER WHEN YOU GAINED A TEACHER.
THEN THIS HAS BEEN A LONG-AWAITED REUNION.
THE HOUR IS LATE, MY SON. PERHAPS ANOTHER TIME.
MASTER, ONCE YOU'VE REMOVED YOUR HEART FROM THE EQUATION...

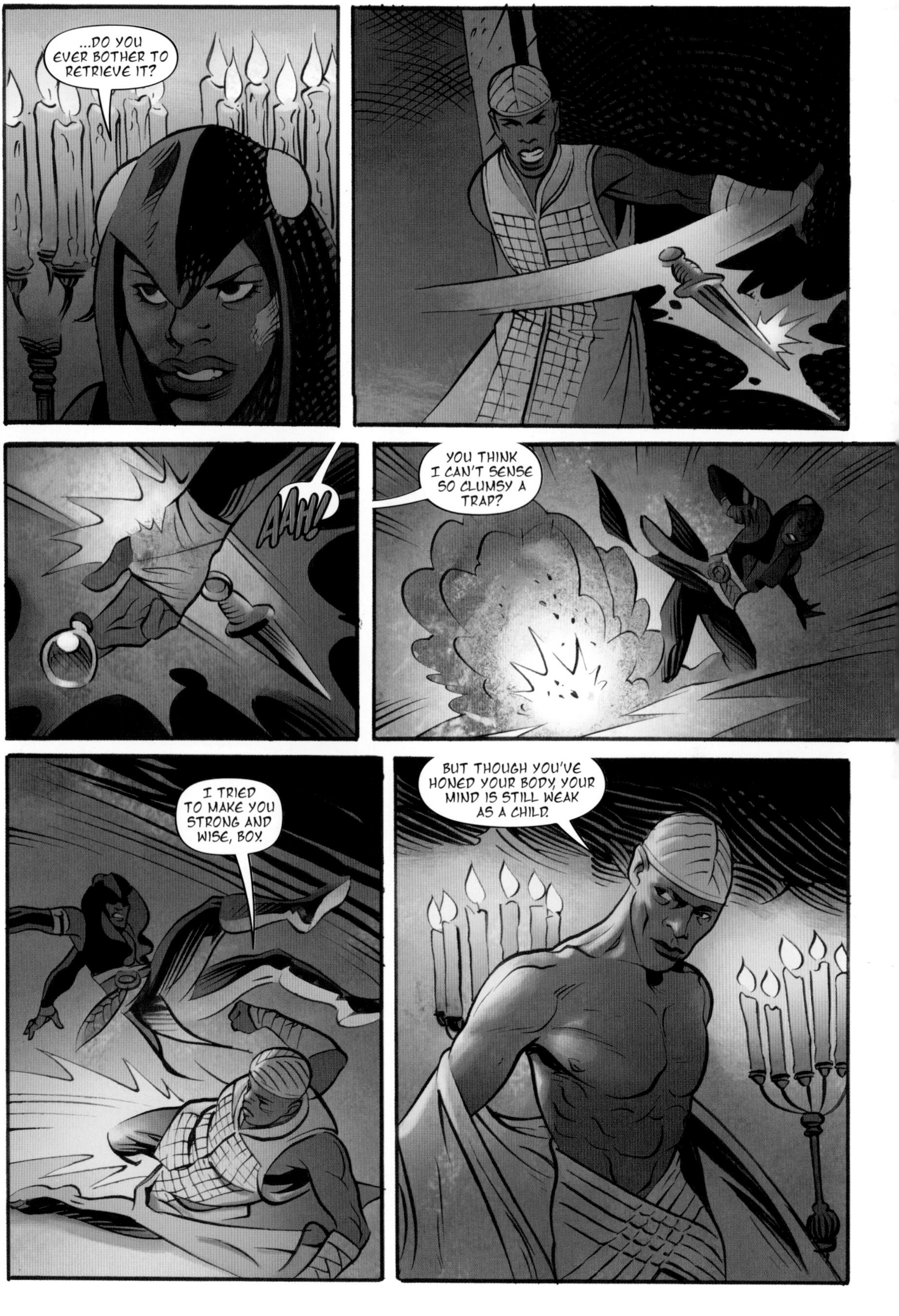
...DO YOU EVER BOTHER TO RETRIEVE IT?
AAH!
YOU THINK I CAN'T SENSE SO CLUMSY A TRAP?
I TRIED TO MAKE YOU STRONG AND WISE, BOY.
BUT THOUGH YOU'VE HONED YOUR BODY, YOUR MIND IS STILL WEAK AS A CHILD.

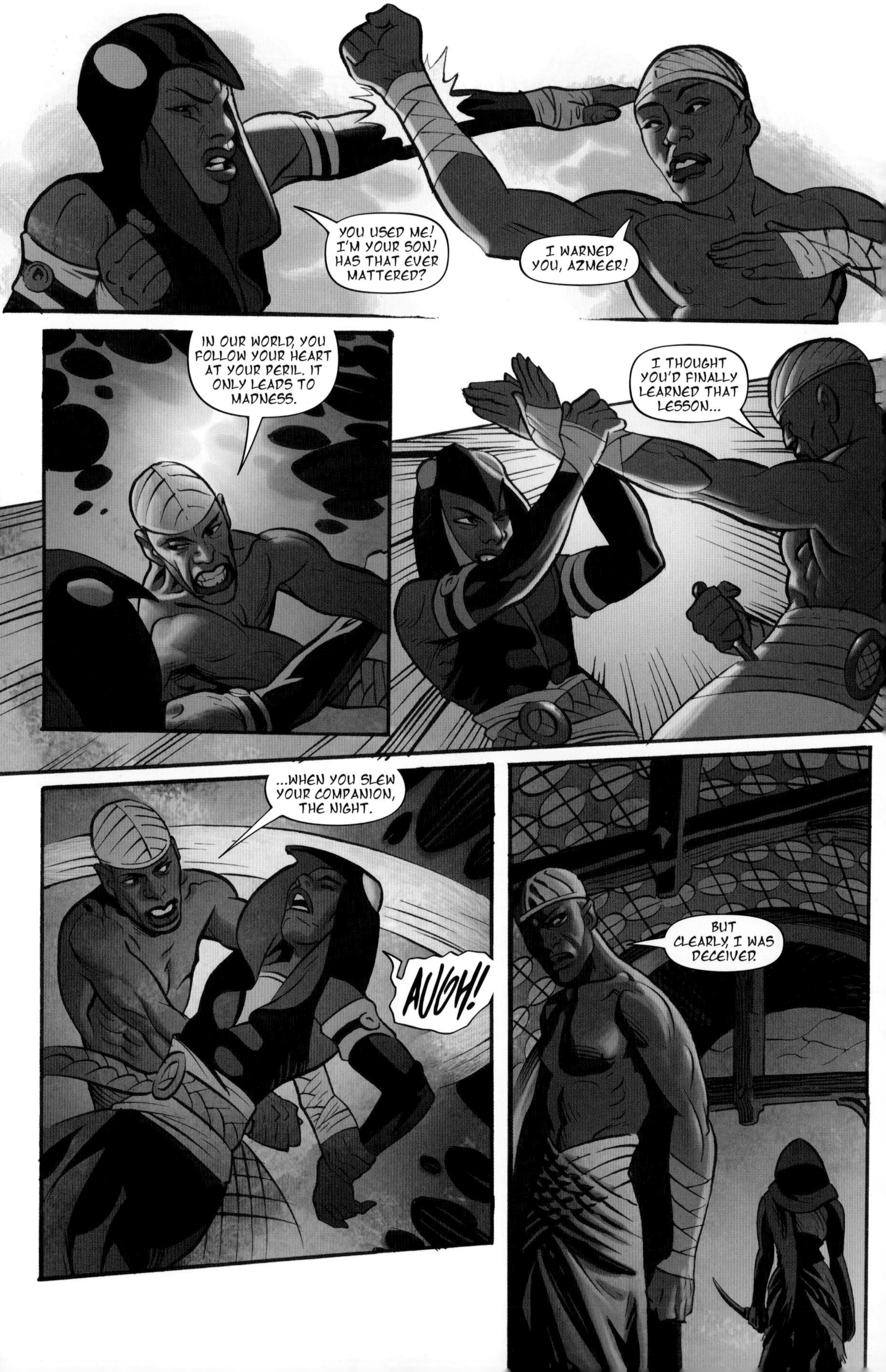
YOU USED ME! I'M YOUR SON! HAS THAT EVER MATTERED?
I WARNED YOU, AZMEER!
IN OUR WORLD, YOU FOLLOW YOUR HEART AT YOUR PERIL. IT ONLY LEADS TO MADNESS.
I THOUGHT YOU'D FINALLY LEARNED THAT LESSON...
...WHEN YOU SLEW YOUR COMPANION, THE NIGHT.
AUGH!
BUT CLEARLY, I WAS DECEIVED.

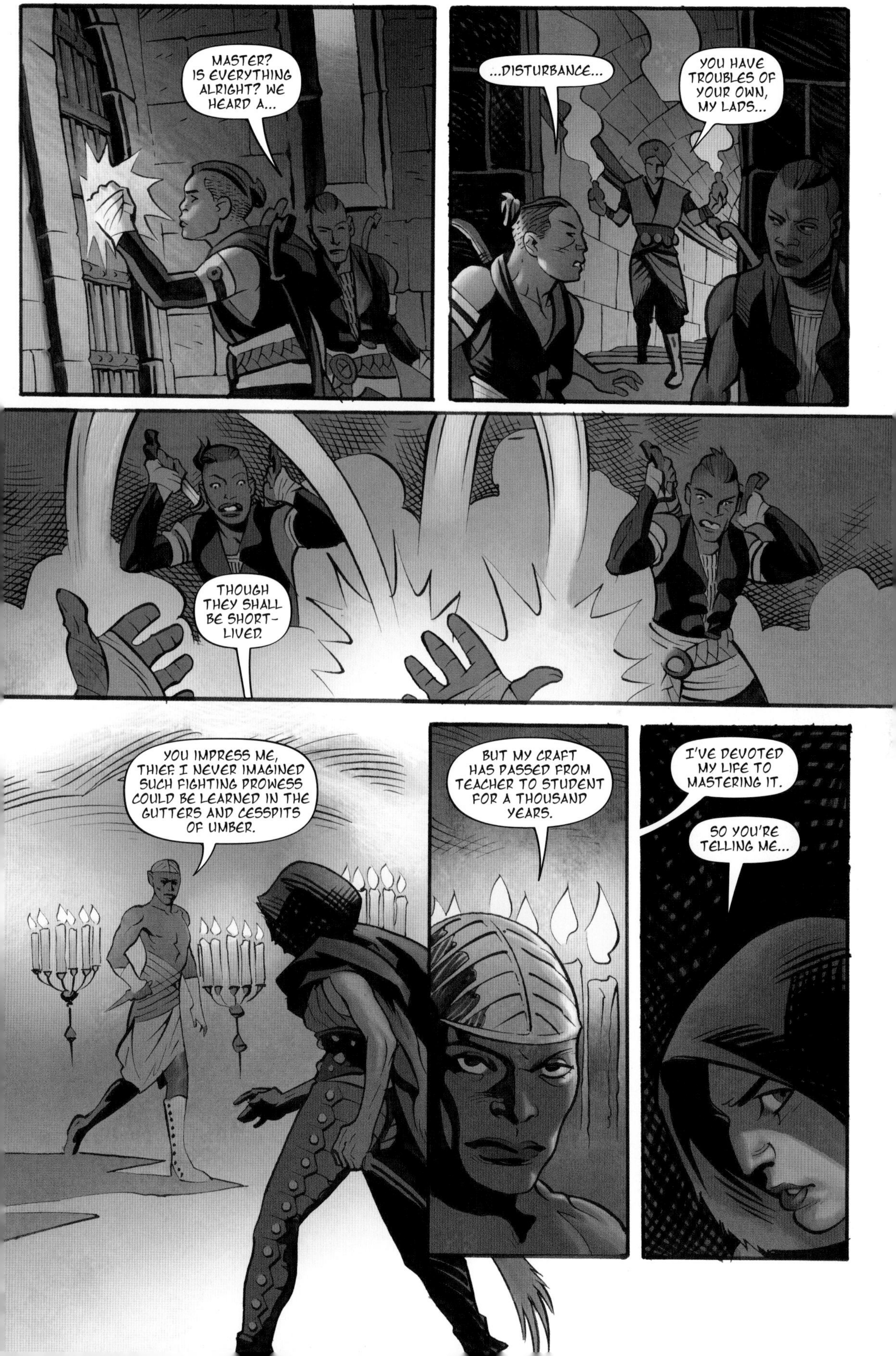
MASTER? IS EVERYTHING ALRIGHT? WE HEARD A...
...DISTURBANCE...
YOU HAVE TROUBLES OF YOUR OWN, MY LADS...
THOUGH THEY SHALL BE SHORT-LIVED.
YOU IMPRESS ME, THIEF. I NEVER IMAGINED SUCH FIGHTING PROWESS COULD BE LEARNED IN THE GUTTERS AND CESSPITS OF UMBER.
BUT MY CRAFT HAS PASSED FROM TEACHER TO STUDENT FOR A THOUSAND YEARS.
I'VE DEVOTED MY LIFE TO MASTERING IT.
SO YOU'RE TELLING ME...

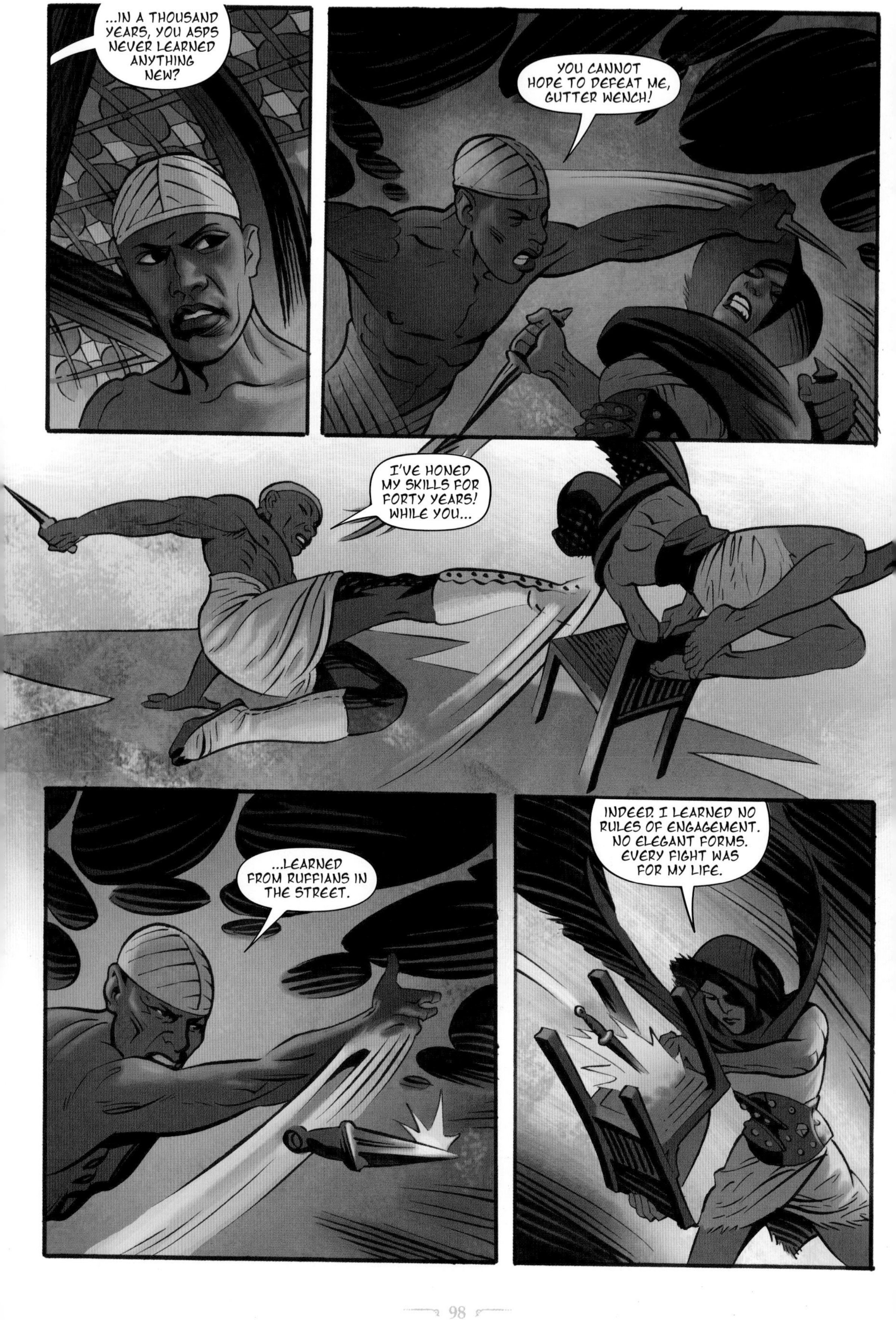
...IN A THOUSAND YEARS, YOU ASPS NEVER LEARNED ANYTHING NEW?
YOU CANNOT HOPE TO DEFEAT ME, GUTTER WENCH!
I'VE HONED MY SKILLS FOR FORTY YEARS! WHILE YOU...
...LEARNED FROM RUFFIANS IN THE STREET.
INDEED. I LEARNED NO RULES OF ENGAGEMENT. NO ELEGANT FORMS. EVERY FIGHT WAS FOR MY LIFE.

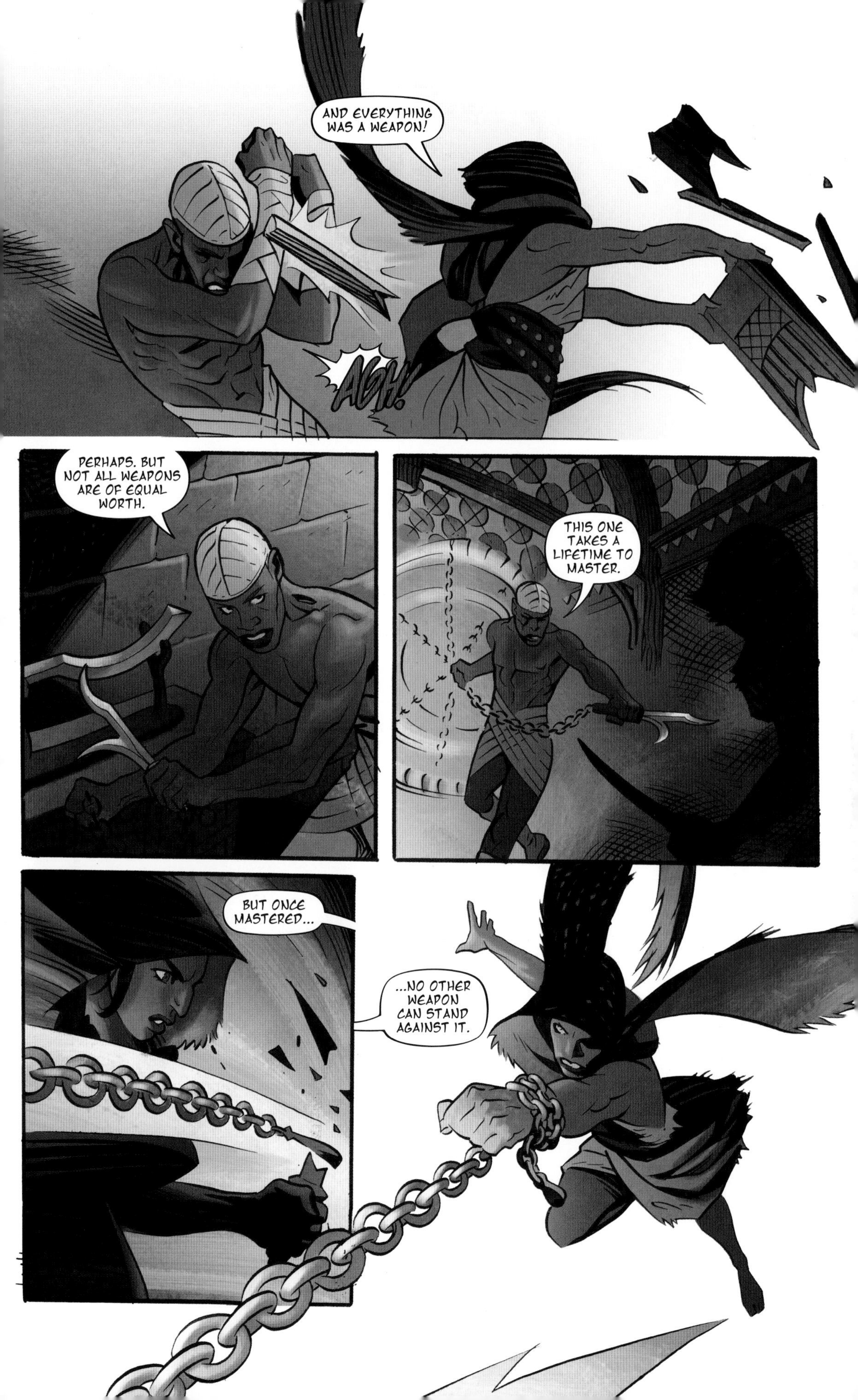
AND EVERYTHING WAS A WEAPON!
AGH!
PERHAPS. BUT NOT ALL WEAPONS ARE OF EQUAL WORTH.
THIS ONE TAKES A LIFETIME TO MASTER.
BUT ONCE MASTERED...
...NO OTHER WEAPON CAN STAND AGAINST IT.

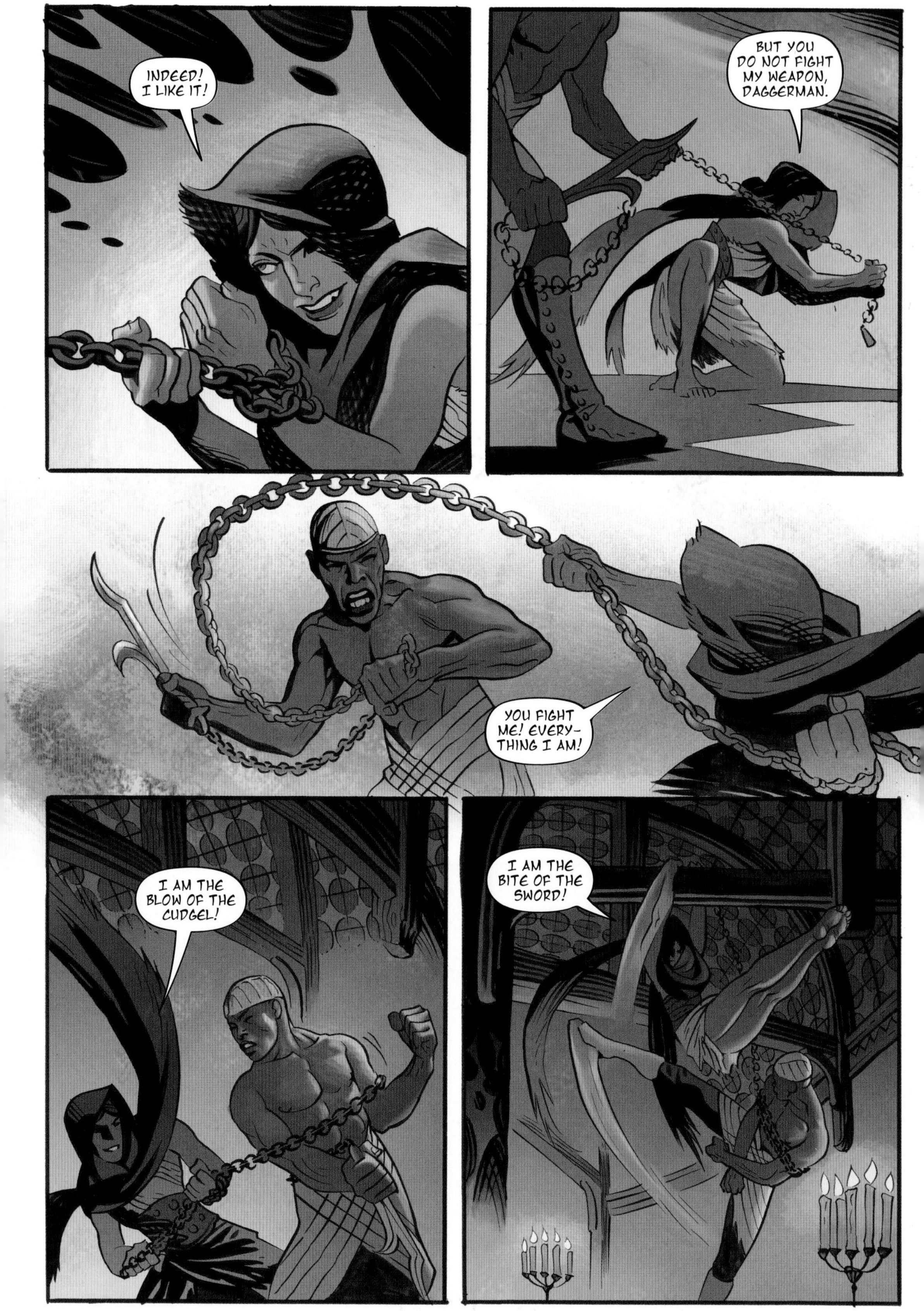
INDEED! I LIKE IT!
BUT YOU DO NOT FIGHT MY WEAPON, DAGGERMAN.
YOU FIGHT ME! EVERY-THING I AM!
I AM THE BLOW OF THE CUDGEL!
I AM THE BITE OF THE SWORD!

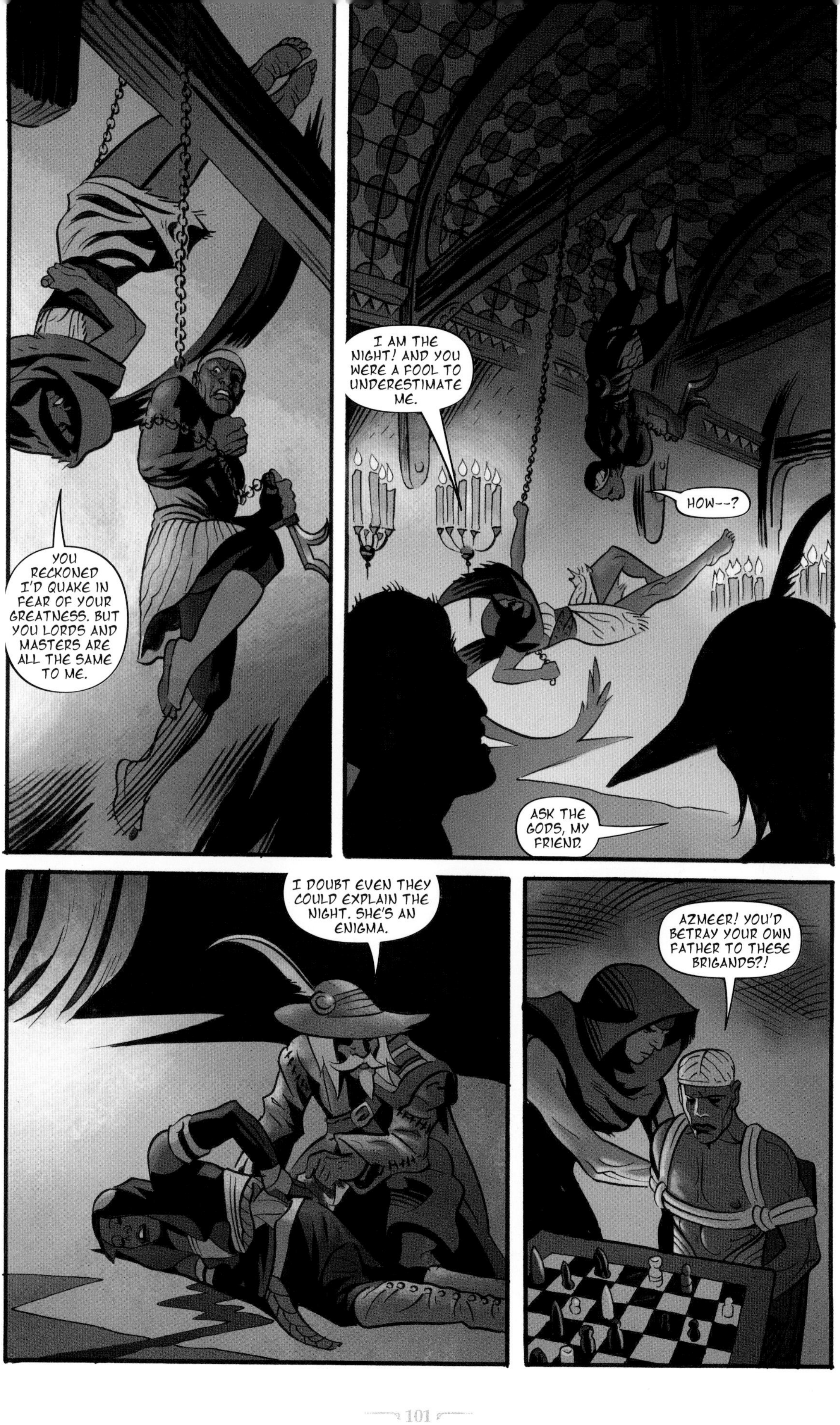
YOU RECKONED I'D QUAKE IN FEAR OF YOUR GREATNESS. BUT YOU LORDS AND MASTERS ARE ALL THE SAME TO ME.
I AM THE NIGHT! AND YOU WERE A FOOL TO UNDERESTIMATE ME.
HOW--?
ASK THE GODS, MY FRIEND.
I DOUBT EVEN THEY COULD EXPLAIN THE NIGHT. SHE'S AN ENIGMA.
AZMEER! YOU'D BETRAY YOUR OWN FATHER TO THESE BRIGANDS?!

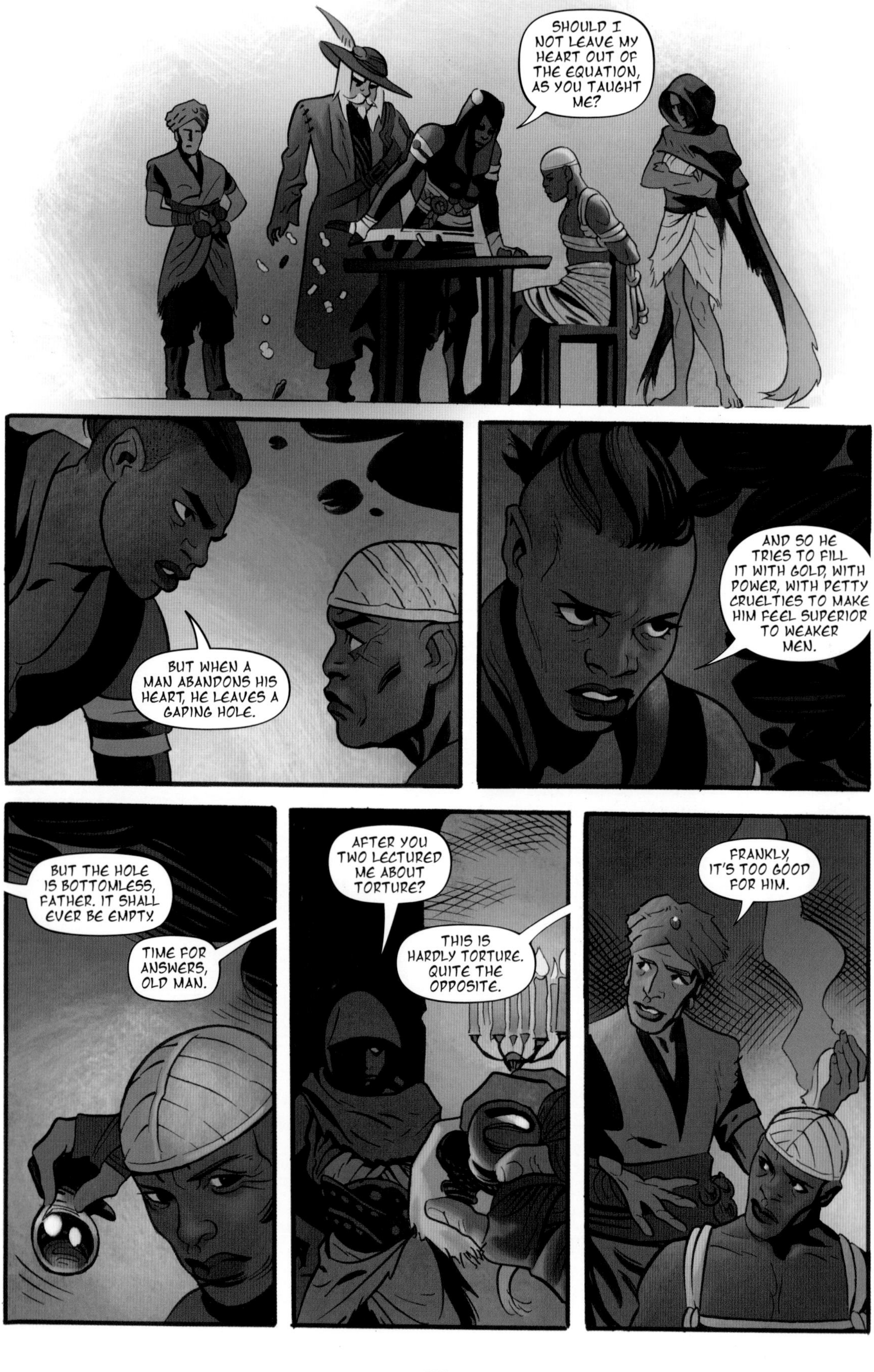
SHOULD I NOT LEAVE MY HEART OUT OF THE EQUATION, AS YOU TAUGHT ME?
BUT WHEN A MAN ABANDONS HIS HEART, HE LEAVES A GAPING HOLE.
AND SO HE TRIES TO FILL IT WITH GOLD, WITH POWER, WITH PETTY CRUELTIES TO MAKE HIM FEEL SUPERIOR TO WEAKER MEN.
BUT THE HOLE IS BOTTOMLESS, FATHER. IT SHALL EVER BE EMPTY.
TIME FOR ANSWERS, OLD MAN.
AFTER YOU TWO LECTURED ME ABOUT TORTURE?
THIS IS HARDLY TORTURE. QUITE THE OPPOSITE.
FRANKLY, IT'S TOO GOOD FOR HIM.

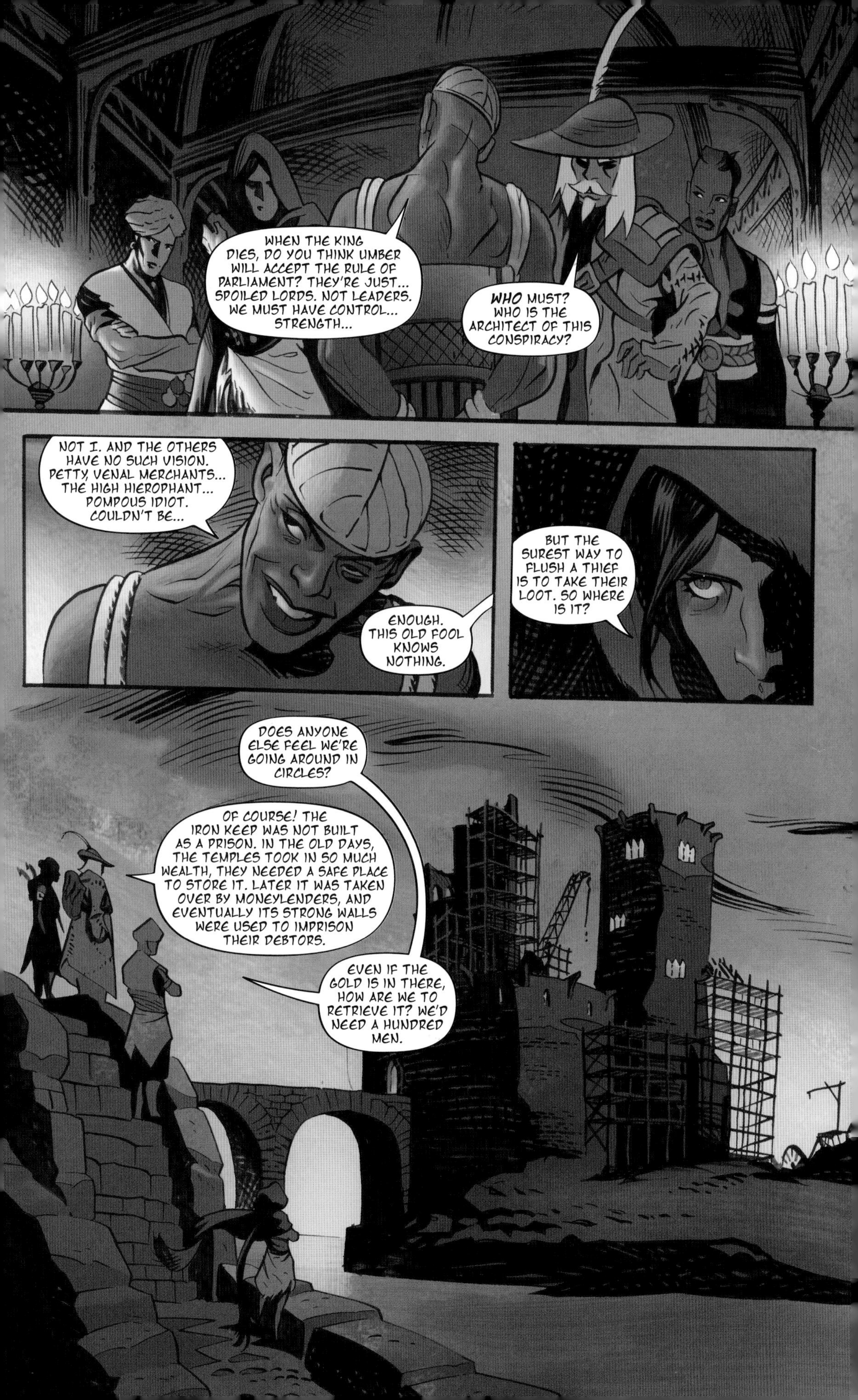
WHEN THE KING DIES, DO YOU THINK UMBER WILL ACCEPT THE RULE OF PARLIAMENT? THEY'RE JUST... SPOILED LORDS. NOT LEADERS. WE MUST HAVE CONTROL... STRENGTH...
WHO MUST? WHO IS THE ARCHITECT OF THIS CONSPIRACY?
NOT I. AND THE OTHERS HAVE NO SUCH VISION. PETTY, VENAL MERCHANTS... THE HIGH HIEROPHANT... POMPOUS IDIOT. COULDN'T BE...
ENOUGH. THIS OLD FOOL KNOWS NOTHING.
BUT THE SUREST WAY TO FLUSH A THIEF IS TO TAKE THEIR LOOT. SO WHERE IS IT?
DOES ANYONE ELSE FEEL WE'RE GOING AROUND IN CIRCLES?
OF COURSE! THE IRON KEEP WAS NOT BUILT AS A PRISON. IN THE OLD DAYS, THE TEMPLES TOOK IN SO MUCH WEALTH, THEY NEEDED A SAFE PLACE TO STORE IT. LATER IT WAS TAKEN OVER BY MONEYLENDERS, AND EVENTUALLY ITS STRONG WALLS WERE USED TO IMPRISON THEIR DEBTORS.
EVEN IF THE GOLD IS IN THERE, HOW ARE WE TO RETRIEVE IT? WE'D NEED A HUNDRED MEN.

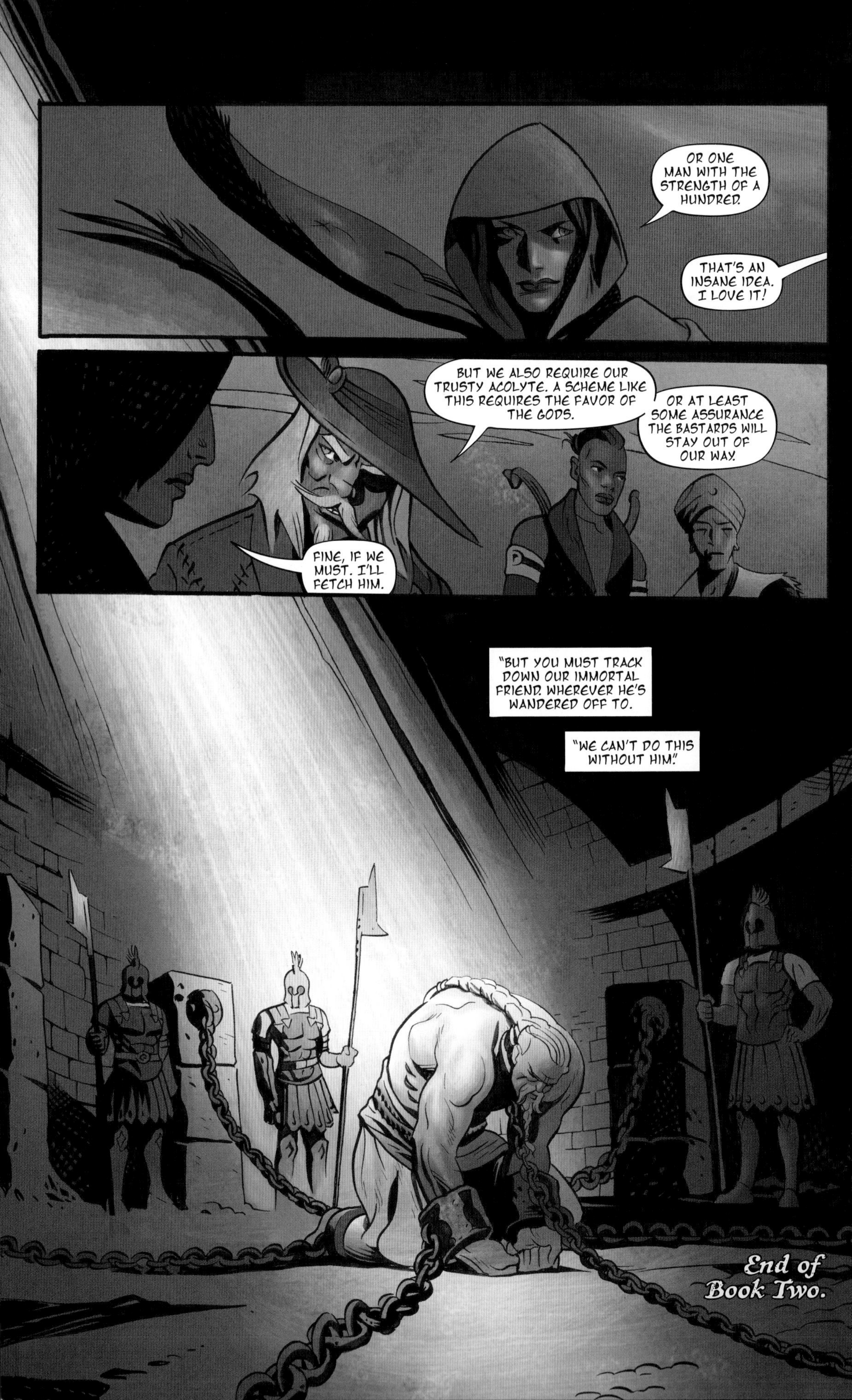
OR ONE MAN WITH THE STRENGTH OF A HUNDRED.
THAT'S AN INSANE IDEA. I LOVE IT!
BUT WE ALSO REQUIRE OUR TRUSTY ACOLYTE. A SCHEME LIKE THIS REQUIRES THE FAVOR OF THE GODS.
OR AT LEAST SOME ASSURANCE THE BASTARDS WILL STAY OUT OF OUR WAY.
FINE, IF WE MUST. I'LL FETCH HIM.
"BUT YOU MUST TRACK DOWN OUR IMMORTAL FRIEND. WHEREVER HE'S WANDERED OFF TO.
"WE CAN'T DO THIS WITHOUT HIM."
End of Book Two.

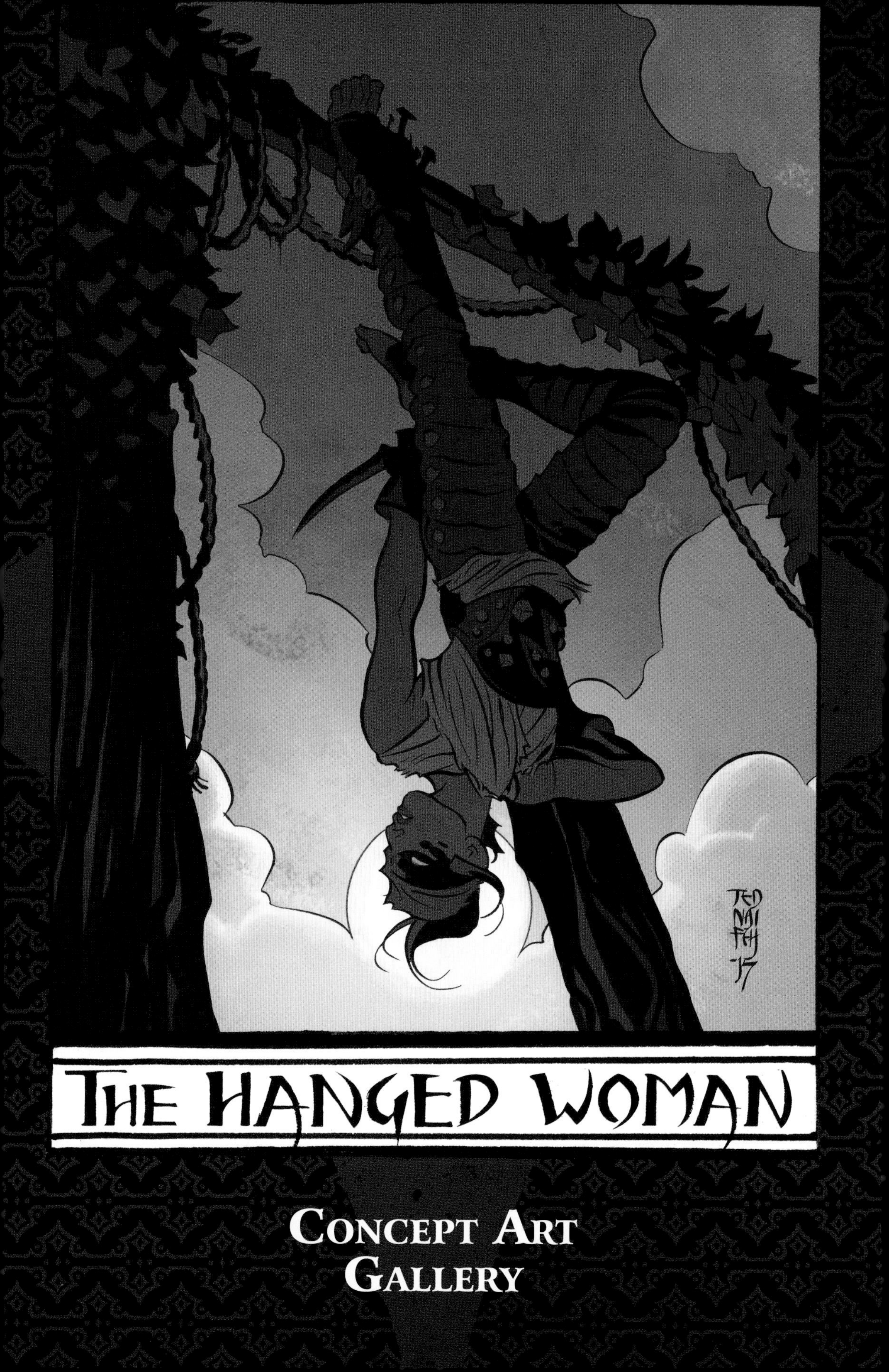
TED NAIFEH '17

THE HANGED WOMAN

CONCEPT ART GALLERY

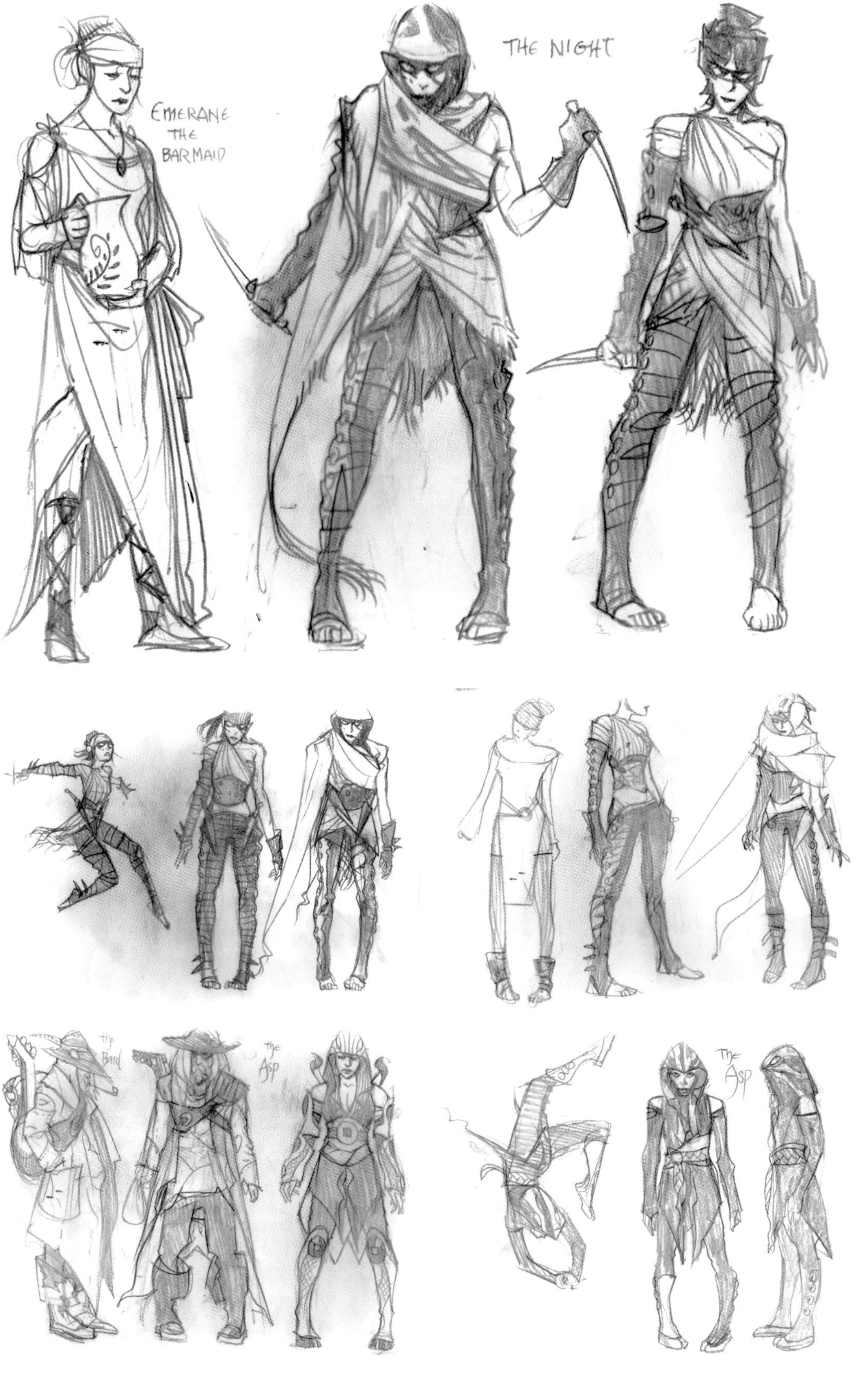
EMERANE THE BARMAID
THE NIGHT
the Bard
the Asp
The Asp

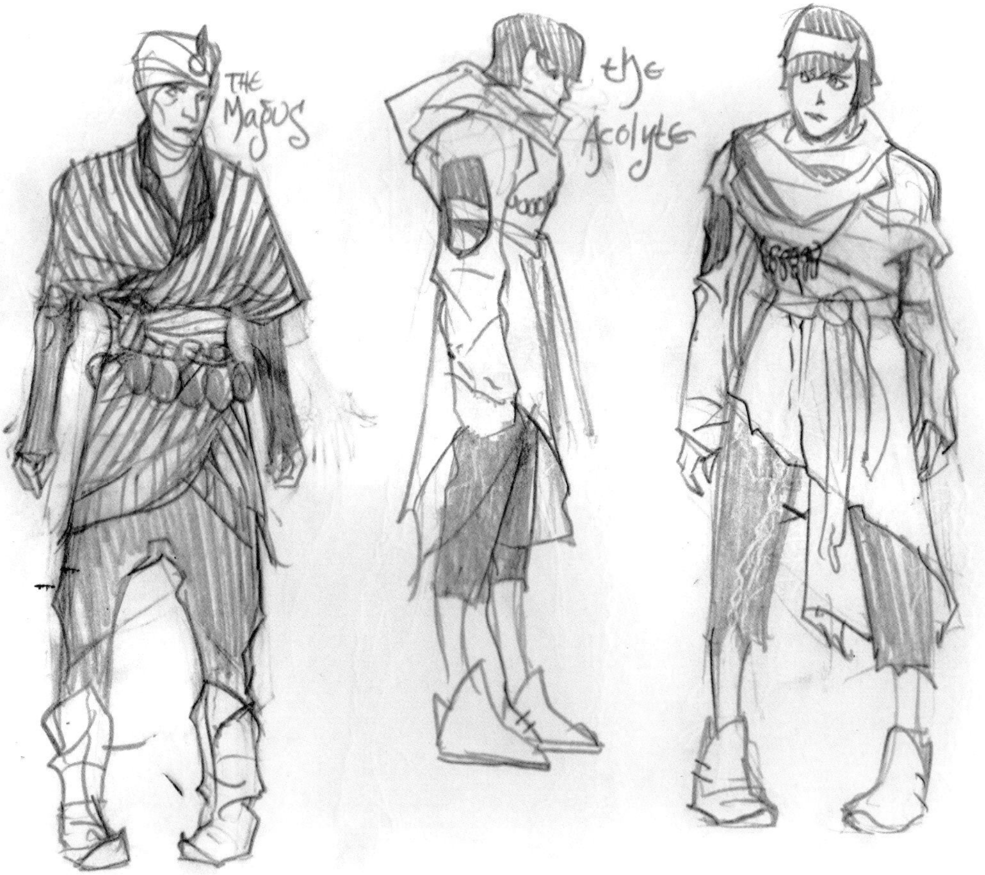
THE Magus
the Acolyte

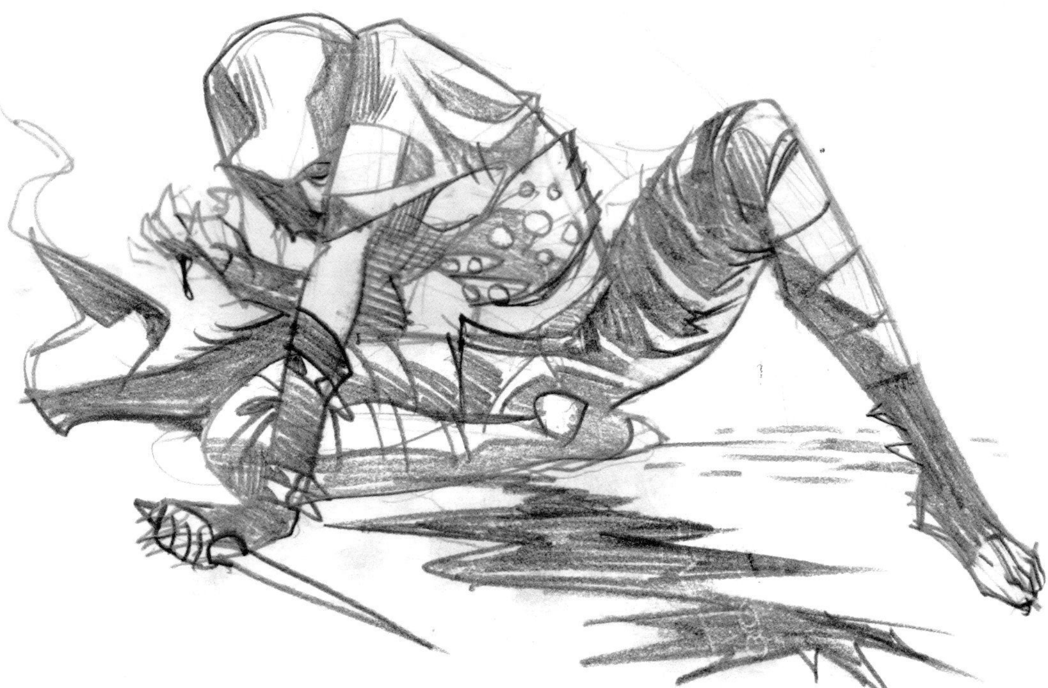

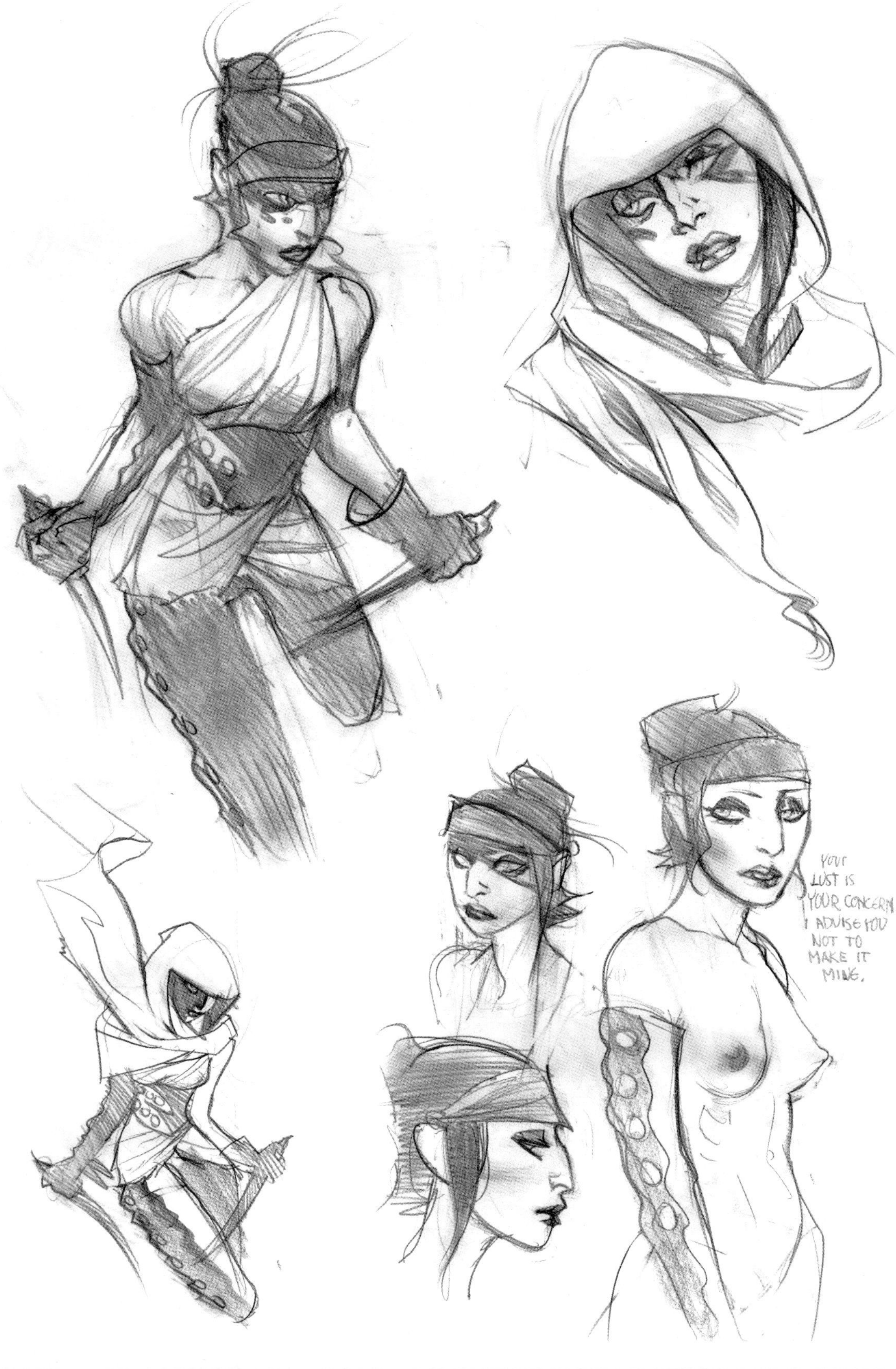
YOUR LUST IS YOUR CONCERN. I ADVISE YOU NOT TO MAKE IT MINE.

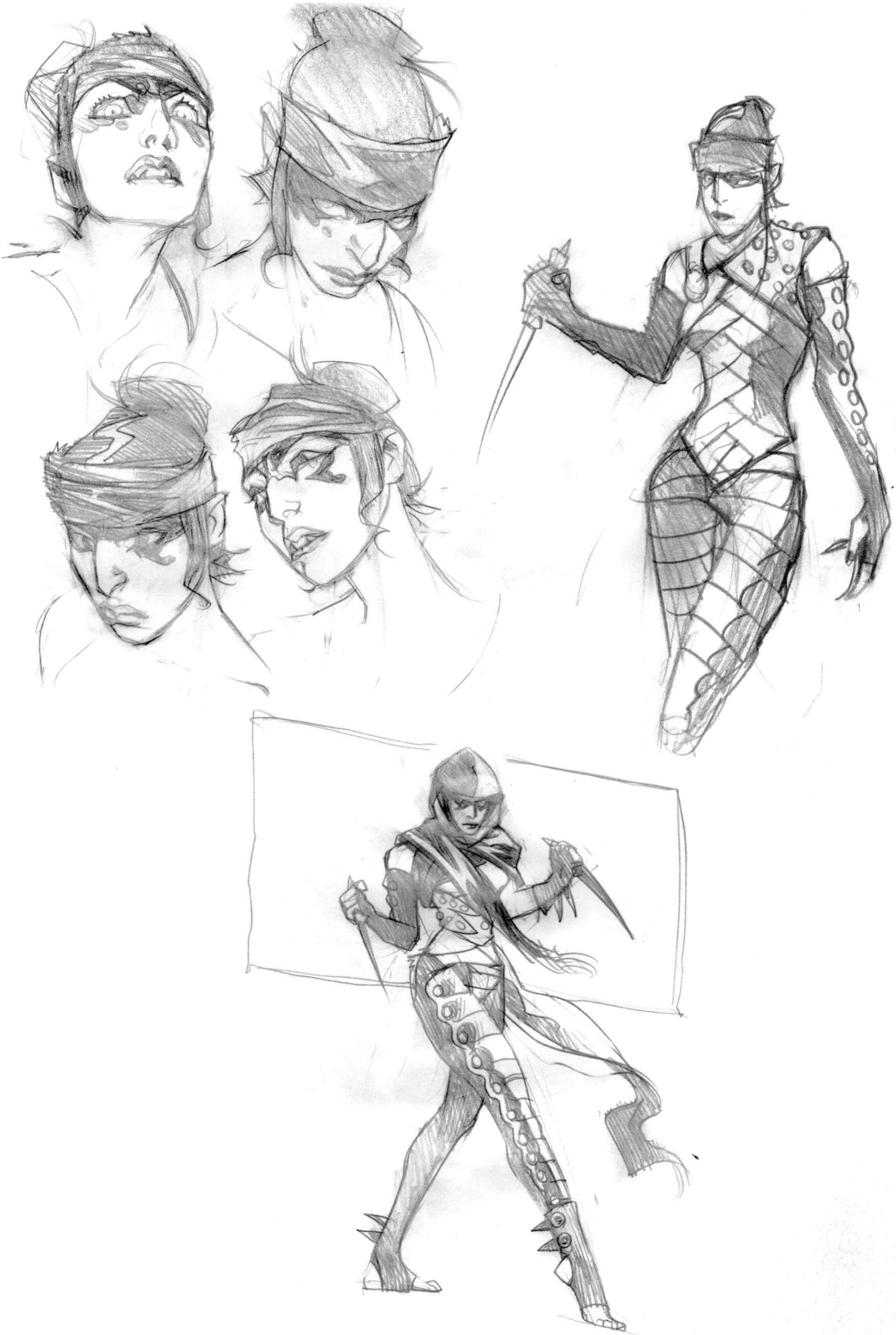

TED NAIFEH

Ted Naifeh has been creating successful independent comics since the late 90s. He co-created *Gloomcookie*, the goth romance comic, with author Serena Valentino, and soon after began writing and drawing *Courtney Crumrin and the Night Things*, a spooky children's fantasy series about a grumpy little girl and her adventures with her Warlock uncle.

Nominated for an Eisner Award for best limited series, *Courtney Crumrin*'s success paved the way for *Polly and the Pirates*, this time about a prim and proper girl kidnapped by pirates who believe her to be the daughter of their long-lost queen. *Courtney Crumrin* now has six volumes, plus a spin-off book, and *Polly and the Pirates* has two.

Ted also co-created *How Loathsome* with Tristan Crane, and illustrated two volumes of *Death Junior* with screenwriter Gary Whitta. More recently, he illustrated *The Good Neighbors*, a three-volume graphic novel series written by *New York Times* best-selling author Holly Black, published by Scholastic.

Recently, Ted has contributed work to many major comics companies, including *Batman* comics for DC, and the horror anthology *Creepy* for Dark Horse. His most recent work for Oni Press was *Princess Ugg*, of which there are two volumes, and *Night's Dominion*.

MORE BOOKS FROM TED NAIFEH

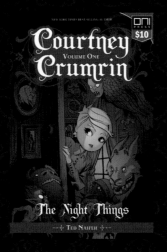

NIGHT'S DOMINION
VOLUME 1
TED NAIFEH

NEW YORK TIMES BEST-SELLING AUTHOR
ONI PRESS
$10
Courtney Crumrin
VOLUME ONE
The Night Things
TED NAIFEH

NIGHT'S DOMINION, VOLUME 1
By Ted Naifeh
168 pages, softcover
color interiors
ISBN 978-1-62010-410-1

COURTNEY CRUMRIN, VOLUME 1: THE NIGHT THINGS, SQUARE ONE EDITION
By Ted Naifeh & Warren Wucinich
136 pages, softcover
color interiors
ISBN 978-1-62010-419-4

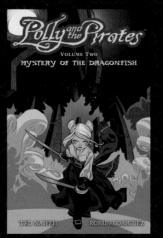

Polly and the Pirates
by Ted Naifeh

Polly and the Pirates
VOLUME TWO
MYSTERY OF THE DRAGONFISH
TED NAIFEH
ROBBI RODRIGUEZ

POLLY AND THE PIRATES, VOLUME 1
By Ted Naifeh
176 pages, softcover
black and white interiors
ISBN 978-1-932664-46-1

POLLY AND THE PIRATES, VOLUME MYSTERY OF THE DRAGONFISH
By Ted Naifeh & Robbi Rodriguez
184 pages, softcover
black and white interiors
ISBN 978-1-934964-73-6

Ted Naifeh's
PRINCESS UGG

Ted Naifeh's
PRINCESS UGG

PRINCESS UGG, VOLUME 1
by Ted Naifeh & Warren Wucinich
120 pages, softcover
color interiors
ISBN 978-1-62010-178-0

PRINCESS UGG, VOLUME 2
by Ted Naifeh & Warren Wucinich
120 pages, softcover
color interiors
ISBN 978-1-62010-215-2

MORE GREAT BOOKS FROM ONI PRESS

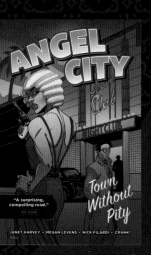

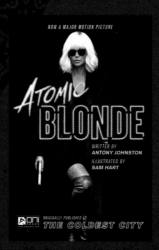

ANGEL CITY
Town Without Pity
"A surprising, compelling read." A.V. CLUB
JANET HARVEY • MEGAN LEVENS • NICK FILARDI • CRANK!

NOW A MAJOR MOTION PICTURE
ATOMIC BLONDE
WRITTEN BY ANTONY JOHNSTON
ILLUSTRATED BY SAM HART
ORIGINALLY PUBLISHED AS THE COLDEST CITY

ANGEL CITY:
TOWN WITHOUT PITY
By Janet Harvey, Megan Levens, & Nick Filardi
168 pages, softcover
color interiors
ISBN 978-1-62010-426-2

ATOMIC BLONDE:
THE COLDEST CITY
By Antony Johnston & Sam Hart
176 pages, softcover
black and white interiors
ISBN 978-1-62010-381-4

FAUNS & FAIRIES
the adult fantasy coloring book
TRUNGLES

HEARTTHROB
CHRISTOPHER SEBELA • ROBERT WILSON IV • NICK FILARDI
"Crime, romance and open heart surgery. Highly (cardiac) arresting." –Kieron Gillen, The Wicked + The Divine
1

FAUNS & FAIRIES:
THE ADULT FANTASY COLORING BOOK
By Trungles
88 pages, softcover
black and white interiors
ISBN 978-1-62010-403-3

HEARTTHROB, VOLUME 1:
NEVER GOING BACK AGAIN
By Christopher Sebela, Robert Wilson IV, & Nick Filardi
136 pages, softcover
color interiors
ISBN 978-1-62010-338-8

THE LIFE AFTER
JOSHUA HALE FIALKOV • GABO
1
$10
10/10

ZANDER CANNON
KAIJUMAX
SEASON ONE

THE LIFE AFTER, VOLUME 1:
SQUARE ONE EDITION
By Joshua Hale Fialkov & Gabo
136 pages, softcover
color interiors
ISBN 978-1-62010-389-0

KAIJUMAX SEASON 1:
TERROR AND RESPECT
By Zander Cannon
168 pages, softcover
color interiors
ISBN 978-1-62010-270-1

ONI PRESS

For more information on these and other fine Oni Press comic books and graphic novels visit www.onipress.com.
To find a comic shop specialty store in your area visit www.comicshops.us.